Spilling the Beans in Chicanolandia

FREDERICK LUIS ALDAMA

University of Texas Press, Austin

Requests for permission to reproduce material
from this work should be sent to:
Permissions
University of Texas Press
P.O. Box 7819
Austin, TX 78713-7819
www.utexas.edu/utpress/about/bpermission.html

∞ The paper used in this book meets the minimum
requirements of ANSI/NISO Z39.48-1992 (R1997)
(Permanence of Paper).

Library of Congress Cataloging-in-Publication Data

Aldama, Frederick Luis, 1969–
   Spilling the beans in Chicanolandia : conversations with writers and artists / Frederick Luis
Aldama.—1st ed.
       p.   cm.
   Includes bibliographical references.
   ISBN 0-292-70967-6 (cloth : alk. paper)—ISBN 0-292-71312-6 (pbk. : alk. paper)
   1. American literature—Mexican American authors—History and criticism—Theory, etc.
2. Mexican American authors—Interviews.   3. Mexican American artists—Interviews.
4. Mexican Americans—Intellectual life.   5. Mexican Americans in literature.   6. Mexican
American art.   I. Title.
   PS153.M4A437 2006
   810.9'86872—dc22
                                                                                    2005029526

Spilling the
beans in Chicanolandia

Conversations with Writers and Artists

Contents

Acknowledgments

I wish to acknowledge but a few of the many scholars who have supported my own work over the years: Henry Abelove, Robert Alter, Chadwick Allen, Mary Pat Brady, Herbie Lindenberger, John Christie, Susann Cokal, David William Foster, Porter Abbott, José Aranda, Kristen Comar, Rafael Pérez-Torres, Alfred Arteaga, Emilio Bejel, Nancy Easterlin, Roland Greene, Patrick Colm Hogan, Seth Lehrer, David Herman, Rafael E. Samuel, Carl Gutiérrez-Jones, Brian McHale, María Herrera-Sobek, José Limón, Jim Phelan, Ralph Rodriguez, José Saldívar, Werner Sollors, Alan Williamson, Deborah Madsen, Robert Warrior, and Lisa Zunshine. Thanks as always to Leke Adecko, Arturo J. Aldama, John-Michael Rivera, Daniel Kim, Cheryl Higashida, Ruben Donato, Vince Woodard, and my many other former colleagues at the University of Colorado, Boulder. Thanks to all of you at the Ohio State University who have so warmly invited me into your fold. Without Marcy McGaugh's patient transcription of many interviews, the Chicano/a voices bound between this book's covers would not have been heard. Finally, I owe much to the generous support of Theresa May, Allison Faust, Carolyn Wylie, Jan McInroy, Liz Gold, and Laura Bost at the University of Texas Press. I hope that this book gives back some measure of the great insight and delight that these Chicano/a creative writers and artists bring to the world.

Spilling the Beans in Chicanolandia

Introducing a Second Wave of Chicano/a Visual/Verbal Artists

Juan Bruce-Novoa's *Chicano Authors: Inquiry by Interview,* which identified a first wave of post–1960s/1970s writers, was followed by a deluge of new Chicano/a voices. Today, Chicano/a visual and verbal artists—novelists, short story and children's book writers, comic-book storytellers, poets, and playwrights, as well as performance and film artists—dazzle mainstream and multiethnic readers and audiences alike; their creatively crafted worlds, born out of a complex Chicano/a point of view, open their readers' and audiences' eyes to new and different ways of experiencing and understanding the world we inhabit. This "second wave" of Chicano/a sculptors of themes and forms has provided us with fresh new visions while fundamentally reshaping the contours of today's American cultural landscapes.

Many of the writers who make up the second wave of Chicano/a crafters of verbal/visual narratives are included here. They represent an array of artists who work in a variety of genres, including novel, short story, poetry, drama, documentary film, and comic book. They have succeeded in creatively reframing reality using strict and compelling means. They have developed an artistic ethos through a creative dialogue with the courageous artists of the first wave, who forged the instruments needed to make starkly visible a Chicano/a experience and imaginary: Alurista, Rudolfo Anaya, Ron Arias, Rolando Hinojosa-Smith, Harry Gamboa Jr., Miguel Méndez, José Montoya, Estella Portillo, Bernice Zamora, Patssi Valdez, and José Antonio Villarreal, among many others.

From this perspective, *Spilling the Beans in Chicanolandia* could be considered a follow-up to Bruce-Novoa's collection of interviews with the first wave of Chicano/a artists (mainly writers). As Bruce-Novoa said, those writers represented "what we can call, perhaps, the first generation or, as Tino Villanueva suggests, the generation of Chicano renaissance writing" (30). *Spilling the Beans in Chicanolandia* also exemplifies the way a later generation of verbal/visual artists deals formally and conceptually with the aesthetic and sociopolitical dilemmas of our society and with the rich landscapes that make up the great canvas of past and present cultural arts worldwide.

Of late, several important interview collections that texture such emergent second-wave writers have been published and should be acknowledged. Bruce Allen Dick's *A Poet's Truth: Conversations with Latino/Latina Poets (2003)* frames its questions around the role of poetry in a range of emerging and established Chicano/a, Puerto Rican, and Cuban poets. Two other collections of interviews that shed new light on the formation of Latino/a writers are Karin Rosa Ikas's *Chicana Ways: Conversations with Ten Chicana Writers (2001)* and Bridget Kevane and Juanita Heredia's *Latina Self-Portraits: Interviews with Contemporary Women Writers (2000)*. These two collections make visible the significant contributions of Latina writers, an especially poignant task given the traditional exclusion of Latina writers from the mainstream publishing marketplace and from traditional American literary scholarship. Although these collections focus on fiction writers and poets, they provide great insight into how Latinos/as generally continue to encounter a racist and sexist society.

Indeed, Latino/a artists face many obstacles when trying to clear the space for creating, producing, and publishing their work. While the representational map has changed significantly since the 1960s, Chicano/a writers, artists, directors, and *pensadores* continue to encounter a deep-seated bigotry in the cultural marketplace. Historically, such bigotry has often worn the garb of "aesthetics" to exclude Chicano/a artists and *pensadores*. In the name of aesthetics—a sense of art containing an inherent beauty—non-Anglo and non-European art has been excluded from the canons of literature, drama, film, and fine art. Not surprisingly, when the first wave of Chicano/a artists and intellectual scholars began to come into their own during the surge of late 1960s civil rights activism, they protested not only social and material inequality but also exclusionary cultural practices: the Eurocentric identification of a lowbrow (bad/street/impure/political) vs. highbrow (good/museum/pure/apolitical) aesthetics. Because this formulation of aesthetics had been deployed by media pundits, editors, and academic scholars to exclude Chicano/a, African American, Asian American, and Native American artists, the new generation linked aesthetics with an Anglo dominance at home and an imperialist stance abroad as well as with a more expanded view of European colonial violence and genocide: its identification of European "culture" as a tool to "civilize" the "savage" New World Other. (Many commentators have also discussed how ideals of "reason"—codified as European—worked to justify the enslavement of indigenous Americans of the Americas as well as Africans.)

Identified as an ingredient in a EuroAnglo-American culture linked to acts of exploitation and genocide, "aesthetics" also came to identify a Western privileging of the individual over the collective. For Chicano/a artist-activists like Alurista, José Montoya, Patssi Valdez, and Harry Gamboa Jr., to disrupt an individualist and highbrow Western aesthetics through collective-based and/or community-focused art was to enact a political activism.

Largely as a result of the gains achieved by the struggles of the pioneer Chicano/a artist-activists, the new wave of Chicano/a authors and artists who came into their own in the mid-1980s was able to explore more freely all available genres and storytelling techniques in their aesthetic reframing of reality. Moreover, the weaving of political concerns into their textual worlds could be lighter and much more nuanced. In the interviews in this book, aesthetics becomes the way a given artist reframes life (personal or other) with a reader/audience in mind rather than an old-school, highbrow vs. lowbrow, exclusionary cultural paradigm. This is not to say that this second wave of artists is not political or that the struggle to clear representational space is over—the literary marketplace is rife with prejudice—but rather that the aesthetic reorganizing of reality does not need to be understood as a form of political activism. As the artists themselves inform us, we need to pay attention to the specific conditions in which society and culture shape a certain artist, writer, or film director and her or his art. Given the present social context, it is necessary to address issues of racism and heterosexism that both Chicano and Chicana verbal/visual artists encounter and that continue to be among their central impulses, the springboards that often propel them into their work.

The many voices represented in *Spilling the Beans in Chicanolandia* shed a different light on verbal/visual art and aesthetics, viewing aesthetics less as an evaluative schema that measures good and bad art and more as it functions to reframe objects (real subjects and real experiences that make up everyday reality), to engage us cognitively and emotionally in ways that will produce pleasure and pain and that might potentially reorient our perspective on those objects—and therefore on reality. As each of the artists discusses, such a reframing of reality does distinguish art-objects from the real world that exists independently. Yet such a reframing, because it offers the opportunity for us to imagine other ways of seeing and empathetically participating, can ultimately connect us to the material facts that make up our reality as lived outside the art-object.

Spilling the Beans in Chicanolandia accounts for these "second-wave" artists, who can now fully partake of the full range of aesthetic devices available to convey an increasingly complex Chicano/a identity and experience. As each artist reveals in this book, the representation of Chicano/a culture had already begun to explode when they began working, offering them the freedom to disrupt representations of Chicano/a identity and experience and unfix it as a static entity. Chicano/a identity is continually morphing, incorporating and rejecting other cultural artifacts and forms. Novelists like Alfredo Véa, Alejandro Morales, and Cecile Pineda, for example, invent storyworlds that depict how cultures have more in common than not when different characters of different racial, ethnic, gender, and sexual identification encounter one another. All of these issues and many more are addressed by the artists figured in *Spilling the Beans in Chicanolandia.*

To put it simply, along with a concern with social issues—usually expressed at the level of theme and characterization—there should be a concern for how a given artist (from novelist to comic-book storyteller) organizes his or her work to give shape to the issues and dilemmas he/she is addressing and to engage the reader's and audience's imagination most effectively. Addressing these issues of aesthetics in the interviews offers readers the opportunity to get a better grasp of the artist and his or her work: the way he or she reshapes and hybridizes genre, manipulates time and space, and textures point of view. The artist does not exist in a hermetically sealed vacuum, cut off from the world; the artist breathes the same air we breathe, suffers the indignities we all suffer, and looks ahead as we all do. However, as an artist, the novelist, poet, short story writer, comic-book writer, or film-maker is committed to transforming the details of the world into a highly organized and beautifully crafted art to engage an audience.

As a response to and engagement with a new wave of verbal/visual artists, *Spilling the Beans in Chicanolandia* aims to give all readers interested in Chicano/a novels, short stories, poetry, comics, poetry, drama, and visual docu-journalism insight into this variegated palette. As such, this collection has a formal pedagogical value. For those of us teaching courses on contemporary Chicano/a literature and film in high school and college classrooms, the collected interviews—including the introduction, which contextualizes the artist and his or her contributions, and the bibliographic information on each artist—could be a valuable ancillary tool for enriching interpretation of primary texts.

There are other publications that have this same pedagogical impulse. In the late 1970s and early 1980s, several introductions to Chicano/a literature appeared, including Francisco Jiménez's *The Identification and Analysis of Chicano Literature* (1979), Charles Tatum's *Chicano Literature* (1982), Luis Leal et al.'s *A Decade of Chicano Literature: 1970–1979* (1982), Vernon E. Lattin's *Contemporary Chicano Fiction* (1986), and Carl and Paula Shirley's *Understanding Chicano Literature* (1988). Since then, there has been a marked absence of comprehensive books on Chicano/a literature; instead, there have been books that take the field for granted to some degree, either focusing on specific genres like poetry or drama or engaging it with other literary traditions, such as Native American literature. Harold Bloom's edited volume of critical essays, *Hispanic-American Writers* (1998), comes readily to mind. So, too, does *U.S. Latino Literature: A Critical Guide for Students and Teachers* (2000). However, Bloom's selection of essays not only covers mostly the first-wave writers—Ron Arias, José Antonio Villarreal, Tomás Rivera, and some Puerto Rican authors—but is too overly invested in his patrilineal-biased "anxiety of influence" agenda. Rather than enriching and complicating our understanding of the Latino/a literary landscape, he reduces it to original (father) versus new (son) binary oppositions. *U.S. Latino Literature* does provide a useful pedagogical handbook that is extremely comprehensive, mapping the grand territory of Chicano/a literature from the late nineteenth century (María Amparo Ruiz de Burton) right up to the late 1980s (Sandra Cisneros). Its long sweep is crucial for understanding the extensive genealogy that predates post-1960s Chicano literary renaissance, but it often misses out on the important details that make up a post-1980s Chicano/a literary landscape.

Students need—and usually demand—to know the big picture. Hence, it is important to present them with a more complete sense of literary genealogy, which is daily filling in newly discovered writers long forgotten. It is significant for them to know, for example, that the first Chicano novel was not born with Villarreal's 1959 publication of *Pocho* but nearly a century earlier with novels such as María Amparo Ruiz de Burton's *Squatter and the Don* (1885). It uncovers retrospective affiliations that shed new light on more recent literary creations, making for a contemporary Chicano/a letters that is growing, as Manuel M. Martín-Rodríguez states, "almost as much toward its past as it is expanding toward its future" (*Life in Search of Readers* 5). It gives a sense of depth and breadth to a tradition of Chicano/a letters. Students and engaged readers of Chicano/a literature need to view this ever-expanding picture. Arte Público's work at recovering a "Hispanic literary heritage" has proved crucial for this effort; its recent anthology *Herencia* (2002), edited by Nicolás Kanellos, traces a genealogy through recovered texts that is as important as the work that has been achieved in recovering an African American literary tradition. (See Manuel M. Martín-Rodríguez's critical overview of the "Hispanic Recovery Project" in his 2003 book, *Life in Search of Readers*.) And José F. Aranda's analysis that places recovered Chicano/a work from the nineteenth century alongside writers like Cotton Mather, has pedagogical value in the way it complicates the picture we have of early American letters (*When We Arrive: A New Literary History of Mexican America*, 2003). *Spilling the Beans in Chicanolandia* focuses on a second wave of Chicano/a writers while keeping in mind that Chicano letters began to form long before *el movimiento* of the 1960s.

As the interviews collected in this book unfold, each verbal/visual artist gives a sense of his or her place within this long line of Chicano/a arts and letters. Each is acutely aware of how earlier forms and themes influenced his or her creations. However, each is also aware that while such a genealogy of Chicano/a arts and letters is extending deeper into the past and is more complicated and varied in genre and storytelling shape than was once thought, much of the influence has not come directly from this legacy—at least in terms of form—but from engaging with all literature, art, film, music, and other genres, regardless of their origin. Yes, these verbal/visual artists are aware that their work is now being read retrospectively within a growing genealogy of Chicano/a arts and letters. Yes, each responds to and develops the work of the first generation of contemporary artists. Yes, all are also equally aware that their apprenticeship as verbal/visual artists has been bound to the work done by many generations of European, American, Latin American, Russian, Japanese, and other writers.

Spilling the Beans in Chicanolandia helps direct us to reading—really reading—Chicano/a novels, poetry, short story, comic books, drama, and docudrama film. Reading well is not synonymous with sleuthing out details that would allow the establishment of a supposed one-to-one correspondence between a character or narrator and the author/director. For this reason, the questions posed to the verbal/visual artists represented here shy away from purely biographical inquiries. There is biography—either in the introductory comments to the artist or in the interview itself—but only to the extent that it serves to flesh out our sense of the artist's circumstances and the particulars of his or her work. The way this information is presented disqualifies any attempt to reduce the aesthetic object created to direct expressions of an author's experience.

The mini-introduction to each verbal/visual artist works in two ways: first, as biographical sketch, and second, to fill in the blanks (thematic concerns, trials and tribulations of publishing or producing, interpretations, etc.) not covered during the course of an interview. The goal is to give as complete a picture of the artist and his or her work as possible by custom tailoring the introduction to the interview and the interview to the questions generated from the artist's corpus. The trick was to relay those insights gleaned from my conversations with writers to shed light on our reading, but not to encourage the author-intention paradigm that ultimately leads to interpretive dead ends. To proceed the other way around—to try to establish a direct link between the author/director and a character or a narrator in a given work—is to run the risk of ultimately ghettoizing Chicano/a creativity and imaginative potential. There are millions of ways of being Chicano/a; millions of representations of such experiences are possible. To write is to create possible worlds, and there are no known limits to those worlds. Luis Rodriguez is a straight Chicano biographically shaped by his experiences in East L.A. in the 1960s, experiences that led him to gangbanging and jail time. However, he is first and foremost a writer: the Luis Rodriguez who could author, for example, a powerful short story told from the point of view of lesbian and straight Chicanas in "Las Chicas Chuecas" (in *The Republic of East L.A.,* 2002). Dagoberto Gilb worked as a journeyman carpenter for sixteen years, an immensely rich experience in the world of labor that nowadays is more and more foreign to fiction writers, and one that has contributed powerfully to Gilb's worldview and his art. Gilb, however, is also the creator of narrative fictions that explore the lives of many in all walks of life. The interviews aim to open readers' eyes to the huge and ever-expanding terrain available to these writers, one that is unrestricted by gender, sexual, racial, or ethnic stereotypes.

The artist, of course, is always at center stage. Without him or her, there is no textual corpus, no literature, no artistic representation, and no creation of possible worlds. However, it is pedagogically important to lead students toward asking questions that extend beyond the author. This is not to propose a poststructuralist "death of the author" paradigm that gives license to read any meaning into a given text. Rather, it is important to help guide students to the way a given story is organized as a composite of elements—point of view, tempo, mood, language, emotions, thoughts, worldviews—by a visual or verbal artist who may or may not have had the same experiences as those represented in what he or she has written. While poems, novels, short stories, comic books, dramatic performances, and docudrama films are saturated with many-layered meanings and thus offer themselves to a variety of interpretations, such artistic works are nonetheless, as the interviewed artists attest, highly organized and deeply thought out constructions; they are not unshaped, endless mounds of mud. And such artistic works impose limits to readers' interpretations. Each of the artists in this collection—in one way or another—addresses the issue of how students can understand how a story engages their imagination at the same time that it disengages them from the inclination to conflate fiction with biography or attested reality, or to give sole credence to an author-intention model of interpretation. So while texts are open to an a priori indeterminable number of interpretations, the literary work of art, as the artists themselves suggest, determines to a certain extent which are legitimate and which are not. With this assumption in mind, each artist speaks to how he or she organizes the elements that make up his or her fictions and poetics (those rhythms, metaphors, and lyrical lines that make up Alfred Arteaga's *dislocasia* and Francisco X. Alarcón's speakerly codex, for example) in order to strike a balance between the reader's engagement and disengagement while he or she is immersed in a fictional world.

The understanding of how contemporary Chicano/a artists balance the social with the aesthetic dimensions that inform their work also leads to more general questions about the social and personal value of imaginatively entering the reframed worlds of Chicano/a novels, short stories, comics, poetry, drama, and film. Why do such Chicano/a artists choose these modes of expression rather than, say, that of a political pamphlet, newspaper or magazine article, philosophical treatise, or ethnographic monograph? As each of these visual/verbal artists attests, innovative narratives such as the novel, comic book, or dramatic production play with showing and telling, time and space, and therefore carry a certain plasticity of form, language, and meaning that is uniquely able to grasp the unlimited variety and richness of the human experience and condition. The novelists, poets, short story writers, and other artists represented here demonstrate how invented narrators and characters, situated in time and place, make choices that are filled with moral dilemmas and that ultimately lead to specific consequences. Through vicarious experience, the reader/audience can enter into those creatively crafted worlds and judge the circumstances and choices, leading to a greater self-understanding and compassion. Each artist, then, in his or her own way, celebrates the reader/audience (White or Brown, straight or queer, male or female) who has the imaginative ability to enter such crafted spaces and acquire impressions, images, emotions, thoughts, knowledge, and experiences that enhance his or her capacity for empathy and appreciation.

Each of the interviews collected here celebrates the craft of writing and visually creating not as a "prison house of language" (in Fredric Jameson's famous and infamous phrase), but as the space of creative emancipation for their people (real and imagined characters and narrators) and also for the reader/audience. It is not that these visual and verbal scribes tell us how to live our lives or even how society should be organized, but their work offers the opportunity for us to broaden our imaginative scope and social purview. Of course, as these artists also comment, not all readers and audiences will be moved by their worlds; many good readers and educated audiences might not be touched by exposure to an artist's work. Nonetheless, the artists continue to create in the hope that, while their work might not make a reader a better union organizer, it can offer a reader the opportunity to learn more about the world and its vast array of human experience and behavior.

Method

Spilling the Beans in Chicanolandia departs significantly in method from other recent collections, such as Ikas's *Chicana Ways* and Kevane and Heredia's *Latina Self-Portraits: Interviews with Contemporary Women Writers,* and their predecessor, Bruce-Novoa's *Chicano Authors: Inquiry by Interview.* First, as already mentioned, the questions posed here to the writers explore both the aesthetic and the sociopolitical, the form and the context. Second, the questions are posed to both Chicano and Chicana, to self-identified straight and queer, and to creators of written, oral performance, and visual works—with no sense of privileging one gender or genre over another. Third, unlike *Chicano Authors* in particular, these interviews took place face-to-face. Bruce-Novoa's fourteen interviews were not interviews in the strict sense of the word. *Interview* (a word dating from the early sixteenth century and borrowed from the French language, derived from the Latin *inter* "between" and Latin *videre* "see") means in essence to meet in person for a conversation in which facts or statements are elicited from both interviewer and interviewee. Bruce-Novoa—and he discusses this candidly— did not have the money to travel and meet with his authors, so he devised a list of survey questions that he then mailed to a mostly straight male cadre of writers. They responded dutifully with eloquent written responses to the same set of twenty-four questions. His questions ranged from "Where were you born?" and "Describe your family background" to "When did you first begin to write?" and "What books did you read in your formative years?" His questions were also designed to elicit information from interviewees about their politics, the way they identified as writers, and their assessment of Chicano literature (including "Who are the leaders among Chicano writers, and why?"). Bruce-Novoa apologizes for the rigid format, asking his reader to keep in mind that "time and finances made it the only recourse." Unfortunately, this lack of means resulted in an artificial uniformity that makes the interviews somewhat staid and, because they all respond to the same set of questions, sometimes redundant.

A direct, person-to-person interview, of course, is the ideal. For this to happen, one must have time and money or be situated well geographically. The more fortunate authors who publish with presses with deep pockets tour major metropolitan centers to sell recently published books. During the making of this book, I was living in both Berkeley and Denver, where I was variously researching, writing, and teaching during the year, so it was simply a matter of keeping a finger on the book-tour pulse and then throwing the net out. The interview with Denise Chávez, for example, took place in San Francisco during her nationwide book tour to promote *Loving Pedro Infante* (2001). Of course, there are many writers and artists who lack such support. However, writers such as Alfred Arteaga, Michael Nava, Lucha Corpi, Francisco X. Alarcón, Cherríe Moraga, Lourdes Portillo, and Cecile Pineda are all Bay Area denizens, making the meetings with these authors fairly easy to arrange. But not all writers tour their work or live within arm's reach. Many of the interviews did require travel. For example, to interview Juan Felipe Herrera, I made a day trip to Fresno, a 400-mile round-trip car journey; to meet with many of the others I took airplanes, often scheduling interviews during vacations with family and visits with friends.

For the personal meeting to go well, all homework must be done. One has to study each writer carefully and all the material that will make up the interview questions: memorize works and dates, determine major thematic components, define formal characteristics, obtain a sense of the worldviews expressed, and take note of writerly trends. This means a huge time commitment that precedes the interview itself. Ideally, one must read all work by a given author; write up notes on style, theme, characterization, and major trends; and then memorize this outline. With a template of the author's work and life set in one's mind, as the interview unfolds, one can plug in elements taken from the outline to direct the flow of the conversation. The interview then becomes both an improvised conversation between the interviewer and the author and a constant process of scripting and re-scripting questions as one moves around the information contained in this memorized template. This process allows one to probe deeply into the author's work, learn of his or her points of view about it, and learn the circumstances in which he or she has written and produced it.

This way of customizing questions that are uniquely suitable for a certain author has another important advantage. Because visual/verbal artists do not always respond in ways that we anticipate, this procedure gives the interviewer the freedom to move away from scripted questions as the situation dictates. So, for example, after an author clearly avoids responding to interpretive questions about his or her work, it is best to move to that part of the interview-template that deals with, say, experiences with publishing. The template also helps the interviewer to be able to move around the author's work—and not always in chronological sequence. Sometimes it is more effective to ask an author about his or her most recent work, in order to grease and move the cogs, than to ask questions about earlier work that may have been written long ago. On other occasions, asking questions about a particularly powerful poem, iconoclastic short story, or even biographical experience works well to jump-start the conversation. On a couple of occasions, I even asked questions about the book cover and insert art—something out of the ordinary line of questioning—as a way to position the authors outside their work so as to gently push them to reflect on their work with critical distance. Finally, the ultimate challenge was to have an informed conversation with the author that best revealed his or her deep wisdom and varied experiences as an artist.

The face-to-face interview usually reveals much more about visual/verbal artists than the words they speak; it gives the interviewer a sense of the artist's worldview and experiences of life, perceived in gestures (the twinkle of an eye, a mischievous smile, quick or slow hand or arm movements, the rubbing of hands, a frown or other indication of seriousness), body markings (tattoos and scars), and poise. Many interviews took place in homes that revealed much about the author's aesthetic taste, travels, indifference or attachment to material possessions, and the environment in which the creating process occurs. Studies and work places ranged from those with several desks used variously to write by hand and to type, to those with one writing surface and a large window. Other interviews took place in cafés, restaurants, and bars that also revealed much about the individual author/artist. When I met with Richard Montoya of Culture Clash, it was in a bustling Latino bar in East Los Angeles; the animated background together with a couple of Dos XX revealed less a parodic performance artist and more an individual moved by a complex—and self-reflexively contradictory— range of human emotions and experiences.

Of the twenty-one visual/verbal artists whose interviews are collected in *Spilling the Beans in Chicanolandia,* some are better known in the main- stream than others, and some are more marginalized within Chicano/a letters than others. However, they fully represent the wide spectrum of verbal and visual art that makes up Chicano/a arts and letters today. There are some obvious omissions. For example, better-known writers such as Ana Castillo, Sandra Cisneros, and Richard Rodriguez were not included. This is in part because they already receive more than their due attention in the academy and mainstream: interviews, scholarly essays, and biographi- cal information abound. While some authors interviewed in this book have become more recognized in the mainstream, others do not get as much play. Often this is the result of their refusal to write according to formula or to fan controversy. The artists in this collection often explore hands-off themes as well as constantly confronting and reforming genre, style, and characterization. Some choose to craft forms in the already marginalized domains of poetry, drama, and documentary film. In a marketplace where hackneyed formulas ensure monetary support and where best-seller lists are almost without exception enumerations of easily digestible narratives—not to mention where overwhelming prejudice rules decisions about publica- tion—the artists collected here have had to surmount huge obstacles to make their work known. It is to be hoped that this collection will assist their efforts.

A few of the interviews collected here have appeared previously in various magazines and newspapers, either as much shortened questions and answers or as interview-essays. For Chicano/a artists especially, it is impor- tant that their work become visible. Publishing interviews and reviews in media with large circulation and teaching their works help to achieve this visibility. Whether it is to sell books or to get audiences out to see drama and film productions, artists need recognition. To create, as these artists remind us, one must have the time to create. This means selling enough novels, short stories, or comic books or producing enough drama and film performances to make a living, or finding a career that pays the bills and allows one the time to write. Some artists take teaching jobs in universities that grant time off during the summer and winter. Others, such as Pat Mora, Cherríe Moraga, and Ricardo Bracho, heavily work the national lecture circuit. Jaime Hernandez of Los Bros Hernandez picks up extra work inking panels for mainstream comic-book publishers. Practicing lawyers Alfredo Véa, Daniel Olivas, and Michael Nava must make time while working jobs far removed from thinking about the crafting of fiction.

To be a novelist, dramatist, or other verbal artist is not only about being dedicated to the craft. It is to choose a difficult and fragile path in life. Of course, the payoff can be great, as these authors attest, for in creating fiction, poetry, comics, drama, and documentary film, they transform the most banal and sublime details that make up everyday life into worlds we can share in and vividly experience. By detailing and inventing new landscapes, they think about our world deeply, offering important insights and treasure troves of experience to those of us ready to listen. *Spilling the Beans in Chicanolandia* provides a forum for such writers.

Thumbnail Sketch of Contemporary Chicano/a Letters

The authors/artists collected in *Spilling the Beans in Chicanolandia* work within a wealth of genres, such as poetry, autobiography, drama, novel, comics, short story, and documentary film. Their careers as artists began as early as the 1980s, and they all continue to publish, produce, and perform today. To understand better the work of those interviewed in this collection, I offer below a brief overview of contemporary Chicano/a letters.

Juan Bruce-Novoa anticipated that, with the arrival of new generations of writers, the concerns of Chicano/a authors would change. This has certainly proven to be the case. He also pointed out that while "the dimensions of that space will alter" (30), such literary *new arrivals* "will not cancel the significance of the pioneering efforts of these first writers, even though their works may be superseded" (30). It is true that many of the authors who made up the first wave no longer write, and it is also arguable that their works have been superseded. However, while the sociopolitical issues that were central to the likes of José Montoya and Bernice Zamora—who sought to make visible the plight of the Chicano in their embracing of a *raza* poetics—might not appeal to readers nowadays, their works certainly continue to provide a reflective surface for authors and artists working today to mirror, with a difference, their own concerns.

Such post-1960s pioneers include, but are not limited to, José Antonio Villarreal, Rolando Hinojosa-Smith, Estella Portillo Trambley, Bernice Zamora, Ernesto Galarza, Rudolfo A. Anaya, Aristeo Brito, Isabella Ríos, Alurista, and Luis Valdez. Their work covers the full range of literary genres, but mostly gravitates around the artistic representation of *la causa:* to texture the migrant worker experience, to depict the alienation and estrangement of urban Chicanos, and to celebrate the symbolic reclamation of the Southwest (Aztlán) by positively evoking a Náhuatl spiritual tradition and an Amerindian heritage. Aztlán functioned as a mythical space that, as Rafael Pérez-Torres sums up in his essay "Refiguring Aztlán" (2000), "served as a metaphor for connection and unity [and also] served to contest notions of national identity and place defined by hegemonic discourses at the social— and most particularly—cultural levels" (103). (As often happens, there are exceptions. Oscar "Zeta" Acosta, John Rechy, and Floyd Salas all wrote narrative fictions that turned away from subjects or themes that had a *raza* sociopolitical agenda.) And as I summarize elsewhere concerning this first wave of critique and resistance, "Chicano/a activist intellectuals sought to intervene primarily at the political and cultural levels" ("Chicano/a Studies," 94). For example, in 1967, Corky Gonzalez published his *raza*-epic poem, "I am Joaquín"; in 1970, Abelardo Delgado published the *Chicano Manifesto;* and in 1971, the Chicano poet known as Alurista published *Floricanto en Aztlán* (with Quinto Sol, the first Chicano press), in which he proposed that a bond be created between aesthetic acts and political activism in order to reclaim territorial rights and thus establish in the Southwest a Chicano nation informed by *mestizo* (Amerindian Aztec/Mayan and Spanish) culture. In 1971, Rudolfo A. Anaya published *Bless Me, Última,* organizing his narrative around dream sequences that work not just as a literary device, but as a way to conjure up the powerful, sociopolitically infused Aztlán iconography of his day (four rivers connecting and the myth of the golden carp).

However, by the end of the 1970s, Chicano critics such as Arturo Islas and Luis Leal were already growing weary of Aztlán as the sanctioned model for Chicano/a artistic expression. In 1974, Islas expostulated in the journal

Miquiztli: A Journal of Arte, Poesía, Cuento, y Canto (published at Stanford University): "More often than not, much of the fiction we do have is document, and sometimes not very well written document. Much of what is passed off as literature is a compendium of folklore, religious superstition, and recipes for tortillas. All well and good, but it is not literature." Similarly, in 1979, in his essay "The Problem of Identifying Chicano Literature," Luis Leal asked, "Why should the Chicano experience be limited to the campesino struggle, the description of life in the barrio, or the social confrontation with the majority culture? Why can it not go beyond to include the universal nature of man?" (3). Though both Islas and Leal reaffirmed the bilingual technique of creating new, bicultural images and forms, both had begun to advocate the need for a truly boundless creative space, where writers and artists could explore all facets of Chicano/a identity and experience, especially within the U.S./Mexican borderland area where culture, history, and racial identification (Mexican, Amerindian, and Anglo) intersected. Both Islas and Leal pleaded in favor of a Chicano-informed literary landscape that would lift "the regional to a universal level" so that it could take its "place alongside the literatures of the world" (Leal 5).

Along with Islas and Leal, Tomás Rivera also wanted to see more literature that explored the multifarious wealth of Chicano/a circumstances, emotions, identities, and experiences, while not neglecting the larger sociopolitical and cultural space in which they were inscribed. In his 1979 essay "Chicano Literature: Fiesta of Living," he wrote, "I should like to focus on Chicano writing as a ritual of immortality, of awe in the face of the 'other'—a ritual of the living, in a sense, a fiesta of the living" (19). While Rivera believed that Chicano/a literature should draw upon cultural origins, he thought it should also reach beyond itself to provide "a perception of the world, of people, of oneself in awe of one's own life and its perplexities, its complexities, and its beauty" (35).

By the early 1980s, the Chicano literary landscape was no longer only of the social protest and/or romanticized Aztlán variety, and it was also less male-centric. One might even go so far as to call the 1980s the decade of the boom in Chicana literature. Of course, the lineage of Chicana writers was illustrious and almost a hundred years old. Thus, María Ruiz de Burton had been active in the late nineteenth century, María Christina García in the early twentieth, and Estella Portillo Trambley, Bernice Zamora, and Isabella Ríos in the 1970s; however, Chicana writers were few and far between and mostly marginalized—if not entirely effaced—within a (male-dominated) Chicano and mainstream literary marketplace.

The appearance in 1981 of the lesbian feminist–charged, woman-of-color–voiced poems, short stories, and essays collected in *This Bridge Called My Back* was a notable refiguring of the literary landscape. Its editors included out lesbian Chicanas Cherríe Moraga and Gloria Anzaldúa, who looked less romantically at the Chicano community and responded more complexly to earlier *raza*-identified binaries such as White versus Brown, male versus female, and queer versus straight. *This Bridge Called My Back* introduced "a powerful new wave of Chicana feminist critique of these essentializing paradigms: in Aztlán one would not heroize men and relegate women to the kitchen" (Aldama, "Chicana/o Studies," 95). All forms of experience and identity were to be embraced. As Anzaldúa would write later in her poetic essay "El día de la chicana" (1993), "To rage and look upon you with contempt is to rage and be contemptuous of ourselves. We can no longer blame you, nor disown the white parts, the male parts, the pathological parts, the queer parts, the vulnerable parts. Here we are weaponless with open arms, with only our magic. Let's try it our way, the mestiza way, the Chicana way, the woman way" (82–83). Many others, such as Cherríe Moraga, Lorna Dee Cervantes, Ana Castillo, Denise Chávez, and Lucha Corpi, experimented with storytelling and poetic form to give flesh to "the mestiza way."

Anzaldúa's 1987 publication of *Borderlands / La Frontera*—a hybrid mix of poetry, prose, and metaphysical inquiry—became the apotheosis of this move away from fixed notions of Chicano/a identity and experience. While *Borderlands / La Frontera* experimented with genre, it was not to be confused with a contemporary, Anglo-identified, postmodernist disaffection. For Anzaldúa, playing with language and form was ultimately to unfix heterosexist histories and metaphysics, and then to anchor once again Chicano/a being within a more radically inclusive, hybrid ontology. For Anzaldúa, then, to deform language and destabilize generic expectation was to intervene into and radically transform heterosexist and racist master narratives. Her textualizing of a borderland ontology (straight/queer, male/female, Brown/White, Spanish/Amerindian) emphasized inclusivity, fluidity, transformation, and transfiguration, radically sidestepping the earlier biological and cultural essentialism of the *raza* nationalist socio-aesthetics.

The decade of the 1990s saw further moves to decolonize and denaturalize the hierarchies between Brown and White, man and woman, straight and queer as well as a more general move to identify a "borderland" Chicano/a letters that would not only reform Western epistemology but also engage with other postcolonial experiences and subject formations. Those borderland writers and intellectuals who began to be active in the 1990s are characterized as border crossers who, as Pérez-Torres describes, function much like the coyote smuggler who moves "people and goods back and forth across aesthetic and cultural as well as geopolitical borders" (246).

The Second Wave
Poetry

Many of the writers interviewed in this collection move freely back and forth between poetry, narrative fiction, and drama. However, some more than others gravitate toward the art of poetry. These include Francisco X. Alarcón, Juan Felipe Herrera, and Pat Mora. (Other writers such as Alfred Arteaga, Cherríe Moraga, Lucha Corpi, Alma Luz Villanueva, Luis Urrea, Ben Sáenz, and Luis Rodriguez are also poets, but arguably their careers have been defined primarily by their work in other genres.) These poets extend a long poetic tradition in Chicano/a culture that has been traced back to the nineteenth-century *corrido* tradition in Mexico and the Southwest. (See José Limón's *Dancing with the Devil*, 1994, and Americo Paredes's *"With His Pistol in His Hand": A Border Ballad and Its Hero,* 1958.) However, as each writer attests, they engage not only with a long and rich history of *poesía mexicana,* but also with the poetic forms that inform American (North and South) and European traditions generally. The Beats, Walt Whitman, Langston Hughes, Federico García Lorca, Pablo Neruda, Adrienne Rich, Elizabeth Bishop, and Angela Davis are all mentioned as influential to these second-wave Chicano/a poets.

Some of the poets included in *Spilling the Beans in Chicanolandia,* such as Juan Herrera and Francisco X. Alarcón, bridge the first and second waves of Chicano/a writing. Herrera and Alarcón both began writing poetry in the mid- to late 1970s, and their first collections of poetry were marked by anger and rage at the social injustices that Chicanos faced every day, from the kid on the street to the migrant farm worker in the fields. They worked within the social protest genre of Amiri Baraka and José Montoya. Herrera's poetic impulse was to link arms with the creative leaders of *el movimiento* like Alurista and José Montoya. Herrera continued to write poetry through the 1980s and 1990s that opened to other themes, such as love, death, and other aspects of the human experience.

Francisco X. Alarcón, Alma Luz Villanueva, and Pat Mora began crafting their poetry sometime after the steam of *el movimiento* had begun to clear. For Mora, poetry was a venue to begin to express a need for recovering and making visible Chicanas' active presence in the making of Chicano culture. She took her lead from first-wave feminist poets like Bernice Zamora, whose poems first began to texture the battleground where women struggled against patriarchal oppression (White and Brown). Much as Villanueva affirms a cosmic womb/maternal/earth iconography in her collection *Blood Root* (1977), Mora celebrates the image of an activist *mestiza* artist/weaver figure in her collections *Chants* (1984) and *Borders* (1986). For Francisco X. Alarcón, poetry was both a celebration of his Amerindian heritage and a venue for coming out as a gay poet. The poetic form allowed him to creatively and powerfully interrogate an otherwise homophobic and heterosexist Chicano/a community. For both Alarcón and Mora, poetry was a forum for complicating the Chicano/a sexual and gendered identity and experience.

Of course, Villanueva, Mora, and Alarcón began to publish their poetry during an exciting time for Chicano/a writers. Poetry slams were becoming commonplace in the Bay Area, New York, and Chicago. Many Chicana poets were getting their work published. Lorna Dee Cervantes published *Emplumada* (1981); Moraga published the first Chicana out lesbian prose-poetry autobiography, *Loving in the War Years* (1983); Ana Castillo published her first collection, *Women Are Not Roses* (1984), followed by her hybrid epistolary poem-novel, *The Mixquiahuala Letters* (1986); and, toward the end of the decade, Anzaldúa's hybrid prose/poetry filled out her path-clearing *Borderlands / La Frontera (1987)*. In spite of the conservative backlash that marked the country politically, the 1980s witnessed the proliferation of straight/queer, male/female, and ex–gang member / college-educated Chicano/a voices. Chicano/a poetry of this period refigured notions of tradition and community and articulated, as Pérez-Torres writes, "a position for itself simultaneously within and without dominant cultural formations" (250).

Dramatic and Performance Art

Three of the twenty-one writers/artists interviewed for this collection work in the realm of drama and performance: Cherríe Moraga, Ricardo Bracho, and Richard Montoya of Culture Clash. (Notably, Denise Chávez, Cecile Pineda, and even Luis Urrea wrote plays early in their careers.) We can locate Moraga's, Bracho's, and Montoya's work within a long history of Chicano/a drama and performance art that extends back to the nineteenth century. The annexation of Mexico's northern territories by the United States in 1858 marked the beginning of the Mexican American theater arts tradition. Mexican American (including California Chicano, Texas Tejano, and New Mexico Hispano) theater evolved as an amalgamation of Mexican street theater arts such as the *carpa* (on-the-road tent theater) and the *zarzuela* (Spanish comedic opera) with a European Bertolt Brechtean brand of sociopolitical drama. Until the 1960s civil rights movements, however, Mexican American theatrical arts did not receive mainstream recognition. In 1965, two Chicano activists—the young, fiery new actor/director Luis Valdez and the powerful farmworker organizer César Chávez—teamed up during California's Great Delano Strike and founded El Teatro Campesino (The Farmworkers' Theater). Valdez used his first-hand experience as an actor/director working with the San Francisco Mime Troupe combined with his knowledge of Mexican drama, history, and myth to train farmworkers after strike hours to perform and write politically savvy, bilingual performances.

Cherríe Moraga, Ricardo Bracho, and members of Culture Clash dialogue with and extend Valdez's improvisational, bilingual theater. We see these connections in Culture Clash's satire and use of the truncated *actos* as well as in Moraga's and Bracho's nod to pre-Columbian myth and iconography. They all variously take up Valdez's *rasquachismo* aesthetic—that parodic recycling of forms otherwise discarded. Of course, each of these second wave dramatic artists variously extends and enriches Chicano *teatro*. Moraga's and Bracho's dramas complexly affirm the role of women and gays/lesbians in the Chicano/a community. Moraga's first dramatic production, *Giving Up the Ghost: Teatro in Two Acts* (1986), celebrated the figure of the *pachuca* as an empowered, resistant woman figure who affirmed a Chicanisma sensibility. Moraga then went on to texture California migrant Mexican and Chicano struggles as well as homophobia and sexism in Chicano working-class families. Her lineage can also be traced back to the first-wave post-1960s playwrights, such as Estella Portillo-Trambley and Luis Valdez. In *Sweetest Hangover* (1997), Bracho offers a powerful glimpse into an urban queer Latino underworld. Bracho and Moraga focus on the struggles of women, gays, and lesbians within the Chicano community. Their scenes and *actos* are directed not only at the racism that pervades an Anglo-identified mainstream, but also at the homophobia and sexism within the Chicano *barrio* and home. Their plays range from the domestic drama to the urban club scene to farmworker struggles.

Culture Clash use satire and humor as well as "site-specific" interviews with people off the streets to affirm the life of the underdog (Chicano, Latino, or otherwise) and to self-reflexively poke fun at Chicano nationalism. Documentary *teatro* dramas such as *A Bowl of Beans* (1991), *Radio Mambo: Culture Clash Invades Miami* (1994), *Bordertown* (1998), and *Chavez Ravine* (2003) satirize our consumer society as well as giving voice to and complicating the diverse array of experiences of peoples of color in the United States.

Novels

With the exception of Alejandro Morales, who published his novel *Caras viejas y vino nuevo (Old faces and new wine)* in 1975, the novelists included in this collection of interviews—Alfredo Véa, Lucha Corpi, Denise Chávez, Michael Nava, Cecile Pineda, Ben Sáenz, and Alma Luz Villanueva (also arguably known as a poet)—all began their careers in the mid-1980s. (Dagoberto Gilb also published a novel, *The Last Known Residence of Mickey Acuna* (1994), but is a writer committed more to the craft of the short story.) These second-wave novelists depart from and dialogue with the novelists of the first wave of contemporary Chicano/a writing.

Each author in his or her own way engages with and challenges those literary conventions—theme, technique, and style—that inform Chicano/a, American, and world literary traditions. Alejandro Morales experiments with a wide variety of forms, from the street-slang style of his first novel, *Caras viejas y vino nuevo* (1975), to the epistolary/journalistic collage of his recent novel *Waiting to Happen: Volume One, The Heterotopian Trilogy* (2001), in which he emplots one-eyed, racially hybrid characters, and he textures cosmopolitan spaces both north and south of the border. In 1986, Denise Chávez published what some have identified as either a composite novel or short story cycle titled *Last of the Menu Girls*. Here Chávez employs the bildungsroman to shape a coming-of-age story of a young Chicana, Rocío. In her later novel *Face of an Angel* (1994), Chávez uses the techniques of stream-of-consciousness narration to shape yet another Chicana character's story. And in her more recent *Loving Pedro Infante* (2001), she reforms the romance genre to complexly characterize a Chicana living on the U.S./Mexican border.

In 1989, Lucha Corpi published her first novel, *Delia's Song*. Like Chávez, Corpi re-forms the genre of the bildungsroman to tell the story of a Chicana who must learn to part from her family to come into a less restrictive way of being a woman in the world. After *Delia's Song,* Corpi turned her attention to the detective novel. In *Eulogy for a Brown Angel* (1992) and *Cactus Blood* (1995), she invented the protagonist Gloria Damasco, who sleuths out crimes with social and political significance. The detective fiction genre proved useful for yet another Chicano writer, Michael Nava. In 1986, Nava published *The Little Death,* introducing his readers to the first gay Chicano lawyer-detective, Henry Rios. The many novels that followed proved to be a huge success until Rios's adventures ended in 2001 with the publication of the last in the series, *Rag and Bone.*

Although Benjamin Sáenz is a poet and writer of short stories, he is also a novelist. *The House of Forgetting* (1997) represents a foray into genre fiction—the psychological thriller. At the same time, it is an allegorical exploration of the effects of colonialism on an oppressed people. The novel opens with the revolt of thirty-year-old Gloria Santos against her kidnapper, an esteemed professor of humanities, who had stolen her from the streets of El Paso when she was seven years old. She has been kept in a kind of "humanistic" captivity in his Chicago home, educated broadly, and given all the accoutrements of an upper-class upbringing. Her escape brings her in touch with a lawyer, Jenny Richard, and a police lieutenant, Alexander Murphy, who befriend her. The novel examines the psychological trauma experienced by the oppressed and the oppressor as Gloria works out her love-hate relationship with the professor and tries to recover her lost culture. Sáenz's themes encompass the alienation and estrangement of modernity but are underlined by a strong commitment to the spiritual power of Mexican culture in overcoming them. Folk Catholicism and Chicano cultural sensibility underwrite the many rituals within his stories—the blessings of water, lighting of candles, prayers to the saints, reverence for the dead, and acceptance of the preternatural—all framed ironically, sometimes humorously, but always with the understanding that ceremony and rite are necessary elements of culture. Spirituality, in Sáenz's hands, becomes an affirmation of the people's resistance to a dominant mainstream culture. It is an identification of an ethnically based poetics that refuses to turn away from its formative symbols, instead embracing the contradictions of its histories to reformulate and reconceptualize a living tradition.

Alma Luz Villanueva likewise works in many different genres, including the novel. In her novels (and poetry) she explores the tense relationship between people and the natural world, especially affirming Latina artists, mothers, and daughters who find their way to the redemptive and transformative power of the earth. *The Ultraviolet Sky* (1988) follows the protagonist, Rosa, as she comes to terms with society's imperfections—a ruined marriage, an unplanned pregnancy, and her son's sexual awakening—through her art. And in *Naked Ladies* (1994) Villanueva gives texture to the pain and suffering of those women who have run-ins with the violence of patriarchy.

Authors Cecile Pineda and Alfredo Véa add significantly to the canon of Chicano/a novels. Pineda's first novels published in the 1980s, *Face* (1985) and *Frieze* (1986), are reminiscent of Isabella Ríos's experimental novel, *Victuum* (1976). Like Ríos, Pineda uses stream-of-consciousness narration and plots devoid of action to explore how myths interweave with and create subjectivity. In a marked shift from these novels is Pineda's *The Love Queen of the Amazon* (1992). Here she employs a parodic narrative voice to texture an action-driven plot that expands the boundaries of an otherwise male-dominated Latin American magical realism. Alfredo Véa, in his novels, *La Maravilla* (1993), *The Silver Cloud Café* (1996), and *The Gods Go Begging* (1999), uses a variety of narrative techniques to expand the notion of what it means to be Chicano. In *La Maravilla*, for example, he weaves into a magical-realist, third-person narrative voice the styles that characterize physics and biology discourse.

In the 1980s and 1990s, many Chicano/a novelists moved into the limelight. Gay Chicano author Arturo Islas moved from a small press with a limited distribution to two larger publishers, William Morrow and Avon. Ana Castillo moved from the *Bilingual Review* to Doubleday, which gave *The Mixquiahuala Letters* (1986) and *Sapagonia: A Novel in 3/8* (1989) glossy, Maya-encrypted cover-art makeovers. Doubleday went on to publish *So Far from God* in 1993, *Loverboys* in 1996, and *Peel My Love Like an Onion* in 1999. And, after first publishing with Arte Público, Denise Chávez signed on with Farrar Strauss for her 1994 novel *Face of an Angel*, which was given a full spread in the *New York Times Book Review*.

Short Stories

Long before Dagoberto Gilb, Luis Rodriguez, and Daniel Olivas began writing short stories, there had been a strong tradition of short story writing in Chicano/a letters. For example, in 1913 María Christina Mena was already writing and publishing her race-focused, sentimental short stories in magazines; and in the 1940s, Mario Suarez published what has become a Chicano classic, "El Hoyo" (1947). By the late 1960s and early 1970s, many short stories by Chicanos/as had appeared in anthologies and Chicano journals such as *El Grito*. These had cleared a space for writers in the 1980s to add to and expand the tradition. In 1983, Pat Mora edited the collection *Cuentos: Stories by Latinas*, which made visible Chicana and Latina (Nuyorican, Cuban émigré) bilingual/bicultural short stories that broke long-imposed silences surrounding sexuality—especially Latina lesbianism. Shortly thereafter, Sandra Cisneros began to invent a variety of empowered Chicana characters, starting with the publication of *The House on Mango Street* (1988). And, during this period, Helena María Viramontes gave narrative voice in her collection *The Moths and Other Stories* (1985) to the shared experiences of young and old Chicanas and Latinas. Dagoberto Gilb also began writing and publishing short stories during this period of canonical growth and expansion. After publishing *Winners on the Pass Line* with Cinco Puntos Press in 1985, he went on to publish *The Magic of Blood* (1993) and then *Woodcuts of Women* (2001) with Grove. In the tradition of Rolando Hinojosa-Smith, Alberto Ríos, and Max Martínez, Gilb's gritty-realistic short stories take place in a variety of towns in the Southwest and gravitate around the everyday life of working-class Chicanos.

While short story writers Rodriguez and Gilb have to a large degree crossed over—one can find them at Borders and Barnes and Noble bookstores across the country—other talented writers like Daniel Olivas find that the publishing world needs only one or two Chicano/a writers for their quota to be filled. Publishing with smaller presses and in journals (print and online), Olivas's powerful short stories dramatically reconfigure contemporary short story topographies and express a complex (often middle-class) Chicano experience and identity. For example, in "A Melancholy Chime," Olivas not only plays with the form of telling the story, but does so to emplot a Chicano professor's experiences living in England and his romancing of an Anglo student. In his story "The Plumed Serpent of Los Angeles," Olivas makes age-old Spanish and Mexican fantastical parables contemporary and urban.

Children's Literature

Although Chicano/a children's literature has become more visible since the 1990s, it has been present in one form or another for some time now. Miguel Méndez's 1979 *Cuentos para niños traviesos (Stories for naughty children)* employs an oral narrative style to shape folk tales of the border. And Rudolfo A. Anaya's collected stories, *The Silence of the Llano* (1982), though read largely by adults, are often told from the point of view of a child and could be read by and/or to children. The same holds true for the early short stories written by Sandra Cisneros and María Helena Viramontes.

The 1990s saw an increase in children's literature written by and about Chicanos/as. In response to the lack of young adult fiction by and about Chicanos, Daniel Olivas turned fact into creative fiction in the writing of bilingual/bicultural experiences of Chicanos in *Benjamin and the Word* (2004). And poet Francisco X. Alarcón has ventured into the world of writing children's literature in the crafting of autobiographically informed, bilingual poetry for children. Poet Juan Felipe Herrera has also turned to writing children's literature. From his first bilingual book, *Calling the Doves: El canto de las palomas* (1995), to *Welcome to Salsaland!* (2002), Herrera's stories deal with real situations such as single parenting and discrimination in the classroom, but are infused with a deep affirmation of Chicano/a culture and values.

While many Chicano/a authors have tried their hand at children's literature—including Denise Chávez with *The Woman Who Knew the Language of Animals* (1992) and Lucha Corpi with *Where Fireflies Dance* (1997)—the author most committed to the craft has been Pat Mora. Although a writer of volumes of poetry and a best-selling memoir, *House of Houses* (1997), Mora has written over a dozen children's books—all of which celebrate what it means to be Chicano/a. For example, in her award-winning *A Birthday Basket for Tía* (1992), she affirms the empowering relationship between grandson and *abuelo;* and in her book *The Race of Toad and Deer* (1995), she gives the tortoise and hare story a Mayan spin.

For these Chicano/a authors, children's literature has the power to engage with young people during their formative years and, therefore, to influence a child's cultural sensibilities and social relations. Alarcón, Herrera, and Mora see their children's stories and poems as a way for Chicano/a children to reconceptualize their identities from pejorative stereotypes to positive communal cultural values. These authors also see their stories as venues for non-Chicano/a children to imagine other ways of existing, with the hope of dispelling prejudice and encouraging cross-cultural understanding.

Other Forms

Since they hit the scene in 1981 with their series "Love and Rockets," Jaime and Gilbert Hernandez, known as Los Bros Hernandez, have extended the rich tradition of cartoon and comic-book art that hails from Latin America and the U.S.—especially the independent tradition informed by R. Crumb. Their stories use visuals (a zoom, a cross-fade, a jump cut, a lap dissolve) as well as narrative techniques (interior monologue, narrative point of view) to engage their audiences and to tell stories of strong and complex Chicano characters living within a U.S. mainstream culture. They introduce readers to characters such as Chelo, the Puritanical town sheriff, and the politically idealistic Tonantzin, as well as the bisexual Chicana characters Hopey and Maggie. Their art has enriched massively the Latino comic-book canon that includes Alejandro Sánchez and Lalo López and inspired those like Jaime Crespo.

The second wave of Chicano/a artists has made waves in visual and verbal journalism as well as in comic-book arts. Radically revising the journalistic approach of Richard Rodriguez (known for his 1982 publication of *Hunger of Memory*) are Luis Urrea (also a poet and novelist) and documentary filmmaker Lourdes Portillo. Luis Urrea explores life at the margins: the lives of people struggling to survive in the Tijuana dumps, depicted in *Across the Wire: Life and Hard Times on the Mexican Border* (1993) the lives of Latinos trying to make it across an increasingly militarized U.S./Mexico border in *Devil's Highway* (2004); and the life of a Chicano traveling through the open roads of the U.S., as he recounts in *Wandering Time: Western Notebooks* (1999). And, as a visual artist using the aesthetics of documentary storytelling, Lourdes Portillo innovates and reframes through editing, mise-en-scène, and musical score to depict the lives of Latinas north and south of the U.S./Mexico border.

Postcritical Cartographies

Alongside this second wave of Chicano/a authors/artists that is rolling across the American cultural landscape is a new generation of Chicano/a scholars who are making their own waves. The earlier cadre was composed mostly of male Chicano scholars—such as Francisco Jimenez, Luis Leal, Roberto Trujillo, Francisco Lomelí, Vernon E. Lattin, and Juan Bruce-Novoa. But since the 1980s, there has been a marked presence of Chicana scholars: Norma Alarcón, Gloria Anzaldúa, Angie Chabrám, Teresa McKenna, Rosaura Sanchez, Tey Diana Rebolledo, María Herrera-Sobek, Sonia Saldívar-Hull, Carla Trujillo, Yvonne Yarbor-Bejarano, Paula Moya, Emma Perez, and Mary Pat Brady. Norma Alarcón theorizes the *mestiza* subject's "provisional identities" as a form of "intervention into dominant Chicano and U.S. Anglo-European discourses of power" ("Conjugating Subjects" 135). Anzaldúa similarly celebrates a queer/straight Chicano/a subjectivity that splits tongues (Spanish, English, Náhuatl, Caló) and resists in its shape-shifting identity. And Sonia Saldívar-Hull identifies a "nuanced global mestiza coalition" with her formulation of a "New Mestiza consciousness" (*Border Feminism* 172). This new wave of Chicana borderland theory seeks to identify an aesthetic and an ontology that is in a constant state of flux and that is, as Carmen Cáliz-Montoro writes, "a battleground of identities" and "a crossfire between camps" (*Writing from the Borderlands* 14).

Along with this re-gendering of a largely male-dominated critical realm arrived a more poststructuralist-informed approach to Chicano/a studies. Ramón Saldívar's *Chicano Narrative* (1990) takes as his lead Jacques Derrida's notion of *différence* to identify how Chicano narrative both moves toward the destabilizing of hegemonic master-narratives that naturalize racial difference and provides new signifying systems in the recovery of residual forms of folk / oral-based epistemologies. For Saldívar, to analyze Chicano/a literature is to decode how the texts speak to a historical reality and against discursively constructed spaces that continue to oppress. By the mid-1990s, Carl Gutiérrez-Jones similarly explored the effects of discursively constructed power matrices present in judicial acts. In his *Rethinking the Borderlands* (1995), Gutiérrez-Jones formulates a Chicano/a text that intervenes and transforms the "objective voice" of legally sanctioned mainstream discourse.

Along with a poststructuralist transformation of Chicano/a studies—especially in the field of literature—came the formulation of a borderland theory. This theory turns critical frames away from the earlier "us versus them" paradigm of analysis and more towards complicating binary oppositions. The borderland theory now active in Chicano/a scholarship largely aims to uncover those intersections where sexuality, gender, and race meet with issues of exile, diaspora, and dislocation. Since the 1990s, there has been a move to identify a Chicano/a postcolonial analytic mode that articulates a borderland theory—the reality of exile within a U.S. homeland—to shed new light on Chicano/a experience and identity. In their essay "On the Borders between U.S. Studies and Postcolonial Theory" (2000), Amritjit Singh and Peter Schmidt celebrate the rich cross-fertilization between diasporic, postcolonial concepts such as hybridity and third space, and U.S. border scholarship. For example, they identify José David Saldívar as a critic alert "to issues of Otherness and creolization in global and transnational contexts" (17). In *Border Matters* (1997), Saldívar brings together Chicano/a scholarship with the British Birmingham Center's cultural studies to formulate a borderland aesthetic and culture. Cultural and biological impurities— much as in the work of Homi K. Bhabha—open up a borderland, a third space of resistance that destabilizes hierarchies of aesthetic, gender, sexual, and racial difference. We see the trend continue with Raúl Homero Villa, who has identified the borderland aesthetic and built spaces in L.A. as "expressive of the practices of barrio social and cultural reproduction" that re-imagine "dominant urban space as community-enabling place" (6). In *Gang Nation* (2002), Monica Brown has used a borderland theory to identify resistance in Chicano and Latino gang literature. In *De-Colonial Voices* (2001), editors Arturo Aldama and Naomi Quiñones articulate a resistant aesthetics of hybridity where Chicano/a and Native American identities and experiences crisscross. And in his edited volume *Violence and the Body* (2003), Aldama reframes U.S. ethnic experiences of technology, the body, and state violence within a "transethnic," globe-spanning, subaltern context.

Several comparative approaches to the recovery and constitution of a Chicano/a canon have appeared. Rosemary King's *Border Confluences* (2004) explores what she identifies as a "geopoetic" expression of the borderland in turn-of-the-twentieth-century novels such as Helen Hunt Jackson's *Ramona: A Story* (1884) and Ruiz de Burton's *The Squatter and the Don* (1885), along with Carlos Fuentes's *Old Gringo* (1985) and Harriet Doerr's *Stones for Ibarra* (1984). In a similar comparative manner, Ann Goldman in *Continental Divides* reads several early Chicano/a texts against those of canonical Anglo authors such as Henry James. And we see a similar comparative recovery method brought to bear in José Aranda's *When We Arrive* (2003), in which he analyzes a variety of Chicano/a border narratives to re-map nineteenth- and twentieth-century American literary history. In a similar comparative vein, but focused on a more contemporary Chicano/a literary scene, Manuel Luis Martinez in *Countering the Counterculture* (2003) builds bridges between the Beats, such as Burroughs, Kerouac, and Ginsberg, and post–World War II Chicano writers such as Oscar "Zeta" Acosta, Ernesto Galarza, and Tomás Rivera to formulate a "new direction for social criticism" (18) and to point us toward new possibilities of what he identifies as a more inclusive "Americano studies" (18).

Along with such Chicana intertextual borderland formulations there has been much progress made in queer Chicana theory. Mary Pat Brady's *Extinct Lands, Temporal Geographies* (2002) moves back and forth through time and space to formulate a radical politics of Chicana feminism. And in her introduction to the collection of essays *Velvet Barrios* (2003), Alicia Gaspar de Alba writes of the need to bring out of the closet *barrio*-based gender and sexuality in an act of recovering an *"alter-Native* culture" (xxi). One method is to affirm the otherwise denigrated figure of La Malinche in the identification of "erotic *travesías"* (xxv) in contemporary lesbian writing. Elsewhere in this collection, M. Teresa Marrero reads Moraga's *The Hungry Woman: A Mexican Medea* (2001) as a "transcultural space" (Greek and pre-Columbian) that maps "a topography of non-heterosexual desire" (290). Marrero identifies other Latino queer/feminist playwrights, such as Luis Alfaro and Caridad Svich, as disrupting stereotypes and "implicit sexual and cultural identities to re-form as fluidly as their art" (293). And Chicana scholar Catrióna Rueda Esquibel writes in her essay "Velvet Malinche" of the need to open up and complicate the field of Chicano/a studies by focusing on representations of Chicana same-sex relationships along with the re-reading of pre-Columbian mythology and popular cultural Mexican iconography. Furthermore, in the anthology *Chicana Feminisms: A Critical Reader* (Arredondo et al. 2003), we see a like postcolonial, feminist, and queer theoretical thrust. For example, in a 2003 essay by Ellie Hernández we see how Emma Pérez's novel *Gulf Dreams* (1996) is an embodiment of a "different historical preaccount of the cultural representation of Chicana lesbian sexuality by making visible the traumatic psychological ruptures of colonial memory in Chicana/o discourse" (155). Hernandez rereads narratives of mythologized origins, seeing La Malinche (*la chingada,* violated mother of *mestizo*) as a foundational act of violence and terrorism that continues to impact gays and lesbians within the Chicano/a community. At the same time, the novel textures and legitimates the coming-out experience of a young Chicana within a heterosexist community.

This new wave of Chicano/a critics has been radically expanding theoretical purviews to complicate readings of ethnic/subaltern textuality and subjectivity. This new wave of Chicano/a criticism aims to build coalitions in the articulation of a borderland space made up of hybrid and diasporic subjects as a way to de-center hegemonic master narratives. These critics emphasize complexity and contradiction, crossings, in-betweenness, and displacement to authorize "the development of a unique sense of self within a white-dominant mainstream that has historically denied the brown subject agency" (Aldama, "Chicano/a Studies" 94).

A Suggestive Bibliography of Chicano/a
Literary Theory Published since 1990

Alarcón, Norma. "Conjugating Subjects: The Heteroglossia of Essence and
Resistance." In *An Other Tongue: Nation and Ethnicity in the Linguistic Border-
lands*, edited by Alfred Arteaga, pp. 125–138. Durham, NC: Duke University
Press, 1994.

Aldama, Arturo J. *Disrupting Savagism: Chicana/o, Mexican Immigrant, and Native
American Struggles for Self-Representation*. Durham, NC: Duke University Press,
2001.

———, ed. *Violence and the Body: Race, Gender, and the State*. Bloomington:
Indiana University Press, 2003.

Aldama, Arturo J., and Naomi Quiñonez, eds. *De-Colonial Voices: Chicana and
Chicano Cultural Studies in the 21st Century*. Bloomington: Indiana University
Press, 2001.

Aldama, Frederick Luis, ed. *Arturo Islas: The Uncollected Works*. Houston: Arte
Público Press, 2003.

———. *Brown on Brown: Chicano/a Representations of Gender, Sexuality, and Ethnicity*. Austin: University of Texas Press, 2005.

———. "Chicano/a Studies." *Encyclopedia of Postcolonial Studies*, edited by John C.
Hawley, pp. 94–96. Westport, CT: Greenwood Press, 2001.

———, ed. *Critical Mappings of Arturo Islas's Fictions*. Tempe, AZ: Bilingual Press /
Editorial Bilingüe, 2006.

———. *Dancing with Ghosts: A Critical Biography of Arturo Islas*. Berkeley: University of California Press, 2004.

———. *Postethnic Narrative Criticism: Magicorealism in Ana Castillo, Hanif
Kureishi, Julie Dash, Oscar "Zeta" Acosta, and Salman Rushdie*. Austin: University
of Texas Press, 2003.

Anzaldúa, Gloria. "El día de la chicana." In *Infinite Divisions: An Anthology of
Chicana Literature*, edited by Tey Diana Rebolledo and Eliana S. Rivero, pp.
82–83. Tucson: University of Arizona Press, 1993.

Aranda, José F., Jr. *When We Arrive: A New Literary History of Mexican America*.
Tucson: University of Arizona Press, 2003.

Arredondo, Gabriela F., Aída Hurtado, Norma Klahn, Olga Nájera-Ramírez, and
Patricia Zavella, eds. *Chicana Feminisms: A Critical Reader*. Durham, NC: Duke
University Press, 2003.

Arrizón, Alicia, and Lillian Manzor. *Latinas on Stage*. Berkeley: Third Woman Press,
2000.

Arteaga, Alfred. *Chicano Poetics: Heterotexts and Hybridities*. Cambridge, MA:
Cambridge University Press, 1997.

Brady, Mary Pat. *Extinct Lands, Temporal Geographies: Chicana Literature and the Urgency of Space.* Durham, NC: Duke University Press, 2002.

Brown, Monica. *Gang Nation: Delinquent Citizens in Puerto Rican, Chicano, and Chicana Narratives.* Minneapolis: University of Minnesota Press, 2002.

Calderón, Héctor, and José David Saldívar. *Criticism in the Borderlands: Studies in Chicano Literature, Culture, and Ideology.* Durham, NC: Duke University Press, 1991.

Cáliz-Montoro, Carmen. *Writing from the Borderlands: A Study of Chicano, Afro-Caribbean and Native Literatures in North America.* Toronto: TSAR, 2000.

Cantú, Norma, and Olga Nájera-Ramírez. *Chicana Traditions: Continuity and Change.* Urbana: University of Illinois Press, 2002.

Castillo, Debra A., and María-Socorro Tabuenca Córdoba. *Border Women: Writing from la Frontera.* Minneapolis: University of Minnesota, 2002.

Christie, John S. *Latino Fiction and the Modernist Imagination: Literature of the Borderlands.* New York: Garland, 1998.

Dick, Bruce Allen. *A Poet's Truth: Conversations with Latino/Latina Poets.* Tucson: University of Arizona Press, 2003.

Esquibel, Catrióna Rueda. "Velvet Malinche: Fantasies of 'the' Aztec Princess in the Chicano/a Sexual Imagination." In *Velvet Barrios: Popular Culture and Chicana/o Sexualities,* edited by Alicia Gaspar de Alba, pp. 295–307. New York: Palgrave Macmillan, 2003.

Foster, David William, ed. *Chicano/Latino Homoerotic Identities.* New York: Garland Publishing, 1999.

———. *Sexual Textualities: Essays on Queer/ing Latin American Writing.* Austin: University of Texas Press, 1997.

Gaspar de Alba, Alicia, ed. "Introduction, Or Welcome to the Closet of Barrio Popular Culture." In *Velvet Barrios: Popular Culture and Chicana/o Sexualities,* edited by Alicia Gaspar de Alba. New York: Palgrave Macmillan, 2003.

———. *Velvet Barrios: Popular Culture and Chicana/o Sexualities.* New York: Palgrave Macmillan, 2003.

Goldman, Ann E. *Continental Divides: Revisioning American Literature.* New York: Palgrave Macmillan, 2000.

Gutiérrez-Jones, Carl. *Critical Race Narratives: A Study of Race, Rhetoric, and Injury.* New York: New York University Press, 2001.

———. *Rethinking the Borderlands: Between Chicano Culture and Legal Discourse.* Berkeley: University of California Press, 1995.

Hebebrand, Christina M. *Native American and Chicano/a Literature of the American Southwest: Intersections of the American Southwest.* New York: Routledge, 2004.

Hernández, Ellie. "Chronotope of Desire: Emma Pérez's *Gulf Dreams.*" In *Chicana Feminisms: A Critical Reader,* edited by Gabriela F. Arredondo, Aída Hurtado,

Norma Klahn, Olga Nájera-Ramírez, and Patricia Zavella, pp. 155–177. Durham, NC: Duke University Press, 2003.

Herrera-Sobek, María, ed. *Beyond Stereotypes: The Critical Analysis of Chicana Literature.* Binghamton, NY: Bilingual Press / Editorial Bilingüe, 1997.

———. *Reconstructing a Chicano/a Literary Heritage: Hispanic Colonial Literature of the Southwest.* Tucson: University of Arizona Press, 1993.

Huerta, Jorge. *Chicano Drama: Performance, Society and Myth.* Cambridge, MA: Cambridge University Press, 2000.

Hurtado, Aída. *Voicing Chicana Feminisms: Young Women Speak Out on Sexuality and Identity.* New York: New York University Press, 2003.

Ikas, Karin Rosa. *Chicana Ways: Conversations with Ten Chicana Writers.* Reno: University of Nevada Press, 2001.

Kevane, Bridget, and Juanita Heredia. *Latina Self-Portraits: Interviews with Contemporary Women Writers.* Albuquerque: University of New Mexico Press, 2000.

King, Rosemary. *Border Confluences: Borderland Narratives from the Mexican War to the Present.* Tucson: University of Arizona Press, 2004.

Limón, José. *American Encounters: Greater Mexico, the United States, and the Erotics of Culture.* Boston: Beacon Press, 1999.

Marrero, M. Teresa. "Out of the Fringe: Desire and Homosexuality in the 1990s Latino Theatre." In *Velvet Barrios: Popular Culture and Chicana/o Sexualities,* edited by Alicia Gaspar de Alba, pp. 283–294. New York: Palgrave Macmillan, 2003.

Martinez, Manuel Luis. *Countering the Counterculture.* Madison: University of Wisconsin Press, 2003.

Martín-Rodríguez, Manuel M. *Life in Search of Readers: Reading (in) Chicano/a Literature.* Albuquerque: University of New Mexico, 2003.

McCracken, Ellen. *New Latina Narrative: The Feminine Space of Postmodern Ethnicity.* Tucson: University of Arizona Press, 1999.

McKenna, Teresa. *Migrant Song: Politics and Process in Contemporary Chicano Literature.* Austin: University of Texas Press, 1997.

Moraga, Cherríe, and Gloria Anzaldúa, eds. *This Bridge Called My Back: Writings by Radical Women of Color.* Berkeley: Third Woman Press, 2001; originally published in 1981.

Moya, Paula. *Learning from Experience: Minority Identities, Multicultural Struggles.* Berkeley: University of California Press, 2002.

Pérez-Torres, Rafael. *Movements in Chicano Poetry: Against Myths, Against Margins.* Cambridge, MA: Cambridge University Press, 1995.

———. "Refiguring Aztlán." In *Postcolonial Theory and the United States: Race, Ethnicity, and Literature,* edited by Amritjit Singh and Peter Schmidt, pp. 103–121. Jackson: University of Mississippi, 2000.

Pesquera, Beatríz M., and Adela de la Torre, eds. *Building with Our Hands: New Directions in Chicana Studies.* Berkeley: University of California Press, 1993.

Rebolledo, Tey Diana. *Women Singing in the Snow: A Cultural Analysis of Chicana Literature.* Tucson: University of Arizona Press, 1995.

Rodriguez, Ralph E. *Brown Gumshoes: Detective Fiction and the Search for Chicana/o Identity.* Austin: University of Texas Press, 2005.

Saldívar, José David. *Border Matters: Remapping American Cultural Studies.* Berkeley: University of California Press, 1997.

———. *The Dialectics of Our America: Genealogy, Cultural Critique, and Literary History.* Durham, NC: Duke University Press, 1991.

Saldívar, Ramón. *Chicano Narrative: The Dialectics of Difference.* Madison: University of Wisconsin Press, 1990.

Saldívar-Hull, Sonia. *Feminism on the Border: Chicana Gender Politics and Literature.* Berkeley: University of California Press, 2000.

Sánchez, Rosa Morillas, and Manuel Villar Raso, eds. *Literatura Chicana: Reflexiones y ensayos críticos.* Granada, Spain: Editorial Comares, 2000.

Trujillo, Carla, ed. *Chicana Lesbians: The Girls Our Mothers Warned Us About.* Berkeley: Third Woman Press, 1991.

Villa, Raúl Homero. *Barrio-Logos: Space and Place in Urban Chicano Literature and Culture.* Austin: University of Texas Press, 2000.

Yarbro-Bejarano, Yvonne. *The Wounded Heart: Writing on Cherríe Moraga.* Austin: University of Texas Press, 2001.

Other Works Cited

Augenbraum, Harold, and Margarite Fernández Olmos. *U.S. Latino Literature: A Critical Guide for Students and Teachers.* Westport, CT: Greenwood Press, 2000.

Bloom, Harold, ed. *Hispanic-American Writers.* Philadelphia: Chelsea House, 1998.

Bruce-Novoa, Juan. *Chicano Authors: Inquiry by Interview.* Austin: University of Texas Press, 1980.

Islas, Arturo. "Writing from a Dual Perspective." *Miquiztli: A Journal of Arte, Poesía, Cuento, y Canto,* Vol. 2 (Winter 1974): 1-2.

Jiménez, Francisco, ed. *The Identification and Analysis of Chicano Literature.* New York: Bilingual Press / Editorial Bilingüe, 1979.

Lattin, Vernon E. *Contemporary Chicano Fiction: A Critical Survey.* Binghamton, NY: Bilingual Press / Editorial Bilingüe, 1986.

Kanellos, Nicolás, ed. *Herencia: The Anthology of Hispanic Literature of the United States.* Oxford: Oxford University Press, 2002.

Leal, Luis. "The Problem of Identifying Chicano Literature." In *The Identification and Analysis of Chicano Literature,* edited by Francisco Jiménez, pp. 2–6. New York: Bilingual Press / Editorial Bilingüe, 1979.

Leal, Luis, Fernando de Necochea, Francisco Lomeli, and Robert G. Trujillo, eds. *A Decade of Chicano Literature, 1970–1979: Critical Essays and Bibliography.* Santa Barbara: Editorial La Causa, 1982.

Rivera, Tomás. "Chicano Literature: Fiesta of Living." In *The Identification and Analysis of Chicano Literature,* edited by Francisco Jiménez, pp. 19–36. New York: Bilingual Press / Editorial Bilingüe, 1979.

Shirley, Carl R., and Paula W. Shirley. *Understanding Chicano Literature.* Columbia: University of South Carolina Press, 1988.

Singh, Amritjit, and Peter Schmidt. "On the Borders Between U.S. Studies and Post-colonial Theory." In *Postcolonial Theory and the United States: Race, Ethnicity, and Literature,* edited by Amritjit Singh and Peter Schmidt, pp. 3–69. Jackson: University Press of Mississippi, 2000.

Tatum, Charles. *Chicano Literature.* Boston: Twayne Publishers, 1982.

Francisco X. Alarcón

n 1954 Francisco X. Alarcón was born in Wilmington, California. This small agricultural town would not be his final destination, however. As he grew up, he and his family moved back and forth across the U.S.– Mexico border, forever in search of that place they could call home. As a little boy in both places, Alarcón felt an outcast: in Mexico he was called a *pocho* ("sell out" to the gringos) and in California a "wetback." To shield himself against a prejudiced world on both sides of the border, Alarcón grew to embrace the power of storytelling—particularly his indigenous Tarascan grandfather's stories of his people's victories, such as taking up arms with Pancho Villa in the Mexican Revolution. From an early age, storytelling provided Alarcón with a sense of empowerment. Along with his grandfather's syncopated and richly poetic stories, his grandmother's Náhuatl dialect, with its distinctive cadence and rhythm, mesmerized him. His ambition: to grow up and become a master storyteller. This deep-seated sense of himself as a storyteller finally became realized when Alarcón began to write and publish poetry in the 1980s. Informed by pre-Columbian traditions, Alarcón's poetic style and content paid homage to his ancestors.

After finishing high school in California, Alarcón sought a venue where he could formally begin to learn the craft of poetry. He attended California State University, Long Beach, where he received a B.A. degree in English (1974). With a keen appetite to continue to hone his craft as a writer and thinker, Alarcón set out to pursue a Ph.D. at Stanford. Once at Stanford, Alarcón was taken under the wing of Chicano novelist, poet, and academic scholar Arturo Islas. However, in spite of Islas's close mentoring, Stanford's strong undercurrents of racism—and homophobia—began to undermine Alarcón's progress as a writer. He pulled increasingly away from the campus, living and writing in San Francisco's Latino Mission District. His vibrant life in Mission District culture contrasted more and more sharply with life at Stanford. To see if he could reconcile his scholarly with his poetic and intellectual ambitions, he traveled to Mexico on a Fulbright scholarship (1982–1983). Here, he discovered that it was possible not only to be an intellectual and a poet without being attached to the university but also to be "out" as a gay Chicano. Upon his return from Mexico, Alarcón cut all ties to Stanford and dedicated himself full-time to writing poetry and to community activism in San Francisco's Mission District.

Alarcón's enthusiasm to shape himself into a poet-intellectual working within the community, however, was soon dashed. This was not, as one might surmise, due to the trauma of his coming out to his friends and family (they readily embraced Alarcón's sexuality) but because of certain events that led to his becoming the target of a judicial and media witch-hunt. In the summer of 1984, he was thrown in jail and accused of the rape and murder of a teenage boy. He was proved innocent of the crime, but the public defamation of his character and the traumatic experience generally of a racist and homophobic police and judiciary system meant that years would pass before his name would be cleared and before he would fully recover psychologically.

After experiencing such a severe extreme of what the human mind and body can tolerate—and with the impulse to find a sense of balance—Alarcón's hand took to his pen. In 1985, he published his first series of out, Chicano-informed verses in *Ya vas, Carnal;* that same year, he published his first collection of poems, *Tattoos.* In both publications, Alarcón had discovered a poetic rhythm and a penetrating, staccato voice that he aimed at a xenophobic and homophobic world. For Alarcón, the black marks on the page that formed into words were less an antidote to his pain than a violent lash against a racist world: "poems / fill up / pages // tattoos / puncture / flesh" ("Acoma: Léxico para desenterrar," *From the Other Side of Night,* 3).

Throughout the late 1980s, Alarcón dedicated his life to activist work and to his crafting of a queer Chicano poetics. His political activism aimed to transform the conditions of Latinos living in the United States, and his poetry aimed to help transform the minds of his readers and to heal his own wounds. In 1990 he published *Body in Flames/Cuerpo en llamas*—the book that put him on the map as a major Chicano poet. In this book, his poet-narrator conjures forth a pre-Columbian mythological imaginary, not just to blur the divide between past and present, but to help heal the violent division of mind from body in a Western, Judeo-Christian society. In "Body in Flames," Alarcón's poet-narrator unifies mind and body:

> I want to abandon
> words
> go and awaken
> the senses
> I want
> no memory
> rather to embrace
> every instant
> to a frenzy
> I want to think
> with my feet
> I want to cry
> with my shoulders
> I want to set my body on fire
> *(From the Other Side of Night, 42)*

Alarcón continued to unify mind/body in *Loma Prieta* (1991), where he positioned the Chicano poet-narrator more explicitly within society: "America / understand / once and for all / we are / the insides / of your body / our faces / reflect / your future."

While Alarcón continued to develop a mythologically resonant poetic voice that expressed a unified sense of mind/body—see his *Snake Poems: An Aztec Invocation* (1992)—he also began to explore a more explicitly gay Latino poetic in his epic love poem, *De amor oscuro* (1991). And, in his more recent collections—*Sonnets to Madness* (2001) and *From the Other Side of Night* (2002)—Alarcón introduced a macabre lyrical style to express a Chicano and queer sensibility. Wanting to share in the storytelling process that his grandparents had shared with him as a child, at the end of the 1990s

Alarcón began writing poetry for Children's Book Press in San Francisco. He has published several highly acclaimed books for children, including *Laughing Tomatoes and Other Spring Poems* (1997) and *Angels Ride Bikes and Other Fall Poems* (1999). Alarcón is the first openly gay Chicano poet to enter the Chicano/a and American literary scene. His poetics run the gamut of content and form, from epics on gay love to sonnets that speak to our everyday, topsy-turvy world.

Frederick Luis Aldama: I want to begin by talking to you about your latest work, *From the Other Side of Night*. I was struck by the jacket cover art of a weeping man lying in a bed of flowers.

Francisco X. Alarcón: I first saw this piece, *El Amante*, painted by the gay Latino artist Tino Rodríguez, in the Museum of Modern Art in San Jose. It spoke to themes of light, love, and the earth that permeate the poems in *From the Other Side of Night*. *El Amante* captured a distinctly Latin American sensibility for the tragic—except here, of course, instead of such a sensibility engendered female, it's male. It was this sense of infusing emotion into the masculine that I sought to convey in my poetry.

That I could use this cover was rather unusual. Usually authors are not allowed to get involved in a book's design. However, just as the editor at the University of Arizona Press gave me the freedom to include poems that expressed a gay Chicano sensibility, so too did the editor take my recommendation for the cover art.

F.L.A.: To a greater or lesser degree, your poetry has always gravitated around themes of love—even passion—between men. Why include more poems that deal with gay issues in *From the Other Side of Night*?

F.X.A.: Yes, I've been very consistently a poet who has given shape to a Chicano homoerotic. In 1985 I came out with my first poems collected in *Ya vas, Carnal*, becoming the first openly gay Chicano poet. The homoerotic that infuses these first poems resurfaced in my third book, *Body in Flames*, as well as the subsequent publication of my two books of love sonnets: *Of Dark Love* and *Sonnets to Madness and Other Misfortunes*. Even *Snake Poems*, which is centrally about the importance of connecting with our ancestral Mesoamerican spirit to survive a racist mainstream, touches on themes of same-sex love and desire.

The new collection, *From the Other Side of Night*, deals directly with a less romantic side of same-sex love and desire. The "night" refers to that period in the 1980s and 1990s when the AIDS hysteria and crisis swept across America. The media made us out to be monsters, forcing us back to be silent once again, and many of my friends in the gay Latino San Francisco community were diagnosed with HIV. Many died without a trace of their achievement. The poems are really a written testament and act of preservation of this vitally alive generation of gay Latino men that were wiped from the face of the earth.

This poetic expression of a complex gay sensibility continues in my new collection of poems, *Deep Song*. Here, I take another step toward the idea that a poet can witness and give testimony to life. While the poems are darker than my earlier work—a sense of mourning and loss pervades—they are also a testament to love. I'm a person that survived the AIDS crisis because I have had a relationship with my partner for the last thirteen years. In a way it was this type of committed and deep love that has saved me. It is the reason I'm alive today. I wanted to convey both the mourning of loss and this affirmation of life in *Deep Song*.

F.L.A.: Why the *"to Madness"* in the title of your recently published *Sonnets to Madness?*

F.X.A.: There is a saying famous among Chicanos: "La locura cura" (The madness of love heals). This is what this collection is all about. Long silenced and neglected, this collection affirms the grief and joy that my people bring to the world. I know for a fact that I'm a gay Chicano poet; I know that I'm going to be neglected, silenced by mainstream America. This is a fact. At the same time, just like others that have been silenced, I'm a part of our country's great promise. That is what this collection is all about—a madness of love. The collection ends with a long canto about hope: the hope that in spite of all the oppression in the world, there might be a time when we will all be free.

In my poetry, I don't separate the personal from the political. I learned this from the Chicana feminist writers Gloria Anzaldúa and Cherríe Moraga. For me, one of the most intimate experiences we can have is sex, and isn't part of this experience love? Perhaps it is within this poetic realm that I can begin to help people see deeply into their selves. That's what I try to capture in my poetry.

F.L.A.: How do you conceive of your use of form—the sonnet, the lyric, the short and long line—in your poetry?

F.X.A.: I am a poet who does not tend to experiment too much with form. This said, I do tend to experiment with the long and short line in my poetry. In my first collection, *Tattoos,* and then in *Body in Flames,* I use very short lines. I believe that you don't have to use very ornate language in order to communicate feelings; to express life and feeling one doesn't need to use a complicated literary language. Poetic form can be very simple and profound. I became attuned to the power of the short poetic form when I discovered this mesmerizing manuscript in Mexico City written by Hernando Ruiz de Alarcón in 1629. Written with short lines and originally in Náhuatl, the poems conveyed concisely and powerfully concrete metaphors and images that moved me deeply. They captured my own poetic sensibility. This is also why I really enjoy reading the short poetic lines of García Lorca and William Carlos Williams; for me, the pleasure comes in the rereading of their short, imagistically suggestive lines. It is the incompleteness of the short line—and not the more complete and imagistically determined longer line—that I'm drawn to. For me, the greater the degree a reader/listener has to fill in blanks in the imagery, the more powerful the poem. The less detail, the more possibility there is for the poet and the reader/listener to meet at the site of the poetic line. For me, then, poetry has always been that art form that allows a writer to engage the reader/listener's imagination with few words.

When I first began to use the short form, I was criticized by many writers. With a bias in modern American poetry toward using the expansive and more narrative-like poetic line, my short line poem didn't go down well—even with fellow Latino/Chicano writers. As a graduate student at Stanford University, for example, when I showed the short-lined poems that were going to make up my first collection, *Tattoos,* to my mentor, novelist and poet Arturo Islas, he responded, "Francisco, these are not poems." And I said, "No, they're not poems. They're tattoos." For me, the short line conveyed precisely just how words, like tattoos, can puncture flesh. I believed that the sharp speed of the short line could best capture that pain of punctured flesh.

This isn't to say that I don't use the lyrical voice and the longer line. I do, on occasion. However, even here I avoid the ornate, opting to create a poetic "I" that is always very accessible—an "I" that is inclusive and not exclusive and that contains multiple voices and selves.

F.L.A.: Why the sonnet form?

F.X.A.: I'm drawn to the sonnet for a number of reasons. I like the idea of taking a European metric form that is traditionally identified with Italian Renaissance and Golden Age Spanish literature and making it my own. In *Of Dark Love* I use the sonnet form for my poetic "I" to express his love for a farmworker in Watsonville. I also find that its dialectical structure is very inviting. If you break the sonnet's fourteen-line structure down—in the Hispanic tradition each line has eleven syllables, and the stanzas appear as 4, 4, 3, 3. The first stanza can be read as your thesis: what you want to state. And then there is a regression in the second stanza. In the third stanza there's an articulation of the antithesis, and by the fourth, there's a synthesis and resolution. In my earlier collection, *Of Dark Love,* there are fourteen poems. Each poem, as a scholar once pointed out to me, is like a line of a long sonnet, concluding with the final poem, that's really like the wrap-up line of a sonnet with its synthesizing of previous oppositions at the end. As Hegel once said of the dialectics of history, it takes place in the poem.

To return briefly to other influences that have shaped my poetry: García Lorca's influence on my poetry is undeniable. (I acknowledge this explicitly in my quoted epigraph to *Sonnets to Madness.*) And Pablo Neruda has been a great influence. Neruda's liberating of the sonnet form from the constraints of rhyme was important and affirmed my conviction that rhyme forces the poem to do something that I don't think is natural. I found Neruda's *100 Sonnets of Love*—his use of concrete images and a lot of nouns as opposed to adjectives—extremely influential. *Sonnets of Madness* is a collection based on the Nerudean sonnet, with its traditional fourteen lines, where I also emphasize the tangible and concrete and where I rely more heavily on nouns and verbs instead of adjectives.

F.L.A.: Sometimes you include line drawings by various artists in your poetry collections. I think here specifically of your epic poem *Of Dark Love.* Even though the drawings are external to the poetry, do you intend them to affect the reader in the same way as your use of word-images?

F.X.A.: Absolutely. I think stark illustrations can provide breaks in the poetry that help pace the poems, add rhythm, and provide that dimension of self-reflexivity: the reader is reminded of his imaginative wandering as it stops and starts again after encountering the black marks that faintly shape a visual illustration.

F.L.A.: Why did you begin to write poetry for children?

F.X.A.: I see my work, including the book for children, as making up one long poem—the poem that is my life. So, for me, there really wasn't a shift here in my conception of myself as a writer.

I've written books as well as led poetry workshops for children in response largely to my sense of giving back to the community. Most children's books are very ethnocentric. In most picture books in the U.S., you would never see the kinds of faces and bodies portrayed like those in my books, that reflect our *mestizo* heritage. It's important for children to see themselves and their families reflected in books. This, to me, is very political. After all, in California one out of three kids is Latino, and the majority of children in L.A. right now are Latinos. Yet, when children go to libraries and open their first books, they don't see themselves. We need to include ourselves in books, so children know that it's okay to be dark-skinned, or to have a nose that is not narrow and turned up like the Anglo noses you see in most children's books.

I also write children's books as a way to reflect on and share my experiences as a Chicano growing up biculturally in California. I was struck by the odd Spanish that was used in the bilingual children's books published by Children's Book Press of San Francisco. I found out that the translator of some of these books was from Spain. I said to myself, "Wow, that's kind of disservice to the community." Here we are in California, and we have millions of Chicano children, yet they have a person from Spain writing and translating the books. I wanted to change this, so I began working as an editor and consultant for Children's Book Press. I then got all my writer friends in the Bay Area involved—Juan Felipe Herrera, Lucha Corpi, and Jorge Argueta—to begin writing for the press, which would reflect more accurately our Chicano/Latino community. When it came to writing my own books, I didn't want to write a traditional narrative. I wanted to write short poems that would be like open doors inviting children inside to play.

Laughing Tomatoes and Other Poems draws from the time when I spent time in Watsonville with the *campesinos* working in the strawberry fields with their children at their side. The second book, *From the Bellybutton of the Moon and Other Summer Poems,* is my version of *Snake Poems* but written for children. Here, I faced a new challenge: how to communicate what I know about the Amerindian tradition and contemporary Chicano life to children? How to write a creative book for children that would be a personal response to the passing of Proposition 227, that made bilingual education almost a crime. One of the images I came up with was the bilingual dog in my poem "Bilingual": At home / we have / a bilingual dog // "guau guau" / he first / greets you / in Spanish / and in case / you don't / understand / him then // "bow wow" / he repeats / barking / in English." It's playful and at the same time it carries a political dimension: that all of life should be free to express itself in a variety of languages. In 1999 I published my third book, *Angels Ride Bikes and Other Fall Poems,* that not only grows out of my experiences as a child in Los Angeles but reaches out to celebrate our culture more generally. In 2002, I completed the magical cycle of the four seasons with the publication of *Iguanas in the Snow and other Winter Poems.*

It's wonderful. I can write poetry that engages all sorts of children, encouraging them to touch, smell, taste, and imagine Chicano culture and experience as it is shaped through Spanish/English word-images.

F.L.A.: That innocence and zest for life present in your children's books is also present in your poetry.

F.X.A.: I think this stems from my having had a very happy childhood. I think a lot of Anglo American poets are weighed down by anguish. And the everyday distress felt by many gay and lesbian poets is often reflected in their poetry. However, identifying gay and Latino was never a source of anguish for me. In 1982, I came out in Mexico City after meeting the gay Mexican writer Elías Nandino; he was eighty-five years old and the last surviving member of the avant-garde writing group from the 1920s, *Los Contemporáneos.* I was on a Fulbright scholarship and was attending an international poetry festival in Morelia when Nandino came up to the podium and mesmerized me with his beautiful homoerotic poetry. It was beautiful. I came out. The more gay writers I met in Mexico—Luis Zapata and Carlos Monsiváis, to name a few—the more I felt empowered as a gay Latino poet. I discovered that while there was a lot of homophobia in Mexico, there was also a strong community of gay/lesbian writers, artists, and intellectuals.

When I returned to the Bay Area after my research trip to Mexico, I helped organize a group called *Los Ocho,* loosely modeling it after *Los Contemporaneos.* Eight of us Latino men, gay and straight—which included writers Víctor Martínez, Rodrigo Reyes, and Juan Pablo Gutiérrez—gathered together once a week. It was during this period that we decided to put together the collection of poetry *Ya vas, Carnal.*

F.L.A.: This was the period also when you were accused of molesting and murdering a young boy?

F.X.A.: Yes, in the summer of 1985 I was subsumed by this living nightmare. I had just quit my job as a tour guide/ranger at Alcatraz Island, and a week later I found myself behind prison bars, accused of murdering a teenager. They set my bail at a million dollars. Community members of the Chicano/Latino Mission District of San Francisco, where I had been active and lived for seven years, managed to organize a defense committee on my behalf. Subsequently my bail was reduced to five thousand dollars. But once I was out, I became a direct target for the media. I kept asking "How could this happen?" and "Why me?" Finally, once the police found their guy up in Oregon, and all the charges against me were dropped, I realized that the whole thing smacked of racism. Even though it was proven beyond a doubt from the very beginning that I had been taking classes and teaching at Stanford during the day and working on producing *El Tecolote,* the bilingual community newspaper of San Francisco, until late hours during the day of the murder, the police wanted to railroad me because I was Latino, out in the community, and a political activist. When I filed a lawsuit against the police for three million dollars for violating my civil rights, it was dismissed in Superior Court because officially they never charged me.

F.L.A.: Did this traumatic event hurt your career as a writer?

F.X.A.: Yes, of course the experience hurt my career. I mean, here I was at Stanford with all these so-called liberals critical of American society, yet when this event became news and I needed some support, they avoided me like the plague: being gay and a supposed murderer was too much for them. No one wanted anything to do with me. This show of hypocrisy is what turned me away from the academy. I dropped out of the Ph.D. program. Later, when I began to apply for jobs as a creative writer, it was like sending letters out into a great void. No one wanted to interview me because of this scandal.

Now, of course, I see all these life and death experiences are an integral part of *Deep Song* and *The Other Side of Night.* In the midst of all this experience, I said to myself, "Well, as a person I died, and I had to transform like a phoenix and become alive again from the ashes." I got through the pain of being accused of one of the worst crimes possible—the abuse and murder of a young person. I survived. My poetry reflects this sentiment of life's struggles and survival in a homophobic and racist world.

F.L.A.: Many of your poems are very introspective. In *Body in Flames,* you delve deeply into the poet-narrator's interior psychological landscape. However, in other collections, such as *Quake Poems* and *Loma Prieta,* the poet's voice reaches outward into the social fabric. Do you see this push outward/pull inward motion as a rhythm that governs the movement of your poetry generally?

F.X.A.: For me, poetry responds to and reflects life. The Loma Prieta earthquake happened when I was teaching at UC [University of California] Santa Cruz in 1989. It was the 19th of October, and I was on the third floor of an office building, on the phone with Rosario Murillo, the First Lady of Nicaragua, when the building began to shake. All my books fell from the shelves, hitting and bruising my body. When I stepped outside, I saw Santa Cruz up in flames.

As a poet, I turned on my mind's eye recorder to feel the experience, then click and record the sounds and impressions. I walked the streets of Santa Cruz taking it all in. That night, I couldn't sleep, so I began writing my "emergency" poems—all to do with movement. I used the title, *Loma Prieta,* not just to identify the earthquake epicenter, but also the site of a Mexican ranch that was taken from the *familia* Castro estate to be developed into a large lumber mill. The title speaks on multiple levels: the raping of the land, the conquest of the Southwest, and now the epicenter of the earthquake. The first version of *Loma Prieta* was printed as a Xerox copy with a cover. As it was passed around by word of mouth, it gained a wider circulation—three thousand or so copies—so I came out with a second edition with an introduction written by Lucha Corpi.

Loma Prieta is very consistent with my other collections, like *Snake Poems*. *Loma Prieta* is centrally about the environment: the idea of paying homage to the motherland. "In front of a house we formed a circle of chairs. We waited for the night, listened to news on the radio. Each after-shock brought us closer and closer. . . . Sometimes we laughed. In hours we went back maybe a thousand years. We were now a small band of mystics. . . ." It's a collection that has to do with returning to the source; it also speaks to the collective spirit. Everybody felt the same energy during that big Loma Prieta earthquake: that felt very mystical and magical.

Loma Prieta is also an indictment of technology. I don't believe that technology is going to provide the answer to all the suffering that we have in the world today. I agree with the Hopi Indians that a long winter is coming, and that technology is just going to bring this winter on faster—a winter that will overwhelm humanity. So in a way I'm very pessimistic. There is much destruction in the world today: in California, where voters have passed anti-bilingual education and anti-immigration initiatives in a state where the emerging majority are Latinos; the wars and the tremendous oppressions that we have today; and of course many of my friends from San Francisco that are gone because of AIDS. At the same time, I know we have to live our lives, so we must celebrate this life. It's possible to write poetry with that sense of life, like the way a child can relate to nature and to spring and to tomatoes. In my poetry, I try to affirm life in all its complexity.

F.L.A.: You've written in a number of different genres, including short stories, straightforward prose, and academic writing. Why poetry as your predominant mode of expression?

F.X.A.: To me, poetry is really magical; it can access and reflect reality in ways that prose cannot. The short poem, as I already mentioned, has the power to say so much with so little. I will spend the rest of my life writing poems, and even still, I will not be able to plumb its depths. For me, poetry opens up that realm of multiple imaginings that you just don't find in prose. Where prose narratives are more closed to interpretation—giving you more detail, for example—poems are more like an open-ended question. I really believe in the power of poetry. Maybe it's the only religion I have now.

F.L.A.: It is certainly a riskier career choice?

F.X.A.: Of course. Certainly, I could've become a very boring academic professor. I was, after all, getting my Ph.D. at Stanford. But, at the end of the day, how many people will read your academic essays or the book that you write to secure your job and get tenure? I would say no more than three or four hundred. That's about it, and that's a generous estimate. Then what? You get tenure, and you move on, and then you die. So, even though this path might've provided more security, I knew it wouldn't ultimately challenge me. So I kept following in the direction of poetry—a direction without a compass. I don't know what I'm going to do next. All I know is that right now I write poetry. To support myself, I teach courses on Chicano/a literature and direct this program of teaching Spanish to native speakers.

The challenge is to continue writing as a Latino gay poet in a world where we are few. Gay Latino poet Rafael de la Campa and lesbian Chicana writers Gloria Anzaldúa and Cherríe Moraga have been some of my peers in this journey. Even though I'm of a new generation that can be out—the older generation like Arturo Islas was always in the closet because he had much to lose in his day—there are still very few of us writing today. And we continue to feel little support from those Chicano/a scholars in the academy. Sometimes the people that call themselves liberators are the greatest oppressors.

I've survived. I'm a survivor. There are many more who weren't able to survive as writers because they didn't have a job that would allow them to write and support themselves. It's a sad thing, but the community might not ever know about these writers.

Writings by the Author
Poetry

Tattoos. Oakland: Nomad Press, 1985.

Ya vas, Carnal. In collaboration with Rodrigo Reyes and Juan Pablo Gutierrez. San Francisco: Humanizarte Press, 1985.

Quake Poems. Santa Cruz: We Press, 1989.

Body in Flames / Cuerpo en llamas. Translated by Francisco Aragón. San Francisco: Chronicle, 1990.

Loma Prieta. Santa Cruz: We Press, 1990.

De amor oscuro / Of Dark Love. Santa Cruz: Moving Parts Press, 1991.

Snake Poems: An Aztec Invocation. San Francisco: Chronicle Books, 1992.

No Golden Gate for Us. Santa Fe: Pennywhistle Press, 1993.

From the Other Side of Night / Del otro lado de la noche: New and Selected Poems.
    Translated by Francisco Aragón. Tucson: University of Arizona Press, 2002.

Sonnets to Madness and Other Misfortunes / Sonetos a la locura y otras penas.
    Berkeley: Creative Arts Book Company, 2001.

Children's Literature

*Laughing Tomatoes and Other Spring Poems / Tomates resueños y otros poemas de
    primavera.* Illustrated by Maya Christina Gonzalez. San Francisco: Children's
    Book Press, 1997.

*From the Bellybutton of the Moon and Other Summer Poems / Del ombligo de la luna
    y otros poemas de verano.* Illustrated by Maya Christina Gonzalez. San Francisco:
    Children's Book Press, 1998.

*Angels Ride Bikes and Other Fall Poems / Los ángeles andan en bicicleta y otros poemas
    de otoño.* Illustrated by Maya Christina Gonzalez. San Francisco: Children's Book
    Press, 1999.

It Doesn't Have to Be This Way. Illustrated by Maya Christina Gonzalez. Mankato,
    MN: Capstone Press, 1999.

*Iguanas in the Snow and Other Winter Poems / Iguanas en la nieve y otros poemas de
    invierno.* Illustrated by Maya Christina Gonzalez. San Francisco: Children's Book
    Press, 2001.

Other

"Oración/Prayer," "Raíces/Roots," "Palabras heridas/Wounded Words," and
    "Fugitive." In *Practicing Angels: Contemporary Anthology of San Francisco Bay
    Area Poetry,* edited by Michael Mayo, pp. 1–4. San Francisco: Seismograph, 1986.

"The Poet as Other." In *Chicano/Latino Homoerotic Identities,* edited by David
    William Foster, pp. 159–163. New York: Garland Publishing, 1999.

"Las repatriaciones de noviembre" and "Acoma: Léxico para desenterrar." In *Pal-
    abra nueva: Poesía Chicana,* edited by Ricardo Aguilar, Armando Armengol, and
    Sergio Elizondo, pp. 14–24, 32–36. El Paso: Texas Western Press, 1985.

"A Small but Fateful Victory" and "Carta a América / Letter to America." In *Light-
    house Point: An Anthology of Santa Cruz Writers,* edited by Patrice Vecchione and
    Steve Wiesinger, pp. 1–4. Santa Cruz: M. Press Soquel, 1987.

Further Readings
Critical Studies

Alarcón, Francisco X. "The Poet as Other." In *Chicano/Latino Homoerotic Identities*, edited by David William Foster, pp. 159–174. New York: Garland Publishing, 1999.

Del Pino, Salvador Rodríguez. "Francisco X. Alarcón." In *Dictionary of Literary Biography*. Vol. 122, *Chicano Writers: Second Series*, pp. 3–7. Detroit: Gale Group, 1992.

Foster, David William. "Homoerotic Writing and Chicano Authors." In *Sexual Textualities: Essays on Queer/ing Latin American Writing*, pp. 73–86. Austin: University of Texas Press, 1997.

———. "The Poetry of Francisco X. Alarcón: The Queer Project of Poetry." In *Chicano/Latino Homoerotic Identities*, edited by David William Foster, pp. 197–216. New York: Garland Publishing, 1999.

González, Marcial. "The Poetry of Francisco X. Alarcón: Identifying the Chicano Persona." *Bilingual Review / Revista Bilingüe* 19, no. 2 (1994): 179–187.

Hartley, George. "Hegemony and Identity: The Chicano Hybrid in Francisco X. Alarcón's Snake Poems." *Studies in Twentieth Century Literature* 25, no. 1 (2001): 281–305.

Muñoz, Elias Miguel. "Corpus of Words and Flesh: *Body in Flames/Cuerpo en llamas*." *Bilingual Review / Revista Bilingüe* 16, nos. 2–3 (1991): 235–240.

Underwood, Leticia Iliana. "Confluencia de textos y voces en la poesía de Francisco X. Alarcón: *Poemas serpiente: Una invocación azteca*." *Explicación de Textos Literarios* 26, no. 2 (1997–1998): 20–43.

Reviews

Ayres, Annie. Rev. of *Angels Ride Bikes and Other Fall Poems*. *Booklist* 96, no. 7 (December 1, 1999): 707.

———. Rev. of *Laughing Tomatoes and Other Spring Poems*. *Booklist* 93, nos. 19–20 (June 1, 1997): 1707.

Hoffert, Barbara. Rev. of *Sonnets to Madness and Other Misfortunes*. *School Library Journal* 47, no. 9 (September 2001): 77.

Kielen, Paul M. Rev. of *Iguanas in the Snow and Other Winter Poems*. *School Library Journal* 48, no. 8 (August 2002): 61.

Nabhan, Gary Paul. Rev. of *Snake Poems: An Aztec Invocation*. *The Sciences* 36, no. 1 (Jan.-Feb. 1996): 40-45.

Quiocho, Alice. Rev. of *From the Belly Button of the Moon and Other Summer Poems*. *Instructor* 111, no. 3 (October 2001): 16.

Alfred Arteaga

lfred Arteaga was born in 1950 and was raised mostly by his mother in East Los Angeles. At a young age, he discovered he had a keen ear for poetic rhythms and lyrical lines, so as soon as he had the means, he took up the guitar. He started playing in a band in his teens. In the late 1960s, Arteaga put his musical career on the back burner to turn his attention fully to poetry. Narrowly missing the Vietnam draft, Arteaga worked in the Los Angeles coroner's office, which not only allowed him to support himself, but also gave him time to work on his craft as a poet. Though disciplined enough to read other poets and experiment with forms and voices, Arteaga knew that he would need more formal training if he wanted to become the abstract, metaphysical poet he intended to be. So he applied and was admitted to the University of California, Santa Cruz, where he earned a B.A. in "Aesthetic Studies" in 1972. Feeling the need for more formal training, he went on to earn an M.F.A. from Columbia University (1974). After a long stretch working at community colleges by day and writing poetry by night, he returned to the University of California, Santa Cruz, to earn a Ph.D. in literature (1987). He has taught creative writing and Chicano/a literature at the University of California, Berkeley, ever since.

Self-fashioned as a Chicano metaphysical poet, Arteaga uses such poetic forms as free verse and prose poems to explore the experience and formation of being in language, space, and time. He abstracts everyday run-ins with love and grief, exclusion and inclusion, confinement and liberation, melancholy and ecstasy, to creatively probe the complexities of existence.

In his first published collection, *Cantos* (1991), Arteaga invents a variety of poet-narrators who variously move in and out of Spanish, English, and Náhuatl to texture Chicano/a subjectivity as formed by a colonial past and a multilingual, postcolonial present. This interplay of languages forms a composite—what he identifies as *"textos vivos"*—that conceives of existence not simply as being in the world but as being formed in relationship to other subjectivities. Arteaga's Chicano-identified poet narrators are the sum of the threads of this intertextual engagement.

In his collection *House with the Blue Bed* (1997), Arteaga turns from some of the more formal verse structures seen in *Cantos* to a poetic-prose riff style in order to convey, as he identifies it in his academic writing, a "Xronotopic Xicano" consciousness.

Aguila negra, rojo chante.
Tinta y pluma.
Textos vivos,
written people: the vato
with la vida loca on his neck,
the vata with p.v., the ganga with
tears, the shining cross. Varrio
walls: codices; storefront
placazos: varrio names,
desafíos, people names.
Written cars, names etched
in glass, "Land of a Thousand
Dances." Placas
and love etched in schools.
Faces of Indians branded
by Spaniards.
Faces of Irishmen branded
by Americans.
Gachupín: he who kicks
with the boot.
Yankee: new man, of the
new world, Yancuic.
Xicano: cantador, namer.

xicancuicatl
floricanto
canto
canto
(20)

In his collections *Love in the Time of Aftershocks* (1998), *Red* (2000), and *Flesh and Verse* (forthcoming), Arteaga foregrounds how the body can shape space and time. In *Red,* for example, his poem "Tentli" unfolds: "Lip is edge, the border demarking in light/and in light of day, desire is that edge,/that border, trim and light" (3). And, in "Love in the Time of Aftershocks: III Cognizance," his poet-narrator moves steadily from abstraction to an embodied experience of space and time: "Because space is always a space between, being nothing without definition, an edge, boundaries, that act always confirms state. The *of what* remains a question in the deep dark of morning before the sun and before any kind of natural life, the *of what* that is cause, even in momentary oscillation from the effect, that is truly the object and subject of physical articulation, like perspiration just then, the question so like a *the* after sensing an echo, physically imprinted momentarily on the auditory organ, beyond the actual hearing, after the spent sound, but the plain physical affect of its former presence" (57).

Frederick Luis Aldama: You are a creative writer and an academic theorist. When did you first conceive of yourself as a writer—creative, academic, and otherwise?

Alfred Arteaga: In the beginning, I guess, is the way to begin. A large part of my early draw toward creative writing—poetry and short stories especially—was the presence of my mother in my life. From day one, she would tell me stories, infusing all of my childhood experiences. I began to think of myself as a writer more tangibly when I was in elementary school. By the time I was in the fifth grade, the short story form had already captured my attention. During this period I had a teacher who encouraged me to sharpen my skills as a short story writer. And, ever since I can remember, I've been attracted to the lyric. Even before I was writing short stories, I used to recite children's poems. I was fascinated with the fact that they rhymed and sounded like songs. I've had this type of children's verse sound in my head ever since. So I've always had a strong sense of myself as a writer; it's truly a part of my being.

Of course later, when I was a teenager, I found that music—especially rock—was a venue to express my poetic lines more publicly. So in junior high, I learned to play guitar and turned to writing lyrics. This is something I continued to pursue in high school. This isn't to say that I wasn't writing more traditionally recognized poetry. I was doing both—and they seemed to feed well off each other.

However, as time passed and the ideas and imagery that filled my poetry became more sophisticated, I found it increasingly difficult to integrate this writing with my music. I could imagine the serious lyric in my mind, but when put to music, it just didn't happen. So when I went to college, I put the music aside and dedicated my time more to the crafting of poetry. I'm still very rhythm-centric. When I sit down to write it's as if I'm about to compose a song: I hear a beat, then build everything on top of it.

In college, I wanted to write poetry and fiction in Spanish and English. Because I didn't speak Spanish growing up, I enrolled in Spanish classes at UC [University of California] Santa Cruz. (My mother and father both spoke Spanish but told me and my sisters that if we were to succeed, we had to speak English—and without an accent. They didn't want us to suffer the same class and race discrimination they had.) Once I was fluent in Spanish, the orientation in my writing changed dramatically. This bilingual writing really freed up my creativity; I found that those protest or romantic lyrics I wrote in English, that sounded sappy and overly sentimental when put to music as a teenager, worked really well in Spanish. You can do the romantic lyric in Spanish without sounding crass. The *bolero* does this with its romantic songs. And studying writers like Pablo Neruda profoundly affected me as a writer. He showed me how one could blend the romantic and political in verse written in Spanish.

After Neruda, and with Spanish under my belt, I no longer shied away from blending the romantic and political in my poetry. Unlike Neruda, though, I mixed my languages up. I was in my twenties when I came into my sense of self as a bilingual poet. It seemed almost natural that my poetry would be mixed-language. It was, after all, in the air I inhaled growing up in East L.A. I always had this intuitive sense that languages were not cleanly divided: the political value of one, the aesthetic value of another, and what you could say in one and not say in the other. Mixing languages in poetry was a way for me to reconcile these unnatural divisions.

The interanimation of languages became my form. In this sense, it wasn't art for art's sake; it was really about exploring how a mixed-language poetics could de-center English as the language that dominated and marginalized Spanish-speaking peoples in this country.

Since my interest in existential philosophy in high school, I've also always been interested in exploring those uncharted territories of the metaphysical in my writing. I think that poetry can be a mode for delving into the metaphysical. Poetry used to do this in the past, and it can still do this today. This interest in philosophy and language and their interaction, along with a sense of poetic playfulness, pretty much informs who I am as a writer today. My latest collection, *Frozen Accident,* is the most overtly philosophical of any of my works. Like all of my work, *Frozen Accident* foregrounds the mixed-language imaginary and has this musically rhythmic undercurrent.

F.L.A.: Can you speak to how your racialized, gendered, and sexualized bodies experience time and space in your poetry?

A.A.: I've always been interested in how our desiring and sexualized body experiences the world. That's why much of my writing is an erotic verse, grounded in the physicality of the body. Whereas a lot of erotic poetry slips into the cerebral and ethereal, which disconnects the body and desire from the physical world, I try not to lose contact with the terrestrial. For me, one of the most densely packed physical spaces is the sex act: bodies coming together to try to bridge that impossible gap that exists between people. So, where in philosophy we try to bridge such impossible gaps intellectually, in sex this bridging happens in a really primal, physical way.

The sexualized body is a great metaphor for what I'm trying to work out in my poetry. I think of sex, for example, as the impossible synchronization of two bodies. In our everyday existence, we try to synchronize with somebody else. We pick up their rhythm to try to understand and communicate with them. We even play against their rhythms, sometimes pushing that other person away. Even though it's muted and obscured by clothing, by discourses, by analysis, or whatever, fundamentally that's what we do as humans. In my poetry, like in sex, I want to strip this everyday process down and make explicit this everyday need to synchronize and bridge gaps.

The act of communication in poetry is an act of reaching beyond the body to the outside. Here, the boundaries of the body—textual and ontological—become really important: the reader/listener's body, the corpus, and the poet/speaker. What happens to the body in poetry? Does it have to disappear? How is it given shape? Can it come out? Metaphorically speaking, one of the ways the body gets out is by the breath of the poet-speaker or the reader reading aloud. That essence of somebody, that comes out in their breath: that shapes language and makes communication in this physical air. This presence that takes shape between two bodies through language and art is in this breath. It's shaped by the body, and you can make sounds with it, but it goes out, and then somebody else picks it up. You see this in my collection *Love in the Time of Aftershock,* where I focus on the spirit and breath.

Breath and spirit are important to my poetics, but so, too, are the other junctures of contact, like the body's surface. Skin functions to keep us in and conditions the way we perceive the outside. This is shaped by skin color and gender morphology. I tend to be fascinated most with bodies in contact that are biologically set up as opposites. The desire of bridging the gap between two differently shaped and racialized bodies in the sharing of surfaces—even in DNA interweaving—fascinates me. Imagine a whole bunch of books coming together as one in a library: well, that's like all the many points of contact—hair texture, skin color—that come together as one when bodies mix. Being *mestizo* like myself means that you're connected all over the place. The *mestizo* is a physical manifestation of the inter-human contact. It becomes a physical manifestation of difference—difference in one, even.

Racialized, gendered, sexualized bodies crossing borders in an attempt to synchronize and hybridize inform all of my work. That's why my poetry and fiction is not just of the body in theme, but also in its form: a spatial embodiment of the chaotics of *mestizaje.*

F.L.A.: Can you talk a little about your theoretical concept of the *heterotext*—the reproduction and the miscegenation of discourses that produces the Chicano/a subject—and your poetry?

A.A.: Coming of age as an adult—becoming a man—was tied to becoming Chicano during the time of *el movimiento*. So my articulation of my sense of self has always been bound to a sense of a *mestizo* identity. Being is being Chicano. When I write theory it is also expression of a Chicano *mestizo* sensibility. My sense of self as *mestizo* is my sense of self as a heterotext: that manifestation of the mixing of Spanish / English / Náhuatl biological and linguistic texts in the formation of the Chicano. It is this heterotextual nexus that I aim to make visible both in my creative and theoretical writing.

F.L.A.: You mix genres and blend styles traditionally identified by the categories of poetry, essay, and narrative fiction. Do you conceive of style and genre as having porous borders?

A.A.: There is a tradition of hybridizing poetry and scholarly essay in Chicano/a letters—especially as seen in the works of Gloria Anzaldúa and Cherríe Moraga, who began doing this in the early 1980s. Poetry is that site where play and serious thought can unfold simultaneously. Poetry can be the place for philosophical and intellectual inquiry. When I was coming into my sense of self as Chicano poet during *el movimiento*, I was also reading a lot of Camus. To me, the boundary between intellectual thought, creativity, and racial identification was extremely porous.

F.L.A.: The first poem that opens your collection, *Cantos,* performs an interanimation of language: what Mikhail Bakhtin has identified in the novel as *heteroglossia*, where multiple languages—and therefore beings—speak. How does theory inform your creative work?

A.A.: Clearly, the biggest philosophical impact on my work has been that of Bakhtin. This, however, didn't happen until I began to read Bakhtin in the 1980s. I was immediately drawn to his work. He addressed this issue of the politics of language I'd been thinking about, giving me the intellectual vocabulary to formulate and comprehend how this worked. His theories helped me to understand the sociopolitical dimension of language.

His theory also helped me get a clearer sense of how multi-voiced literature worked and why poetry had been traditionally identified as single-voiced. He inspired and challenged me to find that multi-voice in poetry. His formulation of *heteroglossia* made me realize that the uni-voiced (or what he calls *monologic*) poem was inherently too narrow and forced. So

I began to explore a poetic form that wouldn't suppress voices, giving into the chaos of language and voice. I began to write poetry that was multilingual and that captured that dynamic interanimation of language that happens between speaker and listener inside and outside the poem. It was poetry that engaged the reader's imagination and that also gave shape to the social and political being-ness of the different speaker-subjects. I think this is why the poet Dante has been extremely important to me. Dante worked in the vernacular during the time when Latin was the official language of the church and of literature. Dante was a writer who understood deeply the politics of language and the importance of popular speech. Bakhtin gave me a language to understand this and so opened up a door into understanding how language and a highly organized poetics can reflect being in the world.

F.L.A.: You also employ the more traditional lyrical form?

A.A.: I do use a variety of forms in my poetry. I get tired of doing the same thing. When I was writing this book based on Dante's *Vita Nova,* I started writing a long cycle of poems. They came so easily, it felt all of sudden that I was doing a parody of myself. So, I just stopped. I didn't want to repeat myself. I didn't want to feel as if I was no longer listening to something fresh and new. I tire of that which becomes too regular and too repetitious. To avoid this, I usually work on at least fifteen different pieces at once. It's what keeps me from feeling stale. Each piece has its own original style and form, with custom-tailored sets of rules that give each its own unique direction and sense of where the poem will go. Different ideas and subjects require different forms of expression. The piece might take the shape of a sonnet, or it might take on forms that I don't even know exist until it takes shape on the page.

Now, keep in mind that the poet doesn't have to make it new all the time. There is real value in not just making something new for the sake of new. There are times when you want to echo—and this might include echoing dead famous white poets or not. And there are times when you might want to revivify a dead tradition.

F.L.A.: You say that you work on a dozen or so projects simultaneously. How do you keep track of each one?

A.A.: Each project has my full interest. When I'm invested in a particular poem or set of poems, I'm fully engaged. It's very difficult to disengage and start something else in the period of a day or so. During the course of a month, however, I can work on multiple projects. In fact, I *need* to be working on several projects. When I began to write what became the collection *Frozen Accident,* it started off as a series of disjointed poems; only after a while did it begin to cohere as a collection and appear to me as one poem.

F.L.A.: After this multiple gestation period you give birth, so to speak, to words and images. How does this gestation begin? How do you conceive of your poetry's place in the world?

A.A.: Events, people, ideas, objects, and life are the seeds. Language-poet Norma Cole and I discussed the odd paradox that while poetry has a physical presence—ink on the page—it is nonetheless without a corporeal presence. That's why things like paper or the poet's signature become so important to us. These physical markings and textures are the poem's bridge into the corporeal world. Even the writing process itself can be a very physical experience; leaking ink all over your hand as you write with a pen—this is the poet's physical connection to the poem. So came some of the ideas that inspired *Frozen Accident,* a collection of poems that foreground the tension between the corporeal and the linguistic dimensions of poetry.

F.L.A.: Why the recurrent images and gestures toward acts of remembering in your work?

A.A.: Somewhere in my work, I say memory is dead. After I had my heart attack and was literally disconnected from the world for six weeks, my sense of memory, my sense of history, my sense of taste, my sense of time, were profoundly changed. After recovering, I began to live my life profoundly in the present. Of course, before this I already had a different concept of time: that time doesn't exist; that it doesn't have reality; that change and movement can be understood and explained spatially without having to refer to time. Time is simply a descriptive device.

Once that happened, it made me rethink everyday existence. For example, what does it mean to be in love with a woman if you don't have time? I began to explore this in my book *Flesh and Verse.* Here, I turn my attention to how love exists within a body/time/space continuum: writing about being in love conceived of as a corporealizing of the masculine/feminine as they interrelate. It is the spatial relationship that matters, and not the category of time. We can conceive of human relationships as either spatially present or not.

As a poet, one has to be open to the body and all its senses *in the moment:* looking, or listening, or smelling, or tasting—whatever. Once this experience has moved into the realm of the past, it's no longer alive and meaningful. That's why memory for me is weak—close to dead, really. It's the way I can see the future—in the sense that the future doesn't exist. You know, for somebody to say, "I'll do this tomorrow," I understand what they're doing, and it's not like I don't, like I'm crazy about this, but it really has no meaning to talk about the future because the future *isn't.* All we're talking about is potential, you know? Or guesswork. So the past is not quite that unreal—I don't deny that I was breathing yesterday—yet it remains totally disconnected from my being in the world in this instant.

F.L.A.: Can you explain your concept of *dislocasia* and how it applies to your work?

A.A.: *Dislocasia* is that sense of being in-between space and time. It's this sense of feeling disconnected from where you are at the moment because of a memory disconnect. Memory gives us this narrative that directs us to where we're going to go in life. This gives us purpose and meaning. So if I were to think back to the narrative memory that got me here, then my very position here right now has meaning. I'm here, and that's just a simple, existential fact. Once this "here-ness" is shaken up, the moment loosens and you have a sense of existing in-between and enter a state of *dislocasia*.

Dislocasia is also to acknowledge the chaotic nature of causality—that the act of trying to pin down a single cause, or a string of causes, is futile. In a state of *dislocasia* you feel that there's no longer any cause, and therefore you discard the traditional and restrictive reasons for existing. You're in a state of limbo where your traditional everyday trajectory—that sense that A to B to C led me to be here right now—is disrupted. I'm simply here.

F.L.A.: How does *dislocasia* differ from the poststructuralist doxa "God is dead"?

A.A.: On one level, they appear to be the same—perhaps that is why Derrida's notion of *différence* interests me. I just don't buy that God exists. I have trouble with belief. However, I don't entirely buy the idea that nothing exists. My interest and study of existentialism early in my life has continued to have a deep impact on my thinking. I think that meaning is in existence itself—in this moment and at this location—and not to be derived from something exterior to the self. This acute sense of the now—not caught up in memory—can allow one to enter into a heightened sense of the present.

F.L.A.: How do you account for the past—memory and myth—in your poetry?

A.A.: I don't absolutely deny the past. I don't deny that those people lived. I don't deny that important texts have been written that make up archives of the past. However, that they exist in the past doesn't make a whole lot of difference. In other words, when you pick up a book and open its pages, you vivify the text. At this precise moment of engaging with the book, it no longer matters if its subjects have been dead for 500 years or three minutes, or are still alive. It is the act of reading that makes that text come alive. In other words, on the one hand, I think that the past—the historical event that shaped consequent events—may account for what I am today. However, by articulating this process in the *now* and in the small world of the poem, and not letting the past paralyze consciousness, I liberate, make active, in the act of re-memorying the past.

F.L.A.: Current scholarship in Chicano/a studies focuses on articulating textual/cultural borderlands that resist and intervene into oppressive political—and discursively constructed—paradigms. Does your concept of memory, *dislocasia,* and the hybrid/*mestizo* self fit into this?

A.A.: Absolutely. If we understand memory and history as composed of multiple trajectories that come together in the individual, then you, me, or anybody else is the sum of a variety of different histories. We might cross borders to come here from Mexico, the border might have crossed us, or maybe we were born here; regardless, we are forced to exist within a society that restricts our expression of our multiple historical pasts and future trajectories. We live in a society that demands that we speak English, for example, and with this demands that we exist as only one history instead of as a composite of interanimating histories. When I teach the novel *Bless Me, Última,* I discuss it not only as the coming-of-age story of Antonio, but also as the story of a young Chicano forced to make choices from a whole lot of competing and intersecting histories. Much like borderland theory—at least temporally speaking—I see the Chicano/a self as composed of multiple sites of history that compete against each other for epistemological control and/or for reproductive rights for cultural genesis. What's important is that the *now* is the site where these different trajectories are being worked out daily, by choices and suppressions and so on. Wittgenstein, Neruda, preconquest texts, you name it—are all trajectories that feed into me in the *now* as a composite self.

F.L.A.: Speaking of multiple trajectories, which one dominates your own sense of identity? Those that identify you as a poet, as a man, as a Chicano, as a theorist, as an intellectual?

A.A.: I think that identifying as a Chicano is an active self-nomination. It's not that you're born to be Chicano and that's your fate. It's an act of self-identification. Namely, if I'm somebody who is actively engaged with the planet in the present, in the here and now, then I make choices and I articulate these choices in the fashioning of my self. The concept that *Chicano* is a fashioned identity—constructed and self-appointed—appeals to me as active and positive. It also allows me to name and affirm the multiple trajectories that make me racially a *mestizo*. In the *now,* this is a stable and emancipating site of self-identification. As far as gender identification, I feel less that it is a constructed identity and more that it is tied to sex; in my experience, gender is pretty much hard-wired and therefore less a site of performativity and play for me.

F.L.A.: How do the different trajectories—as an academic and creative writer—intersect, and when does one become more dominant than the other?

A.A.: I inhabit a border space, if you will, both as an intellectual and as a poet. This is not an easy place to be. That I move seamlessly between poetry and theory works perfectly fine for me, but for those invested in policing borders, it's not so fine. I was fired from the English Department at University of California, Berkeley, because they ultimately didn't know what to do with me; I crisscrossed too many disciplinary borders. Of course, now that I'm in the Ethnic Studies department, it doesn't mean that I'm going to stop doing the poetry and theory.

I think that I have something to contribute to the world, so I'm working on a scholarly book on aesthetics, and I continue to write poetry. As an academic, it affords some opportunities—such as engaging with young people and being exposed to them, and them exposed to me—that allow for the free exchange of thought that can lead to both intellectual and creative projects. This aspect of the academy is very, very appealing. However, as far as those entities that police borders—the administration of the university and department politics—I have no interest in this at all.

F.L.A.: In a world that likes to categorize and classify, do you think that your career as an academic has hindered your career as a poet?

A.A.: Absolutely. First of all, it takes a lot of time being in the academy. It's a real illusion that you're going to get summers off and you're going to write a book. That's a real illusion. It takes a long time just to detox from the environment. Not to mention that transition time necessary to switch your brain from teaching and writing criticism to writing; they're completely different skills. There's also the problem of osmosis: if you spend most of your time in an academic environment, it has a tendency of transforming the way you conceive of yourself; you begin to think and identify as an academic. It's an entire culture that works on you every day to transform you into an academic. After a while, even if you resist, you can't help but begin to see the world from the opposite side of the way a poet looks at the world. When many writers are hired by universities, they tend to teach creative writing classes, but then many leave because they discover that their worldview and writing needs are at odds with those of the university machine. For somebody like me, as far as the university is concerned, I'm here first as an academic and second as a writer. This means that my creative work is not recognized and that, for job promotions and so on, the only work that counts is my straight academic scholarship. For me, it's been impossible to be identified as a creative writer and not an academic in the academy.

F.L.A.: You've mentioned Dante, Neruda—even Wittgenstein and Derrida—as influencing your thought and writing. Are there others?

A.A.: Certain authors and their books have had a huge impact on my writing and thinking. For example, when Alurista's book *Nationchild plumaroja, 1969–1972*, came out, I was really taken by that because I liked the physical fact of the book, the way that it looked, the scripting in it, the way the page numbers worked, the language of it. It all seemed terribly new to me. That's a book that had a really big impact on me.

As I already mentioned, I began reading Neruda in my twenties; his long lines blew me away, showing me that one could both be political and romantic at the same time. Others, like the French Rimbaud, were a big influence; I find myself always returning to "La Bateau Ivre." It never seems old to me. Other writers have been an influence, not in terms of form, but in terms of their lives. Victor Hugo, for example, led a courageous life and represents somebody who proved that you can make a difference in the world as a writer. I mean, sometimes you figure the world needs sweeping, cleaning, destruction, revolution, or whatever, and you're sitting in your office typing or something. However, as Victor Hugo reminds me, one's writing can have an effect. Of course, James Joyce and Emily Dickinson have also proved hugely influential, both in their challenging conventions of form and their unique spirit as writers.

F.L.A.: This leads to my question about your creative and academic work—especially *An Other Tongue*—and its reflection and critique of our present day (neo)colonialism and dislocated postcolonial subjectivity: Puerto Rican, Chicano/a, South Asian, and so on . . . ?

A.A.: The postcolonial understanding of subjectivity, based on the British oppression of the Irish, Caribbean peoples, and those of the Indian subcontinent, has had a huge impact on my intellectual thinking as a Chicano. This is where the theory of the borderland intersects with the work of Franz Fanon and later Gayatri Spivak. I've also learned from the situation of the Welsh in Britain. This is a group of people who are focused on issues of the border and colonialism but who identify a more diffuse form of containment and oppression; it's not as explicit as the example of the British in Ireland or in India. Like the Welsh, my work as a Chicano border intellectual focuses much on the issue of language. This is why Bakhtin's work on language politics has been important—not just in terms of the way I conceive of my poetic line, but also in my theoretical work.

One of the motivations to put together the essays that make up *An Other Tongue* was to take some of the concerns theorized in Chicano/a studies and place them in other contexts. In this way, we could learn from, for example, Tzvetan Todorov's conceptions of borders in Hungary and Gayatri Spivak's formulations of language and South Asian subjectivity, just as they could learn from Chicano theorists like myself.

F.L.A.: Where is the future of Chicano/a studies and the creative work that informs this field?

A.A.: With everything becoming more globalized and new ties being created between otherwise disparate communities—Puerto Rican and Chicano, South Asian and Welsh and Chicano, for example—the field of Chicano Studies has to expand to reflect the changing needs of a changing demographic and also the reconfiguring of creative landscapes. On the other hand, in a department of Chicano Studies—or Ethnic Studies—I think that we need to maintain a strong focus in area studies, but allow for a whole lot of disciplinary border crossing. To talk about this in a broader context, all I can say is that we are witnessing radical shifts in how the world is conceived. The upshot: in my dazed and confused state, it is my poetry, with its permeable borders, bodies, and histories, that offers meaning and insight.

Writings by the Author
Poetry

Cantos. San Jose: Chusma House Publications, 1991.
House with the Blue Bed. San Francisco: Mercury House, 1997.
Love in the Time of Aftershocks. San Jose: Chusma House and Moving Parts Press, 1998.
Red. Tempe, AZ: Bilingual Review Press, 2000.

Other

First Words: Origins of the European Nation. Berkeley: University of California Press, Center for German and European Studies, 1994.
An Other Tongue: Nation and Ethnicity in the Linguistic Borderlands. Durham, NC: Duke University Press, 1994.
Chicano Poetics: Heterotexts and Hybridities. New York: Cambridge University Press, 1997.

Further Readings
Critical Studies

Estill, Adriana. "Mapping the Minefield: The State of Chicano and U.S. Latino Literary and Cultural Studies." *Latin American Research Review* 35, no. 3 (2000): 241–252.

Rodríguez, Iliana. "Alfred Arteaga: Cantos chicanos." *Plural* 22, no. 1 (1983): 76–77.

Reviews

Hepworth, Candida. Rev. of *Chicano Poetics: Heterotexts and Hybridities. Journal of American Studies* 34, no. 2 (2000): 318–320.

Hoffert, Barbara. Rev. of *Red. Library Journal* 126, no. 10 (June 1, 2001): 59.

Pérez-Torres, Rafael. Rev. of *Chicano Poetics: Heterotexts and Hybridities. Contemporary Literature* 39, no. 4 (1998): 675.

Perivolaris, John D. Rev. of *Chicano Poetics: Heterotexts and Hybridities. Journal of Iberian and Latin American Studies* 4, no. 1 (1998): 97–98.

Rodriguez, Ralph E. Rev. of *Chicano Poetics: Heterotexts and Hybridities. American Literature* 70, no. 2 (June 1998): 418–419.

Sticha, Denise S. Rev. of *House with the Blue Bed. Library Journal* 122, no. 19 (November 15, 1997): 58.

Suttaford, Genevieve, Maria Simson, and Jeff Zaleski. Rev. of *House with the Blue Bed. Publisher's Weekly* 244, no. 34 (August 18, 1997): 82.

Thompson, Lanny. Rev. of *An Other Tongue: Nation and Ethnicity in the Linguistic Borderlands. Caribbean Studies* 27, nos. 1–2 (1994): 152–154.

Ricardo Bracho

Born July 18, 1969, in Mexico City, Ricardo Bracho was swiftly transplanted to Los Angeles—the city where he would grow up, come into his Chicano sensibility, and become a successful playwright. Raised in the multi-classed and multiracial West L.A. of the 1970s, with highly educated Marxist-Leninist parents (his mother hailed from Nogales, Sonora, near the Arizona border, and his father from Mexico City), Bracho both came out and came into his writing. His gay Latino artistic sensibility was fine-tuned while an undergraduate at Berkeley and later at Brava Theater Center in San Francisco under the aegis of Cherríe Moraga. Bracho's commitment is both to art and to the community; he co-founded the organization called Proyecto Contra-SIDA Por Vida especially targeting Latino lesbians and gays in San Francisco, worked on AIDS research and prevention in San Quentin Prison, and is working currently on the Blunt Project in New York. His plays, such as *The Sweetest Hangover, Fed Up, Tone Memory, Sissy, Querido,* and *A to B* variously use monologue, nonlinear narrative form, and creative juxtapositions of dialogue and music to explore intersections of race and sexuality.

Always seeking new forms to tell his stories, Bracho has extended his dramatic reach in his recent plays. *Mexican Psychotic,* employs a nonverbal, avant-garde form to chronicle the life of Mexicano artist Martin Ramirez, who came to the United States in the early part of the twentieth century, worked the rails, suffered from a cultural collapse, and after fifteen years of being homeless was put in a mental institution. Bracho is now at work on two interconnected one-acts, one entitled *Horror Movie*—a horror-comedy about racial profiling—and the other entitled *The Dweller*—a drama stylized as a fifties teleplay that follows the life of a writer in New York. His plays have been produced in San Francisco (Brava Theater Center, Theatre Rhinoceros) and New York (INTAR Theatre), and have been read nationally at venues including the Mark Taper Forum, Intersection for the Arts, Pregones, the Ricardo Montalban Theater, and the Exploratorium Museum. He has received two commissions from the Latino Theater Initiative of the Mark Taper Forum and one from the Magic Theater. Bracho has been a participant in the National Endowment for the Arts / Theatre Communications Group Residency Program for Playwrights and the Mabou Mines' Suite Residency, and he has received the Creative Work Fund Award.

Frederick Luis Aldama: Why playwriting and drama?

Ricardo Bracho: Throughout my schooling in L.A.'s unified public school districts, I had done theater, but it wasn't until I took Cherríe Moraga's Chicano *teatro* class as an undergrad at Berkeley that I began to think of it as a career. Her attention to my writing—"There's the poem. That may be the monologue. You really are a writer"—helped kick off my sense of self as a creative artist/playwright. Off campus she asked me to be assistant director to a gay/lesbian youth of color drama program, Drama Divas, she had at Brava [Theater Center] in the Mission District. I did that for six years. This is where I did my old-world/old-school apprenticeship in theater, learning lighting and sound design and operation, and the writing of scenes. This led to my applying for the Creative Work Fund with Brava, which landed me my first grant to write my very first play, *The Sweetest Hangover*. It was after this play closed that I felt like, oh, maybe I am a playwright.

F.L.A.: What was the process of conceiving, then transforming and developing *The Sweetest Hangover* into a stage production?

R.B.: Acting as dramaturg, Cherríe helped me with this process, identifying scenes and monologues that worked, developing main characters, and sculpting and trimming narrative threads to shape this story of an underground house club with its many denizens.

After the production of *The Sweetest Hangover*, I continued my work with Cherríe at Brava, writing another play called *July 19, 1979: The Tide*

Is High—I just changed the name to *Sissy*—that ended up being one of my orphan plays, in that it has had many readings and workshops but has not yet been produced. It was while writing this play that my interest in drama—in dialogue, the real-life, three-dimensional bodies moving and acting in front of people—solidified. I've stuck with it ever since, writing and producing *Fed Up* [Theatre Rhinoceros, 1999], the videograph/two-person play, *A to B* [INTAR Theatre, New York, 2002], and several others still to be produced.

F.L.A.: Can you identify an evolution in your work as a playwright?

R.B.: I feel like each piece organically teaches me its process. In the beginning, too, if I didn't write an idea, scene, or monologue down immediately, I would lose it. So I was always writing in cafes and on buses in the Bay Area; in the earlier writing, I would approach like a machete in the dark. Now I feel much more at ease, knowing that the schema of a piece will come more quickly; I can also carry a play around for a while before writing it. For example, I have a play that's been gestating in me since I moved to New York in July of 2001.

F.L.A.: How has your audience evolved—or not?

R.B.: In the Bay Area, working with Brava, which is such a community-based theater, I felt a lot of support, but the production of *The Sweetest Hangover* didn't make any money. And then my production *Fed Up*, at the predominantly white, gay-focused Theatre Rhinoceros, was like staging something for the enemy on some level: this play is about four gay men of color who basically eat this white gay man. You can imagine, the audience wasn't too happy with the production. My staging in New York of *A to B* has run the smoothest course with the audience's engagement and in terms of production: no director got fired and no actor got sick.

F.L.A.: Is there a significant regional and venue variation that inflects audience response?

R.B.: It's regional, venue, and politics. I've done a play at a feminist theater, a gay theater, and a Latino theater thus far. So you see where I get aligned. And am aligned. And then you also see those strands equally in audience and audience development. And, that I've moved to New York has changed much, so in this sense it is also regional. Because a New York playwright carries more cachet, I get things in New York as a gay Latino playwright that I wouldn't have gotten if I had stayed in the Bay Area.

I mean, even in these difficult economic times, New York's still a city where plays can make money.

F.L.A.: What about the Mark Taper Forum in L.A. and their sponsoring of Chicano/a playwrights?

R.B.: Luis Alfaro and Diane Rodriguez have always been good to me. And they've given me two commissions, but I have no hopes of ever being on their main stage, nor do I think most of the people [do who are] involved in their "minority" programming, if you will. I've never had illusions that my plays would make it to their main stage.

F.L.A.: Do you conceive of a particular audience when you're conceiving and then writing your plays?

R.B.: No theater artist doesn't think of audience. This is our unique realm. It's this relationality to audience that distinguishes our work from sitcom or cinema or dance even. Recently I had a residency at Mabou Mines to develop a new piece (short and silent) about the outsider artist Martina Ramirez, called *Mexican Psychotic.* I began thinking about the audience fairly early on and in very specific ways, taking into consideration how long will it take an audience to read a slide, and how will they deal with this environment where dialogue is not spoken. In other works of mine that are far more verbal and narrative-driven, I want to take them on the ride, and I don't necessarily want to put out all the signposts. I'm always just wanting audience.

F.L.A.: What about the language you use?

R.B.: It sort of depends on the text. I did an adaptation for the Mark Taper Forum of Genet's "Querelle" set in a contemporary Long Beach hustler bar. This is probably the most Spanglish of my plays because, even though most of my plays are multiracial, it's the only one I've written that is majority Chicano. That's how that story is set up, the characters and so on, so that's how that play's language unravels. In *A to B* I had this character, "B," who's this Mexican Indian orphan, but he doesn't speak Spanish—a common occurrence in California—so I didn't use any Spanish in the play.

F.L.A.: How do genre and form come into play in your creative process?

R.B.: I'm very intrigued by genre. After the rambling epic piece about colonialism and cannibalism in *Fed Up,* I really wanted to confine myself to the writing of a two-character play: *A to B.* But I also wanted to disrupt this with voice-overs and videos that were the same characters but done by different actors. And I really wanted to do, like, the most clichéd story I could think of: a love story. In a love story there is a certain narrative formula: the first encounter, the expression of love, the fight, the breakup, the makeup. But I decided to reframe this by telling the story nonchronologically to scramble the stereotypical/archetypical story.

Right now I'm working on a play that's based on the horror comedy genre and another that uses a fifties teleplay as a means of staging. I want to play with that sort of horror comedy in the context of racial profiling 'cause I can't think of anything sort of both more horrifying and more comic. This is how I work with genre.

F.L.A.: How do you first conceive of your story lines?

R.B.: It varies. Sometimes I begin with an image of the character or an image of the stage, and then the story begins to unravel. This is what happened with *Fed Up*. I had in mind an image of Sycorax, Caliban's mother who is spoken of but does not speak in *The Tempest*. That led me to imagine a figure on a diving board on the edge of a proscenium stage, so I ran with that.

F.L.A.: What about your sense of bodies in space?

R.B.: This has been a great challenge—especially the writing down of spatial-object relations on the page; I tend to keep it all in my head. For example, when staging *A to B*, there's a scene with the straight black D.J. and a gay Chicano club promoter lying down to sleep together in a bed, but they weren't really together yet. I wanted to have candlelight, but I couldn't do that on stage. So I had to figure out how to bring that sense of lighting even if it wasn't going to be realistic looking. The challenge of the "Mexican Psychotic" was working with others to collectively direct it and figure out where the slide went in relationship to the bodies on the stage, in relationship to an altar, and where to put the audience.

F.L.A.: How might sex, desire, love, and violence inform a queer Chicano theater poetics?

R.B.: I haven't necessarily been working on a sex-violence interface. Even though *Fed Up* revolves around colonialism and desire and what eating means, I was really trying to imagine what the children of Shakespeare's Sycorax and Tennessee Williams's Sebastian might look and behave like. I get to the question of desire, both on a mundane level—what does it mean to live and love in the bodies and localities in which we reside—

and also at a more epic historical level. I've been in a very gay realm doing that, although I feel like I'm going to start doing a sort of more elaborate both critique and celebration of heterosexuality next.

F.L.A.: Music and film appear to be big influences on your work?

R.B.: Of course, Cherríe is a great inspiration on a day-to-day level; and I'm a big fan of Maria Irene Fornes, Adrienne Kennedy, [Harold] Pinter, and [Samuel] Beckett. Also Caryl Churchill, Christa Wolf, Ntozake Shange, Wanda Coleman. Mao, [García] Lorca, Shakespeare—but only as poets. Miguel Piñero's *Short Eyes* and Pedro Pietri's *Revolving Door Plays*. Edwin Sanchez, Migdalia Cruz, Campo Santo, Red Rocket Theater. I got mad love for Reza Abdoh and Jean Genet. And, of course, music and film definitely inspire me. I have a froufrou, avant-garde taste for film directors like Won Kar Wei, Claire Denis, François Ozon, and Godard. And you hear a lot of music in *The Sweetest Hangover* and *A to B,* which are all about San Francisco's underground music scene—a place I dwelled in for a long time. And *Fed Up* is more of a hip-hop influence piece. I'm very interested right now in the piano. So in *Mexican Psychotic* I have a piano player play *corridos* and *rancheras* from the late nineteenth and early twentieth century; in another play I'm working on a character who's a jazz pianist. Sound is really important to me as the base. It provides the rhythmic drive of the dialogues.

F.L.A.: When do you work on your writing?

R.B.: I am a lazy, undisciplined writer, and New York is an exceptionally and very sort of exquisitely distracting city. I need structures like residency programs and deadlines. I'm more of a pen-to-paper than a laptop writer. Sometimes I can be, like, copiously writing, and then at other times I don't write at all.

F.L.A.: What about other creative forms, like poetry?

R.B.: I feel like I get one good poem a year, and I always think of that as a gift or a blessing, but I can never foresee that. I would die a happy man if I could write a perfect sonnet—in the style of Mark Ameen or Gwendolyn Brooks. I think that Jimmy Santiago Baca and Lorna Dee Cervantes are the Chicana/o poet laureates. I'm not a spoken-word, poetry slam poet. I need to have studied those classical poetic structures (European, Chinese, Japanese, Maya, Aztec) better and harder to be a poet, but I do write creative nonfiction and theoretical essays as well. In that realm I'm down with some of Althusser, Foucault, Spillers; all about Fanon, Benjamin, and Marx; and have enjoyed reading the recent colored intellectual production from New York—Josie Saldaña, Fred Moten, José Esteban Muñoz.

F.L.A.: What about your experience with publishing?

R.B.: Most of my publishing has been in anthologies and magazines on the West Coast, and what you really need to matter in publishing is a New York house backing. I would love to publish my plays, but theater's very hard to have published. And while there's an increased interest in publishing Latino writers, they're not that interested in anything gay. Of course, with *Queer Eye for the Straight Guy* and *Queer as Folk* and *Will and Grace*, it might be a smart move to go to L.A., get representation, and start writing for cable or a network, but this is antithetical to how I was trained as a writer, to so closely wed commercialism and craft.

F.L.A.: Do you have a sense that your work is somehow political?

R.B.: In my early days of writing, I was much more interested in the politics of it before I was ever interested in the craft. I was raised in a very political household, and in my high school I was highly politicized. At Berkeley as an undergraduate, we had all the faculty diversity protests and then both the Gulf War and the Rodney King riots, so politics was in the air we breathed. So we were always reading at demonstrations or fundraisers. Then I began to focus more on the writing and crafting. I'm not one of those writers who thinks that writing is activism or a substitute for activism, or that it saves lives, or that it's necessary like bread and not a luxury. I think it's *foie gras*.

Ricardo would like to note that it was during his undergraduate years at Berkeley that Frederick and Ricardo came into contact while working on the literary journal *IN YOUR FACE*, by and about men of color, edited by Richard Castaniero.

Writings by the Author
Plays

The Sweetest Hangover (& Other STDs). Directed by Roberto Varrea. Produced by Ellen Gavin. Brava Theater Center, San Francisco, April–May 1997.

Fed Up: A Cannibal's Own Story. Directed by Reginald MacDonald. Produced by
    Adele Prandini. Theatre Rhinoceros, San Francisco, May–June, 1999.
A to B. Directed by Ela Troyano. Produced by Michael John Garcés, Max Ferra, and
    Alexandra Vazquez. INTAR Theatre, New York, May–June, 2002.

Films

Artistic Director. *Calle Chula.* Directed by Veronica Majano. San Francisco,
    1997.
Artistic Director. *Drylongso (Ordinary).* Directed by Cauleen Smith. Los Angeles,
    1998.

Essays

Contributor. *Corpus: Vol. 2.* Los Angeles: APLA Publishing, 2004.
Contributor. *Shellac: Issue on Eros and Ethnicity.* San Francisco: Shellac Press,
    2002.
Contributor. *Shellac: The Love Issue.* San Francisco: Shellac Press, 2001.
Contributor. *Virgins, Guerrillas, and Locas.* Edited by Jaime Cortez. San Francisco:
    Cleis Press, 1999.
Contributor. *Poesida.* Edited by Carlos Rodriguez. Philadelphia: Ollantay Press,
    1995.
Editor. *Behind Our Backs/Sumt'n Ta Say.* San Francisco: San Francisco AIDS
    Foundation, 1994.
Co-editor and Contributor. *IN YOUR FACE.* Berkeley: Center for Racial Education,
    1991.

Further Readings
Critical Studies

Delgado, Maria M., and Caridad Svich, eds. *Theatre in Crisis? Performance
    Manifestos for a New Century.* Manchester, England: Manchester University
    Press, 2003.
Foster, David William. *Chicano/Latino Homoerotic Identities.* New York: Garland
    Publishing, 1999.
Muñoz, José Esteban. *Disidentifications: Queers of Color and the Performance of
    Politics.* Minneapolis: University of Minnesota Press, 1999.
Rodríguez, Juana María. *Queer Latinidad: Identity Practices, Discursive Spaces.*
    New York: New York University Press, 2003.

Svich, Caridad, ed. *Theatre: Theory and Practice-Performance.* New York: Palgrave Macmillan, 2004.

Reviews

Aldama, Frederick Luis. Rev. of *The Sweetest Hangover. SF Weekly,* April 16, 1997.

Hurwitt, Robert. Rev. of *The Sweetest Hangover. San Francisco Examiner,* April 14, 1997.

Jacques, Damien. "Hispanic Theater Speaks to the American Experience." *JS Online (Milwaukee Journal Sentinel),* July 19, 2003 <<http://www.jsonline.com/onwisconsin/arts>>.

Muñoz, José Esteban. "Feeling Brown: Ethnicity and Affect in Ricardo Bracho's *The Sweetest Hangover (& Other STDs)." Theatre Journal* 52, no. 1 (2000): 67.

Denise Chávez

Born in 1948 in Las Cruces, New Mexico, Denise Chávez grew up swaddled in her mother's vibrant stories of family adventures along the U.S.–Mexico border. At an early age, Chávez found herself drawn to storytelling. As a young girl, to better understand her aches and pains—including confused feelings toward a largely absent father—she spent long hours in the library reading and writing fiction. In high school, while she continued to write stories, Chávez also found that theater worked well to transform her experiences into something memorable and engaging.

In 1967 Chávez pursued her passionate interest in drama and fiction writing more formally at the University of New Mexico, Las Cruces. In 1970, she produced her first one-act play, *The Wait;* its success opened a floodgate of other one-act plays, including *Elevators, The Flying Tortilla Man, The Mask of November,* and the play that put her in the national limelight, *Women in the State of Grace.* Chávez's plays are informed by her work with Edward Albee and by the Southwestern *santero* and *cuentista* traditions in which she grew up. Each one-act play closely follows a protagonist's psychological transformation and deep revelation within a larger sociopolitical context.

After working with Rudolfo A. Anaya at the University of New Mexico, Albuquerque, and receiving an M.F.A. from Trinity College, Chávez turned her focus more toward the writing of narrative fiction. In 1984, she finished writing a series of vibrantly visual short stories that followed the coming of age of a Chicana, Rocío. The stories were immediately picked up by Arte Público and published as *The Last of the Menu Girls.* This first "novel" (or short story cycle) became a word-of-mouth success, soon showing up on high school and college syllabi across the nation. The book's success fanned an interest in Chávez's writing, and New York literary agent Susan Bergholz helped Chávez achieve publication of her next novel, *Face of an Angel,* in 1994. In *Face of an Angel,* Chávez again explores the everyday struggles of a young Chicana living in a small Southwestern town dominated by patriarchal conventions. Her protagonist, Soveida Dosamantes, tries to eke out a space of empowerment for herself and her fellow waitresses in a small New Mexican town called Agua Oscura by turning to writing. Soveida writes a handbook, titled *The Book of Service,* which she hopes will empower her fellow women. In 2001, Chávez published *Loving Pedro Infante,* which solidified her recognition as a preeminent Chicana writer. In this book she again powerfully portrays the everyday lives of women struggling with passions, melancholia, and love within an often tense and conflictual U.S.–Mexico cultural borderland.

Like a *cuentista,* Chávez has a keen ear for rhythm, and her acute sense of visual detail engages readers, as an oral storyteller would enthrall listeners. To get just the right effect, Chávez spends a great deal of time sculpting, shaping, and refining her writing; sometimes she spends years on a novel. When she launches into a book project, she enters into a trance-like state—what she calls "the dark of the moon"—and then reemerges into the world once again after having given what she identifies as a "bloody birth."

Chávez has won many national awards, including the American Book Award, the Premio Aztlán, and awards from the National Endowment for the Arts, the Rockefeller Foundation, PEN USA West, and the Authors Guild. She continues to live and write in her native New Mexico, where she is also acting director of the Las Cruces book festival and the director of a program that takes writers to prisons and senior homes.

Frederick Luis Aldama: After you finished writing your first book, *Last of the Menu Girls,* why did you decide to publish with Arte Público Press and not one of the big East Coast publishers?

Denise Chávez: First, I was an unknown writer with nothing under my belt and no agent. Second, my creative writing mentor at the University of New Mexico, Rudolfo A. Anaya, suggested that I send the manuscript (my M.A. thesis) out to Arte Público for possible publication. They had already built up a strong list of Latino/a writers, so I sent it to Arte Público. I was incredibly surprised when the director, Nicolás Kanellos, accepted it for publication almost immediately. So that's where the book went.

Towards the end of the 1980s, I realized that I wanted more of a national audience. That's when I decided to pull away from Arte Público. I wanted a wider distribution, so I began to look at larger presses. This coincided with my introduction to Susan Bergholz (Sandra Cisneros's and Ana Castillo's agent) at a reading that Sandra and I did in New York. She agreed to look at my new manuscript. The rest, really, is history.

F.L.A.: Bergholz read *Face of an Angel*?

D.C.: Yes, it was an early version of *Face of an Angel*. By this time, I had several other agents interested in representing me, but I decided to put my faith in Susan. We ended up working on *Face of an Angel* for about seven and a half years. It was so big and so long, like an opera. (My latest, *Loving Pedro Infante,* is, I'd say, more of a chamber piece.) Susan got it placed with Farrar, Strauss, and Giroux. This is when I left Arte Público, who had been good to me in many ways in spite of all the contractual disputes.

F.L.A.: Arte Público has made visible many Chicano/a writers—Sandra Cisneros is a good example. Why, then, leave for bigger, East Coast publishers?

D.C.: Nicolás has helped a lot of Latino writers. It's not that you don't want to stay with a press like Arte Público, but you want to move and expand your wings. With Arte Público, it's almost as if you'd have to stay there and be loyal, or else you'd be unloyal and then have to suffer legal repercussions.

F.L.A.: Now that you've resecured the rights to *Last of the Menu Girls,* who are you going to give the reprint rights to?

D.C.: Well, I haven't decided where to place it. Right now, I'm reworking it and cleaning it up before I even consider sending it out again. I think it still has appeal. It's a coming of age of a young woman, Rocío, in the Southeast and her relationship especially to her mother. My hope is that in its new form, I can publish it as a new edition that will have a wide distribution and reach more people. [Published by Vintage, 2004.]

F.L.A.: On the back cover blurb, Rudolfo Anaya calls *Last of the Menu Girls* a "collage of stories," yet it reads like a coming-of-age novel.

D.C.: I myself do not quite know how to pinpoint some of the writing that I do. I think it could be read as a collage of stories. I have a theater background, and when I was composing the narrative, I thought of each chapter as a theatrical scene with certain movements. "Compadre" is almost like a cinema or theater piece. I have always thought of myself as a performance writer; I think that I've instilled in my writing certain theatrical elements. In chapter five, there are two people talking at the same time; if you read theater, this is a dramatic device used in theater. This, of course, confounds people that are used to a traditional A-to-B, B-to-C kind of fiction that moves in a certain way and has a certain kind of movement and direction. And I also wrote a number of chapters that appear as just voices. They could be lifted literally onto the stage and done as dialogue. So I always feel that my work is very theatrical. And I'd like to think that people read it out loud because I work in a deeply auditory kind of way: I listen to the voices, then play the voices back. If I'm having trouble with a section of a narrative, I'll tape it and play it back to myself. I read it out loud; I'll wander around; I'll meander through this fictional room I've created with mirrors. Some have said that I work in the same manner as Charles Dickens—he also had a lot of mirrors around his studio, and he would prance and dance with his characters.

For me, the characters I invent have to come to life and be in the room in their totality. So, yes, I could see how you might read it as a novel, but you could also read it, like I do, as a theatrical poem.

F.L.A.: You mentioned your theater background as central to your crafting of narrative fiction. Do you still tour your one-woman performances?

D.C.: Oh, I do it from time to time. The last time I did it was in San Antonio with a performance called *Women in the State of Grace*. This performance is based around women characters—from an abused child to an 85-year-old woman in a nursing home. I called the piece *Women in the State of Grace* because I wanted to explore—as I do in all my work—this idea of what it means to exist in a state of grace—in balance with yourself and God and other human beings. So, all of my down-and-out characters are trying to find their balance—their state of grace.

I also create a number of dramatic male characters, as in my play *Santa Fe Charm*. There's the philosopher, Benito Serra, who sits on his little park bench and talks about *la vida*. Then there's the disabled paperboy character, who is 50 years old and yet who sees the world through the eyes of a child.

I don't think there is a division between my theater work and my narrative fiction. So if I wanted to put those characters from *Loving Pedro Infante,* like Theresina Avelard or Irma, into my theater, then I'd simply take certain scenes and workshop them. I see myself as a fictional playwright as well as a playwright who happens to write fiction. This cross-pollinating process is all about one genre spilling over into the other—about rewriting, restructuring, and improvising as I conceive of the process of writing fiction and dramatic performance. It is all about performance: either in prose narrative form or on the stage.

F.L.A.: In *Loving Pedro Infante,* you throw curve balls, characters who speak lines that revise preconceptions of gender.

D.C.: I don't think we do enough as women and as men, and I like to talk about the beauty of the form and the physicalness of Pedro and other men. I like to jolt people. I like to make my readers pause. I like to have the movement in the paragraph. I really pay attention to the endings of paragraphs, like Gertrude Stein. She said the paragraph had great power. I pay attention to that, very carefully. I think this has also been helped by my theater background: the pause, the comic timing, the delivery of a line that flips a preconception over on itself. I work to have this kind of movement within the paragraph that takes my readers for a tumble into some other time and place.

F.L.A.: Men are present in your novels and plays, but aren't women the real focus?

D.C.: Yes, I'm primarily interested in female characters. You know, I come from a very repressed background. My mother was a single parent. She worked as a teacher for forty-two years. Her husband left her. My dad left us when I was ten years old. I had a grandmother that was so embarrassed about her body that she wasn't able to tell the doctor that she really needed to be sewn up after she gave birth; she was so afraid to go to a male doctor because he would see her naked. So she continued to bleed. She died screaming of pain from having developed cancer of the cervix because she was too embarrassed to say, "I'm in trouble. Help me. I'm a woman." So, for me, writing fiction is that place where I can give voice to these women. Who is writing among the Latino writers about sexuality and the abuse that women have to go through and this kind of legacy of cyclical violence and oppression we endure? How can we begin to change patterns, to be aware that, yes, I can go to the gynecologist? Who's going to write the story of my mother's legs? Or my mother's breasts? And my mother's body that was a battleground? My characters come out of such a place—out of such a need to give voice to such experiences.

If Latina authors can't write about our mothers and our experiences as women, who's going to do it? Who's going to talk for those legs and those breasts and those bodies? That's what I say. Who's talking for those people? Somebody has to speak. But it's uncomfortable for people sometimes to read this stuff. I've had men tell me, "If I did not have to read this book in Chicano literature class, I would have never read it. Aren't there any good men out there?" People have asked me, "Can't you write about any good men?" I said, "Well, there are a lot of good men out there. I happen to have grown up in an environment where everybody in my family was alcoholic. What do you want me to write about? What do you want me to write about? Do you want me to show you a perfect world?" I am a writer, so if I want to, I have the freedom to introduce more male characters in future projects. That's what's so beautiful about being a writer. You can change direction, theme, and character focus at will. Of course, your loyal readers might be disappointed, but that's okay.

F.L.A.: Ana Castillo identifies a *Xicanisma* sensibility to counter the presence of a machismo in Chicano culture. Do your characters fit within this model?

D.C.: Yes, I celebrate and affirm a Chicana spirit, but I think that I have a different view of machismo; at least, I think that I turn it into something else in my novels. In the dictionary, to be a *macho* in Mexico is to be a responsible, loyal person that takes care of his family. Yet, look at what people have turned machismo into. And, you know, women can have this positive macho quality. I once wrote that my mom was *la macha grande* because the first macho that I knew was my mother. This isn't to say that I don't respect Ana Castillo; she's been such a great leader, stepping forward and envisioning a bold new world, linguistically and imagistically. My God, look what she's done.

F.L.A.: As they grow into women, characters like Soveida and Rocío feel restricted by their bodies?

D.C.: Right. It's horrible to grow into the body of a woman with your male cousins taunting you about your body. I feel that my major contribution as a writer is to write characters—especially Latinas—that live and breathe, to give them voices to speak as loud and as clear as I possibly can.

F.L.A.: You mentioned this fluid process where you move back and forth between drama and narrative fiction. Can you return to this concept?

D.C.: Well, it's all about fine-tuning, refining, and crafting art. To me, it's like a sculpture. You start out with the raw material and you take away, you chip, you add and refine the features. It's also like painting, "Do I need blue in that corner?" When I was writing *Last of the Menu Girls,* I realized, after I wrote the last three chronological chapters of the book, that they were not to be the final chapters. There were whole chunks of my painting missing. The color wasn't in the corner. So I painted that in at the very last minute. That's why it takes me so long to write a novel.

I'm fearless when it comes to writing. I can write chapter 1 to chapter 10 without a blink of an eye. It is after the writing that I sculpt and texture. This is the laborious part of the writing process for me. Sometimes, too, I work like a psychic surgeon, entering into the body of the text to laser excise a chapter, say, at the end, and put it at the beginning. Or, you might in the refining of the narrative decide that a character isn't going to die, as in *Face of an Angel.* During the six plus years that I worked on that novel, I imagined the character dying. Then, when I was nearly finished, she refused to die. So you surprise yourself in this process of sculpting narrative. Finally, in this process, I transformed a darker, more bitter version of *Face,* what I call my espresso version, into something a little lighter, my caffe latte version.

It's like living in a city or a town: it takes you a while to know the highways and the byways and the place that you want to come and have coffee or where you take your laundry. A novel is like that. You have to live and inhabit that world for a while, then begin to engage with it in a process of continual change: you change and the place changes in this never-ending process. Of course, in fiction you come to a point where you just have to stop and lay down your pen. Even after my novels are published, I still feel that they aren't entirely finished sculptures.

F.L.A.: Perhaps this is why the ending to your novels read as if they are new beginnings? I think of the family celebration at the end of *Last of the Menu Girls,* in particular.

D.C.: Yes, let's face it, Rocío experienced a process of deracination—she cuts herself off from *familia*—that is finally resolved at the end, which is really a new beginning for her, when she embraces her culture in that breaking of the bread with the tamales. It's like spring is coming. You turn over the land so you can plant the new crop, I suppose.

As far as *Loving Pedro Infante,* yes, there is also a sense of new beginnings at the novel's close. There's both a cyclical nature and a breaking of cycles in this novel—a process of embracing and discarding old tradition and patterns that are detrimental to one's health and spirit. I was also exploring the nature of love: friendship and romantic. This cycle, too, of people that you think you love—those phantom lovers—somehow coming into, then disappearing like a haze back out of, your life. My characters also begin to see with clarity those fogs of deception. Like Irma in *Pedro Infante:* she begins to see her supposed friends as they really are. So, while my books are mostly love stories—whether to yourself or to the land or to those people that really matter—they work in these cycles of death and regeneration—beginnings in endings.

F.L.A.: Not only are there friendships and romances in your novels, but all of your characters are survivors: Rocío, Soveida, and Irma, to name a few. How does community help or hinder them in their everyday survival?

D.C.: Yes, a large part of the romance is about surviving and making community. I ask, is it sadder to love somebody that doesn't love you, or is it sadder to be loved by somebody that you can never love? These are some of the questions I explore in my novels, especially in *Loving Pedro Infante,* that's fundamentally a story about adulation. The Mexican heartthrob, Pedro Infante, was a wonderful vehicle to explore the illusion of loving and that kind of adulation. Pedro was beautiful; he was the embodiment of male beauty. And I don't think we talk about male beauty enough. Women don't talk about that, and men feel uncomfortable with it. So to talk about desire and obsession are topics that a lot of people, especially in the Chicano community, still feel very uncomfortable with. And it's been very interesting to work through that.

F.L.A.: At one point in *Face of an Angel,* you suggest that the body is the place that carries memories the longest.

D.C.: Our bodies have markings of experience—the time you broke your leg, say, or when your shoulder was dislocated, that time when I stabbed myself with a pencil. Each marking recalls a situation, event, activity; and I think that we need to acknowledge these. But I don't think we need to dwell on these markings; of course, it's harder for some than others to move on. People that are sexually abused or have alcoholic parents have a difficult time moving from that place. Those that by choice or force linger in the pain—in their markings—are the type of characters that I'm interested in. Soveida's a good example of such a character. Sometimes, moving on means finding that place where you can forgive and accept. I'm interested in how such characters experience grand transformation and change.

Life is change. You have to change, or else you're going to get stuck there. You're going to get mired down in the fact that your father was an alcoholic and I hated him. Come on. He's not here. He's been dead for forty years. What are you going to do? Are you gonna still be stuck there? And so you become an alcoholic. And my father beat me with the whip. Okay, does that mean you have to do it to your own child? When are we going to start breaking those legacies of pain that were given to us by people who were injured by other people who had a cycle of pain because my grandmother was a cold person? Does that mean that I have to be?

Face of an Angel is largely about getting at the pain and trauma that marks the body and psyche. That's why it's such a *hard* book to read. I ended up writing sixty very short, tight, little kernel-like chapters because the reader just can't take much more than that.

F.L.A.: Your novels gravitate around mother-daughter relationships, like Rocío's mother, who helps her recover after a nervous breakdown by making her tacos.

D.C.: The tacos hold Rocío together. They represent, in a sense, the family, the mother's hands making the tortilla to hold you together. You know, with these characters I want to get at the question, what keeps us together? What are those beliefs that keep us together? Who are the people that keep us grounded and together? There are those people who are like mountains in our lives that are solid, and no matter what happens to us, the mountain is there. Without these figures, who are we? What is it that binds us to the earth? What is it that keeps us going forward when everything seems to dissipate and dissolve? Well, I think these are the issues I explore in my fiction.

F.L.A.: Can you speak about some of your influences as a writer?

D.C.: Remember that I have a theatrical background, so I would go to some of the masters of theater: Aeschylus, Sophocles, and Euripides, for example. I read all of those plays. I love those plays. *Loving Pedro Infante* comes out of the tradition of the Greeks—the popular plays that engaged the imagination of a huge audience of all different types of people. Kind of like in Mexico, when all different walks of life would go to the movies in the '30s, '40s, and '50s. Movies were subsidized by the Mexican government, so it was really a popular culture experience, in the same spirit and tradition as Aeschylus and Euripides. I am also greatly influenced by Restoration comedy, Shakespeare—you name it, I've read it all. The Russian writers have been a great influence. . . .

F.L.A.: Chekhov?

D.C.: Yes, Chekhov has been a great teacher. I model my writing after Chekhov, not only in the development of characterization in his short stories, but also plays like *Uncle Vanya* and the *Cherry Orchard*—plays that at one point in my life I even acted in.

F.L.A.: Perhaps García Lorca's plays also had an influence?

D.C.: Yes, the beauty, the magic, the passion of García Lorca. He's an incredible playwright. I also acted in some of his plays in college and in graduate school. I played the bride back then, but I think I've moved on from the bride. Now, I think I'm ready to play the role of *la mama* that I couldn't have done persuasively before.

There were other great influences, like Lillian Hellman—now there's a woman who's got guts; she can tell it like it is. Her play *The Little Foxes*, was like a breath of fresh air. And Ayn Rand's *Atlas Shrugged* was another big door that opened wide for me different worlds and ways to express these worlds.

But finally, the greatest influence was my mother. So when people expect me to say that my greatest influence is someone like Pablo Neruda or someone, I have to say, excuse me, but I didn't read him till I was in college. The biggest was my mother, who kicked ass.

While my mother wasn't much of a writer when I was growing up—she became more of a poet in her later years—she was just an incredibly strong, forceful woman who allowed us to dream dreams and let us know that we could do anything we wanted to do. She was also a great reader and encouraged us to read. It helped that my aunt had an incredible library in West Texas. It was so damned hot that we'd read during the day and sleep outside on these little cots behind the family's grocery store. So in a way my mythological and my mythic characters were not any of the writers. My own family and their stories rivaled anything that I would have ever seen in any fiction.

My mother's own life was a piece of fiction. Her first husband was accidentally poisoned by a druggist. He was given the wrong prescription. He died across the courtyard from her, three days after my half-sister was born. Who needs fiction with this? And then she was mourning for nine years, dressed in black. This was a woman who lived it all: a schoolteacher in a little, small mining town in West Texas whose husband was poisoned. I mean, who needed fiction?

F.L.A.: Your family has deep roots in New Mexico?

D.C.: My dad is originally from Socorro, born in what is called "Little Mexico." But my mother's from West Texas. I consider myself a Mexicana/Tejana. West Texas is a wild place—a spirit-filled world that combines the dark and the light, the yin and the yang. If I hadn't grown up in this place that is a blend of Mexico and the U.S., a blend of the light and the dark, and that's full of spirits and energy, I would be nothing as a writer. I would surely be a lost person.

F.L.A.: Would you consider yourself a border writer?

D.C.: Yes, and I do consider myself a border writer. In fact, I'm working on a novel right now that I set in a small town on the border between Mexico, Arizona, and Texas; my towns are usually small because they want to get bigger—like my protagonists. My protagonist is a 64-year-old immigration officer on the brink of retirement, and of course it's a love story. It's the book that I've always wanted to write.

F.L.A.: You set your novels in the everyday and not in some mystical never-never land. In *Loving Pedro Infante,* you mention Stephen King novels, the Dr. Atkins diet, and so on, along with your invention of Chicana characters with roots in Chicano cultural traditions.

D.C.: I love popular culture. There's a place for all of that in my fictions. That's why I make room in my novels for Elvis and Pedro Infante impersonators. It's also a way of complicating stereotypes that Chicanos/as are somehow not a part of mainstream popular culture—in fact, to take stereotypes and twist the image around to complicate how we are represented. I'm not afraid to go there. I'm not afraid to admit that I had a subscription to the *National Enquirer* for six years. And, I admit, I'm a big Jerry Springer fan. See, I think that's part of being a writer: to not be squeamish about life, and that includes popular culture. I'm willing to look at things that people aren't willing to, and that's what the writer does. We are willing and able and unafraid and, without trepidation, able to look at things very deeply, and I don't care what it is—the pleasant, the unpleasant, the ecstatic, the divine. I look around and record all the things that fill up my world. Certain people and events stand out. Later, when I write and want that quick phrase, that jingle, or to jar the reader, I turn to these moments—these memory markers. Popular culture is a great resource to build up a store of memory markers that later help create big narrative pictures.

F.L.A.: In your novels, much learning and teaching takes place, not in the, say, high-brow arena of higher education, but within the everyday—popular culture, the kitchen, and other places.

D.C.: Well, I think you are so sensitive to have picked up that. Teaching goes on everywhere in life: a mother teaching her child how to roll tacos—"You want to have the dark side in, so that the tacos look really nice on the outside"—is a form of cultural learning and intergenerational exchange.

I think, too, that my characters, in their acts of teaching and learning, are preservers. They're keepers of our tradition and culture, just as my novels educate and preserve tradition. I also think that my novels open the door for others to understand our culture. (You know, my editor did not know what a *piñata* was when I started working on *Loving Pedro Infante*.) Maybe you've never been there before. Maybe you don't know what it is to dance salsa or to eat the food that you're going to eat, but hey, go in there with your heart open, your eyes open, to enjoy and to learn. And that's what I want my books to be.

F.L.A.: Have your books been translated and published in Mexico?

D.C.: As we speak, *Loving Pedro Infante* is being translated in Spanish to be sold in Mexico. We'll see how it flies there. Aye, I hope some of Pedro's Infante's fans and family don't come after me. I'd love to travel in Mexico and read it *en español*. *Face of an Angel* has been translated into German; it's called *The Lost Year,* I think. The translation of this novel must have been a real feat, with all of its *caló* and its different story lines.

F.L.A.: Your books have traveled as far afield as Germany. Have Chicano/a writers finally crossed over into the mainstream?

D.C.: I think that we still have a long way to go. We still need more translators from the Southwest (and not New York City and Miami) to translate our work, and we need more diversity across the board: more Latino editors and writers. I look with longing for that Vietnamese Mexicano novel that's going to come out of East L.A. I can hardly wait for that. And I look forward to all of those people that are coming out of Des Moines, Iowa, and Los Angeles, and Chicago. I think it's a very exciting time to be a Latino writer—not only a Latino, but a multicultural woman writer from the Southwest. I'm just a wave. I'm just a wave in the ocean. It's going to be great. It's a very interesting time, for women writers. The power of Latino literature right now is that we are writing with voices that are fresh, passionate, and energetic. We are writing stories that matter.

F.L.A.: As a Tejana/Mexicana Latina who has "made it" as a writer, what might you advise the next generation of Latino writers?

D.C.: To write as honestly as possible, not to hold back, to let it go, to look at your past to see your future. To look at your ancestral demons very closely, then put them to rest. Stand firm because life is going to ram at you. It's going to present you with quite an adventure. Write with honesty and integrity.

Writings by the Author
Novels

The Last of the Menu Girls. Houston: Arte Público, 1986. Reprint, New York: Vintage, 2004.
Face of an Angel. New York: Farrar, Straus, 1994.
Loving Pedro Infante. New York: Farrar, Straus and Giroux, 2001.

Children's Literature

The Woman Who Knew the Language of Animals. Boston: Houghton Mifflin, 1992.

Further Readings
Critical Studies

Castillo, Debra A. "The Daily Shape of Horses: Denise Chávez and Maxine Hong Kingston." *Dispositio: Revista Americana de estudios comparados y culturales* 12, no. 41 (1991): 29–43.

Chávez, Denise. "Novena narrativas y ofrendas nuevomexicanas." *The Americas Review* 15, nos. 3–4 (1987): 85–100.

———. "Poems." *The Americas Review* 15, nos. 3–4 (1987): 65–83.

Davis-Undaino, Robert. "Denise Chávez." *Hispanic* 14, no. 4 (April 2001): 88.

Delgadillo, Theresa. "Denise Chávez, *Face of an Angel.*" In *Reading U.S. Latina Writers,* edited by Alvina E. Quintana, pp. 37–50. New York: Palgrave Macmillan, 2003.

Galehouse, Maggie. "Macha Woman." *New York Times Book Review* 106, no. 19 (May 13, 2001): 17.

Ganz, Robin. "Sandra Cisneros: Border Crossings and Beyond." *MELUS,* Special Issue: Varieties of Ethnic Criticism 19, no. 1 (1994): 19–30.

Heard, Martha E. "The Theatre of Denise Chávez: Interior Landscapes with 'Sabor Nuevomexicano.'" *The Americas Review* 16, no. 2 (1988): 83–91.

Kester-Shelton, Pamela, ed. "Denise Chávez." *Feminist Writers,* pp. 194–196. Detroit: St. James Press, 1996.

Lanza, Carmela Delia. "Loving the Mother: Feminine Spiritual Spaces in the Writings of Ana Castillo, Denise Chávez, Tina DeRosa, and Carole Maso." Ph.D. dissertation, University of New Mexico, 2001.

Lopez, Adriana. "Chávez Hunts for Translator for Her Book, *Loving Pedro Infante.*" *Library Journal* 126, no. 13 (August 2001): 7.

Rivera, Rowena A. "Denise Chávez." *Dictionary of Literary Biography,* Vol. 122, *Chicano Writers,* pp. 70–76. Detroit: Gale Group, 1992.

Saldívar, José David, and Rolando Hinojosa, eds. *Criticism in the Borderlands: Studies in Chicano Literature, Culture, and Ideology.* Durham: Duke University Press, 1991.

Reviews

Gagnier, Regenia. Rev. of *The Last of the Menu Girls. Feminist Studies* 17, no. 1 (1991): 135–149.

Nericcio, William. Rev. of *Face of an Angel. World Literature Today* 69, no. 4 (1995): 792.

Ott, Bill. Rev. of *Loving Pedro Infante*. *Booklist* 97, no. 16 (April 15, 2001): 1532.

Slade, Tomelene. Rev. of *The Last of the Menu Girls*. *School Library Journal* 38, no. 12 (December 1992): 35.

Interviews

Balassi, William, John F. Crawford, and Annie O. Eysturoy, eds. *This Is about Vision: Interviews with Southwestern Writers*. Albuquerque: University of New Mexico Press, 1990.

Clark, William. "Denise Chávez: 'It's All One Language Here.'" *Publishers Weekly* 241, no. 33 (August 15, 1994): 77–80.

Ikas, Karin Rosa. "Denise Chávez." In *Chicana Ways: Conversations with Ten Chicana Writers*, pp. 45–64. Reno: University of Nevada Press, 2002.

Kevane, Bridget, and Juanita Heredia. "The Spirit of Humor." In *Latina Self-Portraits: Interviews with Contemporary Women Writers*, pp. 33–44. Albuquerque: University of New Mexico Press, 2000.

Mehaffy, Marilyn, and AnaLouise Keating. "'Carrying the Message': Denise Chávez on the Politics of Chicana Becoming." *Aztlán* 26, no. 1 (2001): 127–157.

Lucha Corpi

Born in 1945 in Jáltipan, Mexico, Lucha Corpi grew up in a small town enveloped by rich tropical sounds. As a child she heard more than the noises of birds and animals: she heard the syncopated rhythms of people speaking Zapotec and Spanish. She was especially attentive to her grandmother's voice as she would recount stories to young Corpi (along with her eight siblings) of grand adventures and bygone eras.

Before becoming a writer, Corpi trained variously to become a concert pianist, a dentist, and a teacher. Playing the piano was her great passion, but just before she was to enter Mexico City's famous music conservatory, her father strong-armed her into studying dentistry. In defiance, Corpi not only stopped playing the piano (the sounds of which her father greatly enjoyed) but also took the first opportunity to distance herself from her father's reach. In 1964, she married a man who was on his way to study at the University of California, Berkeley. By the early 1970s, she realized that she wanted more than to be a housewife. She divorced her husband, enrolled at Berkeley for a bachelor's degree in comparative literature, and began to write poetry. To make ends meet and help support her daughter as a single mother, she also began teaching English as a Second Language.

Poetry became an important creative outlet for Corpi. It was through poetry that she was able to understand better the tensions between being raised a Mexican Catholic, with rigidly defined gender roles, and working as an educated, single mother in the United States. In 1976, Corpi published her first poems in a collection titled *Fireflight*. She wrote in Spanish and used a formal, short-line verse to express the deep conflicts and emotion she felt as a Latina—unable to identify culturally as Mexican or American, and facing racism and sexism in her everyday life. Her subsequent publication, *Palabras de mediodía: Noon Words,* put her on the literary map both in the United States and in Mexico. Here, for example, Corpi complicates the image of Malintzen, viewing her not as a traitor of the indigenous peoples, but as a complex female figure within Mexican legend and history: "Once, you stopped to wonder / where her soul was hidden, / not knowing she had planted it / in the entrails of that earth / her hands had cultivated— / the moist, black earth of your life" ("Marina Virgen," 121). Her early poetry inspired many Chicana feminist authors, including Cherríe Moraga, Ana Castillo, Norma Alarcón, and Gloria Anzaldúa.

By the end of the 1980s, Corpi's journey as a feminist Latina poet had brought her to a crossroads, and she chose a new direction to travel. Encouraged by editor Nicolás Kanellos at Arte Público Press, Corpi wrote and published her first autobiographical novel, *Delia's Song* (1989). In it, Corpi experiments with narrative voice and storytelling form to tell the story of Delia Trevino's journey from being caught in the web of domestic life to becoming an empowered author of fiction. *Delia's Song* not only put Corpi on the literary map as a gifted novelist but also whetted her appetite for more. Turning to the mystery/detective genre, in 1992 she published *Eulogy for a Brown Angel,* introducing her readers to a political activist Chicana detective, Gloria Damasco. This Chicana detective would reappear in *Cactus Blood* (1995) and *Black Widow's Wardrobe* (1999), sleuthing out murders and cases of social injustice. She has recently embarked on the writing of children's books, publishing the well-received *Where Fireflies Dance,* which colorfully revisits her childhood in Jáltipan, Mexico.

Frederick Luis Aldama: When did you first begin to become aware of language and its power to communicate?

Lucha Corpi: I grew up in an environment rich with language, community, and communication. When I was little, my grandmother would speak in Spanish and some Náhuatl, which she called Mexican. She also understood and spoke some Zapotec. I remember being fascinated by the language because it was so rhythmic; I didn't understand a word, but it was so musical-sounding. And my father loved to recite poetry and listen to music of all kinds. There was poetry everywhere in Veracruz. The local newspaper was filled with politics, stories, myths, and legends. Improvisation and poetic rhythm was in the air we breathed. On the streets, a verse would roll off one man's tongue and another man would respond in verse to try to one-up him.

F.L.A.: When did you begin to write creatively?

L.C.: I was in the third grade, and because I already knew how to read and write well, my teacher decided to give me a challenge. One day, she decided to teach me how to recite poetry. So I began to memorize, then recite, the lines in a certain way, which later my music teacher told me was called "phrasing." I was also taught how to use all kinds of gestures to move patriotic poems along. Because my father objected to my reciting only patriotic poetry, my teacher began to teach me other kinds of poetry. From then on, I developed a deep love for poetry—even though it would take twenty-four years before I would begin writing my own poetry.

As far as my interest in writing crime novels, it goes back to when I was seven or eight years old. My father, a self-taught man who worked for the National Telegraph Company, would ask me to read him any part of the newspaper except the crime page; he had very poor vision and needed a couple of cornea transplants. This sparked my curiosity. So, even though he would hide the crime page from me, I would always find it and read it on my own. Though I didn't understand many of the details, crime stories have always intrigued me.

When I was much older and a single mother living in Berkeley, I began to write poetry. I wrote poetry with the same intensity that I had when studying and playing the piano as a teenager. In fact, my training in music seemed to complement my poetry writing. After years of writing poetry, I turned to the novel form. Unlike poetry, I realized, writing novels required long-distance endurance. You just have to go on and on, and it doesn't seem to finish until you put the final period in. You beg, you pray that it will be over soon. And then, when it's over, you cry.

F.L.A.: You lived in Berkeley during the free speech and civil rights movements of the late 1960s?

L.C.: Yes, this experience was in and of itself an education. It was during this period that I rediscovered—largely via my husband's interest in literature and philosophy—the joy of reading. That I could never become a dentist, as my father wanted, was confirmed. We are born to do something in this world. In some way, I had to travel north to Berkeley—to leave the place where I was born, my culture, my community in Mexico—to find my reason for being in the world. Berkeley was the first big step in this journey to become a writer.

F.L.A.: At Berkeley, you studied for a degree in comparative literature. Was it during this period that you began to more formally study and write poetry?

L.C.: I never took creative writing classes. In fact, to this day, I have never taken a workshop. Towards the end of the 1960s, I began to write poetry more formally, as a way for me to express my feelings; having just divorced my husband, it was a way for me to talk about my feelings and work out emotional contradictions to an audience outside of myself. I was a young mother with a two-and-a-half–year-old, coming to terms with my Catholic Mexican heritage while living in the U.S. as a Latina. I turned to poetry as a way to work through these conflicts and to find strength to persevere. However, a formal instruction in literary criticism taught me how to be my own editor—quite essential for a writer to have.

F.L.A.: Did you feel as if you were living in exile?

L.C.: It was exactly like being in exile. I was in a strange land and yearning for more than just a domestic family life for myself; I wanted to do something with my life but knew that this would go against everything I'd been told to believe. I was angry at my Mexican heritage, yet I was still very drawn to it. After my father died in 1971, and I worked through the pain and grief of his loss, I felt as if something had opened up for me. Suddenly, it seemed as if I couldn't stop the poetry from flowing. Out of this period I wrote what would become the much-anthologized poems "The Marina Poems."

After "The Marina Poems," I kept writing one poem after another, sustaining this writing habit for ten years. It verged on the manic. I truly felt at the time that if I stopped writing poetry, I would just stop living. I wrote from ten o'clock at night to about midnight every day during this period. That's when I finally said, perhaps I am a poet.

So, living in so-called exile cleared that space for me to transform the personal into something bigger and to find my voice as a poet. It was a pause in the grand journey when my experiences and my feelings clicked into place and I found an electrically charged poetic voice. I then spent years learning to harness and nurse this raw energy. This included learning to heal myself and face my fears.

F.L.A.: You wrote your poetry in Spanish?

L.C.: Yes, I was writing in Spanish. I think I will always write poetry in Spanish. I have written a couple of poems in English, but I prefer Spanish. For me, the language of poetry is the language you learn at home. It's the language you use to express your emotions. It's what you've been taught, what you learn since you're a child. So that language for me is Spanish. When I'm moved, when something really touches me very deeply, it's the language that first comes to mind. I write my fiction in English, the language I dream in.

F.L.A.: As a poet and novelist, you have had to make a living as a teacher?

L.C.: I've been a public school teacher now for nearly thirty years. I started teaching for the Oakland public schools in the years between getting my B.A. from Berkeley and an M.A. from San Francisco State. I needed a job. I had a child to support, so I accepted this teaching position for $10 an hour, which was a lot of money for me at the time. I had no idea what I was walking into. I was teaching mostly Latino adults, who lived in Oakland, just about everything: from sewing and English grammar to teaching poetry and letter writing in Spanish. After a month, I realized that not only did I like the challenge of teaching, but also it was a place that offered refuge from a chaotic world. When the door shut to the classroom, whatever problems I had in my own personal life were shut out. I became totally absorbed in teaching.

F.L.A.: Can you talk about your transition from poetry to the writing of novels?

L.C.: As I mentioned, during a ten-year period, I wrote poetry without a break. And then one day I couldn't write any more poetry. I tried and nothing would come. During this period when I couldn't write, I developed an ulcer. This writer's block lasted two years. It was a painful period for me. In search of answers, I started reading writers like Virginia Woolf and Kate Chopin and other feminist writers. Their prose inspired me to write narrative fiction. And by the mid-1980s I began writing short stories in Spanish that were published in Mexico and won some prizes. Inspired by a dream I had in English, I wrote my first story in English, called "Shadows on Ebbing Water." I sent it to the Chicano literary contest at Irvine, where it won first place.

Winning the Irvine contest didn't mean much to me. I had no intention of staying with fiction. In fact, I considered writing short stories only as a push through my writer's block to return once again to my poetry. I did go back to poetry after those first couple of stories, writing the poems that made up my second collection, *Variaciones sobre una tempestad / Variations on a Storm.* But I must have been bitten by the fiction bug because I found myself suddenly writing and rewriting the story of a young woman living in Berkeley in 1968. The story grew and grew. Like a little bonsai, I would cut and trim, and then it would grow some more. I wasn't sure I was ready to write a novel. I was still somewhat timid as a writer in English, but I knew that I owed it to the characters to finish the story.

F.L.A.: This shaped into your experimental novel, *Delia's Song*?

L.C.: Yes, and as you know, it's filled with soliloquies, extended interior monologues, and surreal scenes. Of course, in the mystery novels that I write now I don't play as much with technique because I'm working within a different genre.

F.L.A.: Was James Joyce an influence when writing *Delia's Song*?

L.C.: Yes, Joyce provided a model for the form of *Delia's Song*, providing the guide for me to better understand how to give it shape and texture. After all, you need an Irishman to wake up the English language.

F.L.A.: Was it difficult to publish *Delia's Song*?

L.C.: At first I wasn't sure I wanted to publish it. I met up with the director of Arte Público Press, Nicolás Kanellos, at a conference in Boston, and he asked me if I'd been writing more poetry. I told him that I had just finished a novel. He insisted that I send it to him for his opinion. So I sent it to him. And then, months later, he told me, "I think we can publish this book." I said, "But I need an editor." "No, no, no. It's fine." And so it was published.

I think if I rewrote *Delia's Song* with what I now know about the craft, it would be a much better novel. It's now out of print. So I have all the rights, but I don't intend to publish it again until I have a chance to rework it again.

F.L.A.: After *Delia's Song,* you made the shift to the mystery/detective novel?

L.C.: It's all because of that crime page (the "red page") that I mentioned earlier that my father tried to keep me from reading. That's when I fell in love with the mystery story. That's when it all began. Later, as a teenager, I loved reading the Conan Doyle series. I've always been drawn to mystery stories, and ever since I can remember, I've wanted to write them. So, after *Delia's Song*—really an apprenticeship in character development—I started writing my first mystery novel, *Eulogy for a Brown Angel*. Even before I finished it, I felt that I had fulfilled my dream of writing a mystery.

F.L.A.: You chose to stay with Arte Público when publishing *Eulogy for a Brown Angel*. Is this partly because Chicano mysteries aren't that commercial?

L.C.: I chose Arte Público for two reasons: first, because I feel that no matter what else we do we have to somehow support our institutions. They've always been there for me—right from the beginning. And so now I'm giving back. Second, because I want my books to live long after I'm gone, and Arte Público is dedicated to making sure Latino writers continue to be read.

F.L.A.: Tell me more about your influences—especially regarding your mystery series?

L.C.: Certainly Gloria Damasco is not the first Chicana detective in American literature. The first one was written by Marcia Muller, a detective fiction writer in Santa Barbara whose protagonist is a Chicana. And there's the San Francisco–based writer Gloria White (her mother's Puerto Rican), whose detective is of Mexican ancestry. Perhaps people refer to Gloria Damasco as the first Chicana detective in American fiction because she is so deeply grounded in Chicano culture and politics.

F.L.A.: You're working on a new novel. Is this part of the Gloria Damasco series?

L.C.: Well, it's not a series anymore. The series pretty much finished with the third novel, *Black Widow's Wardrobe*. I want to constantly challenge myself, so I decided to stop the series with *Black Widow's*. I can't truly say that I won't write another Gloria Damasco mystery. I'm sure that if she comes calling in the middle of the night with a new adventure, I will surely listen to what she has to say. But now I'm writing a novel set in Berkeley, Oakland, and Denver during the Black Panther Party and Chicano civil rights era in the Bay Area and Denver. It is told from the different perspectives of two different detectives. They're all trying to solve the same mystery, but they don't know it. Each point of view has to be handled in every chapter; then it finally pushes through at the point when they all realize they're working on the same case. This novel, *Crimson Moon,* is scheduled for release in March 2004, also by Arte Público Press in Houston.

F.L.A.: In 1997, you published *Where Fireflies Dance* with Children's Book Press. Can you talk about this a little?

L.C.: Just as I'd decided that I wanted my work to live long after I die, and to be a Latina writer known for making a difference, so, too, I decided to write children's literature. It's also an act of making sure that cultural knowledge is passed down to the next generation. Interestingly, I get more royalty from my children's book than I get from all my novels put together. So it's worked out pretty well in that respect. Of course, I still have to work as a teacher to make a living. I could never live off my royalties.

F.L.A.: This same year you also edited a collection of personal essays by Latina writers like Cecile Pineda, titled *Máscaras,* with Third Woman Press. Do you think it's getting better for Latinas to publish in this country?

L.C.: Oh, absolutely. Yes, more and more. Not long ago, there were only two or three writers that were really visible, like Sandra Cisneros, Ana Castillo, and Julia Alvarez. Now you see more and more Latina writers being published by mainstream presses. I have to say, though, while more of us fiction writers are being published, there is still a gaping hole in the Latina poetry scene.

F.L.A.: Have you ever felt that Chicana writers have formed a members-only club?

L.C.: I suppose I've never paid much attention to this clique. I accept all Latina writers wholeheartedly. I accept myself as one. My political affiliations definitely qualify me. So for me there is no question I belong, yet sometimes I also feel as if I'm on the margins of everything. I write poetry in Spanish. I write Chicano mysteries in English. I identify as neither Mexican nor American. I suppose the most important challenge for me, and the reason why I don't think too much about this members-only club, is that I'm mostly interested in challenging myself as a writer. That's why I try new genres and experiment with technique. You can educate your readers about racial injustices in the themes and characters you portray, but ultimately, for me, the novel has to be a good read, so I don't follow any set agenda—political or otherwise.

F.L.A.: What genre do you feel most at home in?

L.C.: Poetry. That's my home; that's my voice. That's what I was born to write. We've been too long apart and now it's time to go back to it. But poetry is very elusive. It's a very jealous lover. That's why I think the very best poets are only poets, like Neruda. In fiction, the story takes you from day to day. It carries you. No matter how tired you are or what interruptions you might have in your life, once you start, and you get enough quiet time, you can always go back to the story.

There are some great Chicano poets, like Francisco Alarcón. But there are those like Gary Soto whom I stopped reading long ago because his poetry lately seems to lack substance and has become somewhat formulaic. Mostly, I find today's poetry to be a rehash of what's already been said before. I recently read Sarah Cortez's *How to Undress a Cop,* and I was quite moved by her terse, gritty poetry. But most other poets' works I've read lately lack substance; the Mexico City poets writing in Spanish are too abstract and dense to enjoy. We're at a point where I feel that most poets have lost that sense of discovery, that sense of being vulnerable. There is no longer that desire to travel into the unknown—that place where you get ulcers or your heart beats faster. You have to make yourself vulnerable as a writer. You have to constantly take risks. Maybe you will slip and fall flat on your face and your nose will be bloody, and everybody will know it, but if you don't do that you risk losing that vitality as a writer.

Writings by the Author
Poetry

Fireflight: Three Latin American Poets. Translated by Catherine Rodriguez-Nieto. Berkeley: Oyez, 1976.
Palabras de mediodía: Noon Words. Translated by Catherine Rodriguez-Nieto. Oakland: El Fuego de Aztlán, 1980. Houston: Arte Público Press, 2000.
Variaciones sobre una tempestad / Variations on a Storm. Translated by Catherine Rodriguez-Nieto. Berkeley: Third Woman Press, 1990.

Novels

Delia's Song. Houston: Arte Público, 1989.
Eulogy for a Brown Angel. Houston: Arte Público, 1992.
Cactus Blood. Houston: Arte Público, 1995.

Black Widow's Wardrobe. Houston: Arte Público, 1999.

Crimson Moon: A Brown Angel Mystery. Houston: Arte Público Press, 2004.

Other

Where Fireflies Dance. Illustrated by Mira Reisberg. San Francisco: Children's Book Press, 1997.

Ed. *Máscaras.* Berkeley: Third Woman Press, 1997.

Further Readings
Critical Studies

Alarcón, Francisco X. "Lucha Corpi: Poeta Solar." *Metamorfosis* 3/4 (1980/1981): 111–113.

Brinson-Pineda, Barbara. "Poets on Poetry: Dialogue with Lucha Corpi." *Prisma* 1, no. 1 (1979): 4–9.

Bruce-Novoa, Juan. "Lucha Corpi, poeta." *Plural* 23, no. 1 (1994): 17–22.

Curiel, Barbara Brinson. "Lucha Corpi." *Dictionary of Literary Biography.* Vol. 82, *Chicano Writers,* pp. 91–97. Detroit: Gale Group, 1989.

Kessler, Elizabeth Rodriguez. "New Texts in Chicana Studies." *NWSA Journal* 10, no. 3 (Fall 1998): 213.

Pearson, Carol Elizabeth. "Gender, Genre, and Resistance in the Works of Lucha Corpi, Angeles Mastretta, and Claribel Alegría." Ph.D. dissertation, University of New Mexico, 1999.

Raso, Manuel Villar, and María Herrera-Sobek. "A Spanish Novelist's Perspective on Chicano/a Literature." *Journal of Modern Literature* 25, no. 1 (Fall 2001): 17-31.

Rodriguez, Ralph E. "Cultural Memory and Chicanidad: Detecting History, Past and Present, in Lucha Corpi's Gloria Damasco Series." *Contemporary Literature* 43, no. 1 (Spring 2003): 138–170.

Reviews

Alamilla, Nan. Rev. of *Máscaras. Signs* 25, no. 1 (1999): 255.

Gladhart, Amalia. Rev. of *Cactus Blood. Letras Femeninas* 22, nos. 1–2 (1996): 254.

Hoffert, Barbara. Rev. of *Noon Words. Library Journal* 26, no. 10 (June 1, 2001): 59.

Menard, Valerie. Rev. of *Black Widow's Wardrobe. Hispanic* 13, no. 5 (May 2000): 80.

Ordóñez, Elizabeth J. Rev. of *Delia's Song. Letras Femeninas* 16, nos. 1–2 (1990): 158–161.

Soto, Gary. Rev. of *Palabras de mediodía / Noon Words. Revista Chicano-Riqueña* 9, no. 1 (1981): 76–77.

Interviews

Binder, Wolfgang. "Lucha Corpi." In *Partial Autobiographies: Interviews with Twenty Chicano Poets,* edited by Wolfgang Binder, pp. 75–92. Erlangen, Germany: Verlag Palm and Enke Erlangen, 1985.

Carabi, Angels. "Belles Lettres Interview: Lucha Corpi." *Belles Lettres: A Review of Books by Women* 7, no. 2 (1992): 48–53.

Ikas, Karin Rosa. "Lucha Corpi." In *Chicana Ways: Conversations with Ten Chicana Writers,* pp. 66–89. Reno: University of Nevada Press, 2002.

Pérez-Erdélyi, Mireya. "Entrevista con Lucha Corpi, poeta chicana." *The Americas Review* 17, no. 1 (1989): 72–82.

Dagoberto Gilb

Dagoberto Gilb was born in Los Angeles in 1950 and was raised by his Mexican single mother. In high school, he worked in an industrial laundry, in a warehouse as a shipping clerk, and as a graveyard shift janitor. During college, he worked as a stock boy and a salesman in department stores. After his college years, he became a professional carpenter. He spent his days breathing cement dust and nailing forms as a journeyman union carpenter working on high-rises in and around Los Angeles. His desire to become a published writer transformed his life as a working-class Chicano into something bigger than himself.

In the early 1980s, Gilb sent a short story to *The Threepenny Review*. Much to his joy, the magazine's editor, Wendy Lesser, wrote him back quickly saying she loved his work, and she began to publish his short fiction regularly. Gilb's work began to take shape as a collection, and he soon won his first literary prize in California, the James D. Phelan Award. Gilb moved with his family to El Paso, and there the newly formed Cinco Puntos Press received a grant to publish his work. In 1985, *Winners on the Pass Line* reached a wide audience, and so did his Chicano working-class protagonists (from plumbers and carpenters to mechanics) and their everyday experiences on and off the job site. In one of these early stories, "Where the Sun Don't Shine," we learn the complex reasons why the Chicano character Sal puts up with a racist, unskilled Anglo foreman. In 1993 the University of New Mexico Press published *The Magic of Blood*—a collection that adds twenty or so stories to *Winners* and includes even more working-class Chicano characters. After the success of *The Magic of Blood* (winner of the PEN/Hemingway

Award and a finalist for the PEN/Faulkner Award), Gilb's fiction caught the eye of Grove/Atlantic's new owner, Morgan Entrekin. In 1994 Grove Press published *The Last Known Residence of Mickey Acuña,* a novel employing an unassuming, unreliable narrator (his trademark) to tell the story. Here, Gilb plunges his readers deep into the troubled psyche of Acuña as he tries to live anew in an El Paso YMCA. Gilb returned to short fiction with *Woodcuts of Women* (2001). In this collection of ten short stories, he sharpens details and widens his scope to flesh out a panoply of working-class characters. For example, in "Mayela One Day," Gilb's narrator and protagonist is street-smart and wise beyond his years. He muses on one occasion:

> I'm in a city called El Paso. I could point it out on a map. Right here, here it is. There is longitude, latitude. For most this is enough, a satisfactory explanation. But say we don't use all these imaginary concepts. Say there is no west of or east of or north of or south of. Forget all that. Forget these legalistic boundaries. No Texas here, no Mexico there, no New Mexico. Forget all that. Here's the river. Here are mountains. A sky above.
> *(19)*

Frederick Luis Aldama: So what is your latest writing project?

Dagoberto Gilb: It's a collection of about forty essays that I've amassed over the last twenty years or so. Some I wrote for the National Public Radio program *Fresh Air.* Others appeared in magazines like the *New Yorker,* and I've included the one from *Harper's* and ones reprinted in *Best American Essays.* There's a piece I did for the *L.A. Times* about undocumenteds crossing the U.S.–Mexico border. You name it. The collection is broken into four categories: culture, women, family, and work. I titled it *Gritos,* which I had a little trouble explaining the meaning of to my editor at Grove. In part, he was reacting to my reputation as a bad boy, always causing trouble—he didn't understand what a *grito* was and thought it meant that I wanted to scream at Anglos; the other part was that he just didn't think it would sell because it's a Spanish word. Any Chicano knows what a *grito* is; it's a word like *taco.* I asked César Martínez to do the cover art. He's from Laredo; he's famous for his paintings of *pachucos.* I want the cover to be an image of a *grito,* but not of an old, sour-looking *mariachi,* like, singing. What I'm thinking of is like a face with one of those cartoon bubbles popping up above, saying "Gritos."

F.L.A.: You had the artist Artemio Rodríguez do all the art for *Woodcuts for Women*?

D.G.: Yes, and Artemio is an incredible artist, too. He deserves more attention. I showed a couple of his drawings to the editors at Grove when I was putting *Woodcuts* together, and they loved them. Then Artemio ended up designing the drawings for the interior of the book, even though he didn't use his regular folk art style. The drawings he did do for the book worked nicely to complement what people think of—I say misunderstand—as my "realism."

F.L.A.: The collection of essays, *Gritos,* seems to be a departure from the short stories you're known for.

D.G.: Well, in a way they're a departure, but in a way I've always been writing essays. And I've been asked to write a couple of newspaper op-eds. The last one I did was a piece on Steinbeck for the *New York Times.* It's just that most people don't know about my essays; they only know my short fiction.

On the other hand, it's kind of ironic that with all the short stories that I've published—over fifty or so—none have made even a mention in the yearly *Best American Short Story* anthology, whereas I've gotten two reprinted in *Best American Essays.* I get the prizes for the essays, but I'm better known as a short story writer? Maybe this new collection will change that image, although I see myself as a fiction writer. I wrote the essays because people ask for them, and when they do, they offer money.

F.L.A.: Writing the essay is a different process from writing the short story?

D.G.: The only difference is that nonfiction is based on fact—call it "truth"—whereas the writing of fiction is all about making it up, inventing, lying. I mean, in fiction, I might make this room we're sitting in right now blue instead of the white that it is, or I might mix it up with two or three other places that I've seen or read about. In an essay, I'd be more careful about representing its true color and shape.

"Truth" is just as fascinating to me as fiction is. Even when you represent things as they are, they can be just as bizarre. I did a piece for *Harper's* called "Blue Eyes, Brown Eyes" that I wrote for our local, regional magazine *Texas Monthly.* Talk about reality being bizarre. *Texas Monthly* is like frat boys with rich parents, and though I was asked to write this piece, the editor wouldn't run it unless I dumbed it down. Even in this day and age, even if you're a known writer publishing in places like the *New Yorker,* if you're Mexican, you still can't be included in their magazine unless you're dead or a gangster or a boxer—or you have to be fixed by them, in my case. It's a mixed-up world, but it's also still racist in this "highbrow" Texas, what I think of as that magazine's apartheid world. When I turned in the story to *Texas Monthly,* I was assigned a young assistant editor who felt he had to explain to me how to open an essay, who felt no qualms or reluctance in talking to me like he knew more about writing than I did. (I archived this correspondence at the Southwestern Writers Collection because it was so incredible.) Here's this, like, twenty-five-year-old kid telling me how to write, even though I've probably been publishing since before he was born. He told me that I put my readers in some dream-like trance. Wow, I thought, thank you. But he meant that was a bad thing. I almost fell over my chair. I said to myself, what, he wants me to wake the readers up for a commercial break? Anyway, yeah, there's a lot of shit in the world that makes the world we live in sometimes even more bizarre than fiction.

F.L.A.: I want to talk to you about *Woodcuts.* Can you talk about the different responses it generated when first published?

D.G.: I had no expectations, but what shocked me most was how patronizing the responses were in the Texas media, even when the reviews could be seen as "positive." There was only one newspaper that really treated me like a serious writer. I thought maybe it was because people don't know how to respond to sex in the stories; they tend to go all giggly and a-twitter when you write about sex, so they don't know how to treat it. What's strange is that sex isn't even the main focus of the collection. So I thought, maybe it's my bad-boy image: you know, Dagoberto's always fighting, and if he's not fighting, he's fucking. They took it as like a "Latin lover" book, or whatever the hell it is they think. If someone like Norman Mailer writes about sex, the critics still don't simply sexualize him, they talk about his brains, his intelligence, even if they don't like what he has to say. But with mine, it was like the book was only about my own raw, native, sex-crazed juices. That's a kind of racism, cultural or whatever you want to call it.

F.L.A.: What about the response nationally?

D.G.: That is interesting. Outside of Texas, the critics took the book seriously and talked to me. I even did an interview on *The News Hour with Jim Lehrer,* where I was asked intelligent questions. I had gotten so in the defensive mode after the Texas critics that it took some time to adjust. The only exception was the *Washington Post,* where the reviewer ripped the book apart in a very odd way that I still don't entirely understand—like she was pissed at her own life and discussing situations that weren't even in the book. That was the only bad review I got nationally. Everything else seemed to be good. What was also interesting is that the story "Snow," which I thought was one of my best, the people seemed to understand the least. It is a transitional piece for me from my trademark "gritty realism" to a more surrealist style. But that's all right.

F.L.A.: Where does your inspiration come from when you write your stories?

D.G.: It usually comes from some incident that I experienced or something I've seen or heard happen. Then I just mix it all up and make a story. I write based on experience, on living, more than I do my beliefs or what I imagine.

F.L.A.: Why return again and again to the working class setting in your stories?

D.G.: Because until very recently I've been a working person, working hard since I was thirteen years old. I started working for my dad, who was the floor superintendent of this industrial laundry in downtown L.A. There were a lot of Mexicanos, workers from Central America, and black people—mostly just poor people that worked for minimum wage. I didn't grow up with my dad, so I always knew him as a boss. That was my relationship with my father: he was an ex-Marine, of German descent, raised in Boyle Heights. Then I worked construction for sixteen years. I was twelve years in the Carpenter's Union—its health plan paid for one of my sons' births. That's how I paid for my kids to grow up. I guess what I'm trying to say is, I can't avoid writing about working people—and I don't know why I would. The workplace is central to my short stories. I don't even think of it as a "setting"; it's not some self-conscious literary choice, or whatever, I insert to make some intellectual point.

F.L.A.: Do you feel at odds with creative writing programs?

D.G.: I never imagined I'd be teaching creative writing at a university. [Texas State University–San Marcos] I wasn't one of those who came to writing through a college setting. I went to college, studied philosophy and religion, and the rest of the time I worked jobs. It wasn't till I was a journeyman carpenter that I decided to write fiction seriously. At the time, I thought you just sent in your work to editors of magazines and you got published that way. So that's what I did: I just sent my work out. And I was lucky because though nobody recommended me and I wasn't at a big university, I got published anyway. It was six o'clock in the morning and I put my story "Where the Sun Don't Shine" in the mail on the way to a construction job. Next thing I know, it was accepted at *The Threepenny Review.* That was my first big publication, and it sort of changed everything. As I kept publishing with *Threepenny,* I was told how no one believed I could be a construction worker, Mexican, and write without Wendy Lesser (the editor) editing me severely. So pompous and offensive. Anyway, this is how I started, and how I began to think of myself as a writer. I didn't have the college workshop experience. I worked construction and pumped out stories.

F.L.A.: You won the James D. Phelan Award for *Winners on the Pass Line.* Can you tell me a little about this and the collection?

D.G.: Not exactly, because the book came after the prize. It was a real transition point for me. The prize committee flew me up to San Francisco and had a lunch at the Mark Hopkins Hotel—exciting for me. Suddenly, I went from being a construction worker to a *writer* in a public way. Cinco Puntos Press came into existence with a grant to publish the stories I'd submitted to that prize, which became *Winners on the Pass Line.* It's more like a poet's chapbook—a smaller book of fiction. It did help my writing career. It got its first review on National Public Radio's *All Things Considered.* It might have sold a little better, but it ran into distribution problems. The book was in one bookstore in the entire country when it was reviewed on NPR; it was a bookstore in L.A., where I was working construction, where I had dropped off ten copies. They sold nine copies the day the NPR review aired.

F.L.A.: What were you doing during the eight or so years between publishing *Winners* in 1985 and *The Magic of Blood* in 1993?

D.G.: I was publishing a lot and working, raising my family. Even though I won awards for my writing, I had no creative writing credentials; I didn't have any of the normal connects in the system. So, though I kept publishing stories in magazines and journals, no one was interested in publishing a collection. I was being rejected by the very top person at every New York publishing house. They all said no, they can't sell this guy. You know, here I was, a young man fit from working high-rise construction jobs, who could even pick up cute women, and they couldn't think to take a picture of me, the only writer in America who worked as a high-rise construction worker? What do you mean, they couldn't sell my book? I couldn't understand it. I'd win another prize, and still nothing would happen, and still I kept getting published regularly in some of the better literary magazines. At one point I was becoming the most honored, un-book-published writer in America. It was becoming a distinction. In some warped way, I was kind of liking it.

F.L.A.: So how did you get your break with Grove?

D.G.: I had been turned down by just about every major East Coast publishing house, and I was tired of fighting, so I decided to commit what seemed like literary suicide because I wasn't going to be published by New York City. I dug up a query letter from the University of New Mexico Press and decided to send it to them. They got back within a week, excited that I was going to give them my stuff. I'd given them what were two collections of fiction, and we pulled out about a hundred pages of stories, and that was it.

When *The Magic of Blood* came out, literary prizes came, and all of a sudden I started going to New York and Washington, D.C., and Boston. I realized that it wasn't because of my lack of skill that I had been rejected by the big publishers, but that I myself and what I wrote about was invisible to editors on the East Coast. It didn't hurt that I also won a Whiting and was nominated for a PEN/Faulkner (Philip Roth won it). It was stunning because no university book ever gets chosen for that award. Nothing against New Mexico Press, but for the record, getting these awards was my own doing. Though they swore they would, they never sent *Magic* to those prize committees; I did. I found out because I called one of the judges to make sure he'd received the book. Not one of the three award contests had been entered, so I went straight to the post office and mailed the book out myself. I won the Texas Institute of Letters's best book of fiction and the PEN/Hemingway and was a finalist for the PEN/Faulkner.

The awards changed my life. I had written a novel, and my agent was shopping it around. Even after I'd been to New York, the novel was still being nitpicked at, so I told her to tell everybody they got two weeks or I'm giving it to New Mexico (they were enthusiastic and wanted it). Right at the end of the two weeks, I got a call from her, and she told me that Grove Press wanted the novel. I was in shock. That was the press that published all the writers I loved to read, that my brain grew up on. It published all the outcasts, weirdos, and bad kids: Juan Rulfo, the Beats, John Rechy, Genet, Burroughs. It was like a sort of little miracle. If there was anyplace I felt I belonged, it was Grove.

F.L.A.: Grove picked up your novel *The Last Known Residence of Mickey Acuña*. Then what?

D.G.: Two things happened. First, because *Magic of Blood* did well and I got lots of media attention, when the novel came out, people were already prepared to receive it. Second, I have this habit of, like, screwing everything good up. And I did. I had some personal problems and had to run. So I bought this truck with a $200-a-month payment, put everything I owned in it, and hit the road—ended up living in Austin, Texas.

F.L.A.: What about the novel's reception?

D.G.: It was received okay, though I don't think many understood it because it's weird and intended to be weird. It has started popping up in literature classes. I don't think it's taught in Chicano literature classes. In fact, Chicano teachers still don't get it, probably because it doesn't have any of the usual Chicano props or any of the banners that everybody wants to see in Chicano fiction: gangbangers and/or campesinos, like that. I write about Chicanos living in urban places like El Paso and L.A., and who work in factories and construction sites. But because we have so few images of what it means to be a Mexican American in this country, I think people didn't know what I was doing. Then there is my name, "Gilb." We're all used to seeing Cisneros, Anaya, and Rivera on the Chicano literary menu, kinda like tacos, enchiladas, and flautas, but what's a "Gilb"? How do you eat that? You know? So they're all, like, what the hell is that, who the hell is he?

Interestingly, the German reviewers really got the novel—that it was a story simply about a down-and-out guy living on the U.S.–Mexican border in a struggle with mental and economic borders. They understood that all the characters were struggling while crossing all kinds of real and imaginary and economic borders. In the States, nobody would ask me anything intelligent about the book.

F.L.A.: You mentioned writers who use Chicano props. Who are some Chicano writers who you think avoid this?

D.G.: One of the things I used to love about Rolando Hinojosa is that he'll tell stories about everyday life; he'll have salesmen and bankers. He isn't concerned only with gang signs and the hippest slang.

F.L.A.: When you made your so-called suicide leap with *Magic of Blood*, weren't you a little bitter about those Chicano writers who were using all the props to sell their fiction to mainstream America?

D.G.: I came up as a writer with Sandra Cisneros. I watched her rise to heroic heights. I don't have anything against her success, but she worked through the flow of the university system. It's done her well and meant a ton to the community, too. To me, she's like a literary activist, making our community care about reading. But if you look back over the history of authors in and out of the system, writers before the 1970s wrote outside the academic system. Then in the 1980s, you started to see more and more writers graduating from writing programs like Iowa or Stanford. You had to go to school and have the credentials so that people took you seriously. Now it's so entrenched, it's like I'm so wild because I had a regular job and was writing. If you're not in the system, they don't know how to take what you're doing. Today, when people write a bio line on me for a paper or magazine, they don't want to mention that I was in construction for sixteen years, only about the teaching jobs I've had these past few years. That's serious; the other isn't. But look, we're all still fighting to get into mainstream acceptance: that hasn't really changed very much. In my case, because I didn't work the university system as a writer, I'm still less known as a writer for those whose only knowledge is through it.

F.L.A.: Do Chicana writers participate in this institutionalizing of writing?

D.G.: I think what happened was that the academic world took control over what Chicanos read and write, and for years they were favoring feminist stories because most of the professors are women—even making people write that slash in: "Chicano/a." It's a phase, even understandable. But I do hate that "Chicana/o." So I say, "I give up. I'm a Chican*a* writer.

I don't want that slash shit anymore. I hate it. So you just call me a Chicana writer." It just shows you how much they've been in power. If I look around at my generation of Chicano writers who've been pushed forward—males New Yorked, so to speak—I can only think of a couple: Jimmy Baca, and the poet in El Paso, Ben Sáenz. So, because of the focus on Chicanas, I think it is harder for Chicano writers right now.

F.L.A.: Did your experience at college studying philosophy and religion affect your writing?

D.G.: When I was in junior college, I wanted to be sort of a half-breed Hegel. I read fiction on the side; didn't write at all. In fact, I flunked English. But I really wanted to be smart, so I studied philosophy. For me this was like going to the source. Also, you could read a page of Plato, and that was considered serious reading. A page at a time was more my speed.

F.L.A.: So when did you figure out that you liked to write?

D.G.: Basically, to be a writer you have to be kind of fucked up. I didn't see writing fiction as studying. I thought of it as a job. I loved hearing stories, I felt like I had thousands of stories to tell, and then one day I thought I could write a novel and make money, even. I looked at that annual *Writer's Market* book, read success stories, and started working on a novel.

F.L.A.: A critic once referred to you as the Chicano Bukowski, and you identify as a Grove Press author?

D.G.: That's awful flattering. Yeah, I like Bukowski's publisher, Black Sparrow. He offered to publish me a long time ago, but it was like they were going to take a year and a half or more to get the book out, so I said no.

F.L.A.: As a Chicano and as a writer, do you feel you have a responsibility or a role to play?

D.G.: First, let me say, it's a dumb choice to be a writer! What a miserable, poor job. On the other hand, I think my job is to write, and I like doing my job. Today, I put in an hour and wrote a page, so I did my job, and now I can go have fun. Instead of reproducing, I'm trying to produce. I'm trying to not fuck up anymore. And in some sense I don't really like that question, just because I think it is what people expect: that you're supposed to have a "role" and be someone "good." That's dumb. I'm a writer, so I'm not running for office or sainthood—those are different professions. Of course I stand up for political causes, but as far as my fiction goes, I'm more fascinated by the mystery, which isn't about time or politics. I believe all writing is unavoidably political. Writing about working people, for example, is unavoidably political—it means that a certain class of people is being paid attention to, that another class wants to not pay attention to.

One great thing about being a writer is that, unlike a lot of careers, as you get older, you don't get closer to ending your career; you get more mature and more material and, if things go well, more respect. Tolstoy and Dostoevsky didn't write their best books until the end of their lives.

Writings by the Author
Short Stories

Winners on the Pass Line. El Paso: Cinco Puntos Press, 1985.
The Magic of Blood. Albuquerque: University of New Mexico Press, 1993.
Woodcuts of Women. New York: Grove Press, 2001.

Novels

The Last Known Residence of Mickey Acuña. New York: Grove Press, 1994.

Essays

"Blue Eyes, Brown Eyes: Mexican-American Man Visits Mexico." *Harper's Magazine* 302, no. 1813 (June 2001): 57.
"Sentimental for Steinbeck: Honoring the Workers' Writer on His Centennial." *New York Times,* March 18, 2002, p. A27.
"Spanish Guy." *New Yorker* 78, no. 9 (April 22, 2002): 166.
Gritos. New York: Grove Press, 2003.

Further Readings
Critical Studies

Bahr, David. "Dagoberto Gilb: A Lust for Life, Down and Dirty." *Publishers Weekly* 250, no. 3 (January 15, 2001): 48.
Beuka, Robert, and Gerald Kennedy. "Imperiled Communities in Edward P. Jones's *Lost in the City* and Dagoberto Gilb's *The Magic of Blood.*" *Yearbook of English Studies,* Vol. 31 (2001): 10–23.

Broun, Bill. "Lives of Working Men." *TLS, the Times Literary Supplement* 5144 (November 2, 2001): 22.

Christie, John S. "Crowding Out Latinos: Mexican Americans in the Public Consciousness." *MELUS* 26, no. 2 (2001): 267–271.

Fox, Claire. "Fan Letters to the Cultural Industries: Border Literature about Mass Media." *Studies in Twentieth Century Literature* 25, no. 1 (2001): 3.

Thompson, Jean. "What Men Want Women to Want: A Story Collection Focuses on Males, Females, and What They Think about Each Other." *New York Times Book Review* 106, no. 3 (January 21, 2001): 11.

Tonn, Horst. "History's Remains: Performative Appropriations of the Past in the Short Fiction of Dagoberto Gilb." In *Re-Visioning the Past: Historical Self-Reflexivity in American Short Fiction,* edited by Bernd Engler and Oliver Scheiding, pp. 383–390. Trier, Germany: Wissenschaftlicher, 1998.

Reviews

Donahue, Peter. Rev. of *Woodcuts of Women. The Review of Contemporary Fiction* 22, no. 1 (2002): 143–145.

Nericcio, William. Rev. of *The Last Known Residence of Mickey Acuña. World Literature Today* 69, no. 4 (1995): 794–795.

Saez, Barbara J. Rev. of *The Magic of Blood. MELUS* 22, no. 1 (1997): 159–163.

Interviews

Gabbard, Dwight. "A Short Talk with Dagoberto Gilb." *Short Story Review* 4, no. 4 (1987): 4–5, 15–17.

Jaime Hernandez (of Los Bros Hernandez)

The Hernandez brothers, Jaime (born October 10, 1959) and Gilbert (born February 1, 1957) are from the farming community of Oxnard, California, where they were raised along with their older brother, Mario (born April 18, 1953), by their single mother. The brothers grew up with comics; their mother harbored a great love of them. They also grew up in a multiracial community—a place of tense racial relations (between Anglos and Chicanos especially) but also a place of much cultural cross-pollination. The brothers grew up with a strong sensibility of both Mexican culture and alternative Americana: punk rock music, lowrider cars, and, of course, comics. This mélange of cultural influences informed directly the storymaking and inking that went into their debut comic book in 1982, *Love and Rockets*. With their brother Mario playing more of a supportive role in the process, Jaime and Gilbert became quickly known as "Los Bros Hernandez"; their stories kept flowing and their readership kept growing.

Over three decades of storytelling and inking, "Los Bros" have brought forth a vivid and rich array of stories that follow a pantheon of Chicano/a, Anglo, African American, and other characters who have become familiar to readers across the nation. While many of the stories are inspired by the punk rock music and everyday Chicano *barrio* culture of their Oxnard neighborhood, one can discern many other creative influences, including films and novels. To turn their creative vision into individual stories with their own unique style, Los Bros work side by side (though less often than they once did, now that Gilbert is in Las Vegas and Jaime in Los Angeles). Jaime's *Locas* series, for example, uses few lines and many visual details to flesh out the lives and adventures of Southern California bisexual Chicanas Hopey and Maggie and their run-ins with various elements of U.S. society, from bigoted police to jealous boyfriends. In another of Jaime's series, *Hoppers 13,* he plunges his readers deep into the lives of working-class Chicanos, Asian immigrants, punk rockers, and gang members who inhabit Barrio Huerta—a place on the outskirts of Los Angeles. In Gilbert's more text-heavy *Heartbreak Soup* series, we move back and forth across the U.S.–Mexico border as he textures vividly the lives of characters like the puritanical town sheriff, Chelo; the political idealist, Tonantzin; and the hedonistic entrepreneur, Pipo.

Investing their graphic stories with the density and visual sophistication of novels—using such techniques as flashbacks and flash-forwards—and with an ear for the rhythms of all varieties of speech, Los Bros have cultivated a large national readership and won numerous awards (for example, Harvey Awards for Best New Series and Best Cartoonist). Their stories at once complicate and simplify the everyday experiences of multiethnic and multigenerational Americans and continue to be hugely inspirational for other Latino/a and Chicano/a comic-book artists.

Frederick Luis Aldama: Why the comic book for Los Bros instead of other narrative forms like the short story or novel?

Jaime Hernandez: It's pretty much because we grew up with comics. From early on, I liked drawing; it was my favorite form of art. I wanted to draw comics my whole life, and I wanted to tell stories and make characters. So making comics seemed like the perfect medium to tell what I wanted to tell; it involved drawing and storytelling. It was the perfect means for expressing myself in stories, and it was inexpensive.

F.L.A.: When did you realize that it was something you wanted to make a career out of and to make a living?

J.H.: A couple of years after *Love and Rockets* came out, it started to become something I could support myself with. Of course I was pretty young then, and I didn't need much to survive. But I was lucky because, as my needs changed and I wanted to support myself a little better, so did the comic grow in popularity.

F.L.A.: Did you have to do other jobs to support yourself when you first began publishing *Love and Rockets*?

J.H.: I was twenty or twenty-one and was still living at home as a bumming punk rocker. I had moved out for a couple of years, but I had gone back due to lack of funds.

F.L.A.: How did you come into the idea for drawing and writing the stories in *Love and Rockets*?

J.H.: I liked drawing rocket ships, superheroes, and things like that when I was younger, and that's why you see a lot of them in the early comics. But it also came out of the life I was living growing up in the barrio in Oxnard, California, filled with low-rider and punk culture. It was a fascinating world where punk and *cholo* came together and that most of the world didn't know about. This was a story that needed to be told, and no one was doing it in comics, so we took the lead.

F.L.A.: Is *Love and Rockets* a collaborative process with your brother Gilbert?

J.H.: We just share the book. We never collaborate, but we inspire each other just by working side by side.

F.L.A.: Chicano barrio and science fiction, low rider and punk: has it been difficult for you to write stories about Chicanos that don't fit into any one box?

J.H.: I was always more of a rock 'n' roller, whereas my childhood friends were into soul and funk. I listened to this white-boy music and so was kind of an outsider; I always felt like I was somewhere on the outside, looking in at my life and my neighborhood. If you're inside it, you kinda don't get to observe it much; if you step back a little bit, you can see how it relates to the rest of the world and how the rest of the world relates to it. I got the best of all worlds.

F.L.A.: In 1981 you submitted your first issue of *Love and Rockets* to be reviewed by *Comics Journal*?

J.H.: We were looking for cheap publicity, because we didn't know how to sell our own little black-and-white comic that we made ourselves. So Gilbert sent it to them to get a review. We thought, even if they didn't like it, it would be free advertising. So we just went for broke, said "Screw it," and sent it in. They liked it and because they had been planning to publish their own comic series (Fantagraphics), it was perfect timing. We helped them take off.

We never had time to fail. We were ready with our idea and knew where we wanted to go with it, so when it took off, we were ready to produce.

F.L.A.: Much time has passed from 1981 to today. Have you noticed big changes in readership, distribution, and so on, with the Chicano or ethnic-themed comic?

J.H.: It's a lot better than it was in '81, that's for sure. There're a lot of Latino artists out there doing all kinds of work; it's kind of hard to keep track. It's pretty cool because I feel like we had something to do with that. I'm partially set in my ways, and the world I created has become so vast that I don't look outside that often to see who's coming up, but I do know there are a lot of great upcoming artists; a lot are still toying with this dead superhero thing, though. This doesn't inspire me too much. I prefer a more personal vision.

As for readers, today we have a big Chicano readership. There was a young Chicano who told me that when he saw our comic and read our names, it just blew him away 'cause he couldn't believe there were Chicanos doing comics. That made me feel really good, that I could at least get it out there and spread the word.

F.L.A.: Why black-and-white drawings?

J.H.: The black and white was an economic issue. We couldn't afford to do a color comic because it would have killed us. And we wouldn't sell. That's how it started out. But I've always been a fan of black-and-white things like *Mad Magazine* and all the underground comics that were in black and white. So it started out because of economic necessity, then ended up becoming art.

That's kind of the story of comics in the first place. Comics were first created in the '30s as a kind of disposable art. They were reprinted newspaper strips that you read like a newspaper and then threw away. Then they became a collector's thing. That's sort of how we started. We just took what we could afford and turned that into something.

F.L.A.: Can you speak a little about how you conceive of your stories?

J.H.: Well, since I deal with an ongoing series of characters, the story pretty much evolves as they mature. It's the characters that determine the story's direction. They make the story. This character's going through their thirties, so what can I make them go through? It's only once in a while that I have an actual story idea that I fit the characters into. It's usually the other way around: I fit the story to the characters.

F.L.A.: What's that process between what you imagine and the final inking of the story?

J.H.: I'm mostly self-taught, so what I do might be considered very primitive. I start off with a loose, partial script. I never script out a whole story at once. Usually the script starts with a basic beginning of a story or middle of a story, and then I fill in the pictures and words, that then take on a life of their own. This is what actually ends up giving shape to the whole story. It's very organic.

Most creators start with a script, and then they start doing layouts that they then put on the paper. After I've put something down, like a loose dialogue, I draw directly on the paper. I edit it as I'm drawing it on the paper in pencil. And then when I'm finally comfortable with what I see, I start inking. But I try not to jump the gun. I've done stuff that could have been edited down much better, but because I jumped in too fast and finished it, I realized afterwards that it could have been better if I'd thought about it more.

There's a real art to figuring out how to describe a scene and how you move from one panel to the next. You don't want to give too much or too little detail. As far as characters, I just throw them out there. I don't try to force you to like Hopey. I just give you Hopey, and it's up to you to engage with her. I think that's a big part of the art of crafting comics—that you only give so much, and you trust your readership to do the rest.

F.L.A.: Were underground comics—those that tell stories of America's underbelly—a big influence?

J.H.: I didn't see a lot of them growing up. I was still a little young, mostly reading superhero and Archie comics. The ones that I did notice were the ones my older brothers were reading, like Crumb. What I really liked about the underground comic was the freedom—that the authors were doing exactly what they wanted without any editorial pressure or a big company to tell them yes or no.

They represented the underdog: that was interesting to someone growing up Chicano. You're never in first place. You're always in second or third, so you just fight harder, telling yourself, I'm gonna do this. I've got nothing to lose. I don't have as much to lose as people on top. It's not so much written down. It's in the spirit of the actual work and with the confidence to do this without you telling me whether I can or can't.

F.L.A.: Los Bros have taken risks, like using untranslated Spanish in *Love and Rockets* as well as depicting some erotic, sexual content.

J.H.: America hates this stuff, so guess what? We're gonna do it—because we can. It is easy for us because we really don't have the FBI cracking down on us. We're not really that dangerous. We're not seen as dangerous. Who knows? We may be inspiring something bigger than the comic along the way—which is not such a bad thing.

F.L.A.: Why the shift from the early to later *Love and Rockets,* from the use of the fantastical and science fiction style to a barrio realism?

J.H.: This was a conscious shift. I wanted to start doing more serious work, so the dinosaurs and robots got in the way. I never hated doing them. I loved drawing all kinds of goofy and weird stuff, but Gilbert and I made a decision that we wanted to take a harder, grittier path. I mean you don't care if someone's going to get shot when there's a dinosaur outside the door. Its message can't be that serious. I wanted to put reality in front of my readers as best I could.

F.L.A.: *Love and Rockets* is serious—Hopey and Maggie have run-ins with the police, and you depict the violence of *la migra*—but it's also about family conflict and struggle within the Chicano community.

J.H.: Our Chicano culture is so rich and has so much to offer that I've barely scratched the surface. I want the whole world to experience it. I've made it my job to make everybody understand it without watering it down and without trying to protect the readers' feelings. Whether they understand it or not, the comics aim to communicate a vision of the Chicano community so readers can see what it's really all about.

F.L.A.: There are aspects of the Chicano community that some would rather not see—for example, your portrayal of the lesbian relationship between Hopey and Maggie. You've received criticism for this?

J.H.: When they tell me I'm doing it wrong is when I get a little irked. I'm portraying a community that's complicated. That's why I make the characters people first, more than anything. I've become a pretty good observer of people. So that's what I focus on. It's always the characters first. Everything falls into place after that.

I guess the whole mission is just to present the truth of a world that we know or that we've witnessed and that a lot of people try to ignore. I guess the main thing for Los Bros is try to bring as much truth to our stories as we can. That's the most important, next to entertaining. I mean, even if we're doing serious stuff, we're still entertaining readers.

F.L.A.: Your stories are very melodramatic.

J.H.: I'm very much a romantic at heart. I'm a very sentimental person, but I know that if I just let the floodgates open, I would be creating the sappiest stuff in the world. To keep a balance, I have to rein in the sentiment. But every once in a while, I like to turn on the faucet and blast. Without insulting them, I like to manipulate my audience a little just to draw them in. I'd like to think that I know pretty well how to step in and step out with the melodrama. But I try to keep a balance between the serious and the sentimental because I don't want to cheat the audience.

F.L.A.: Who is your audience?

J.H.: In the early days, when we first started, our comic was supported by professionals. Comic professionals. They supported and encouraged us. Then we started to build an audience. We had a large female as well as male readership that was mostly white and of college age. (I would say that even today mostly white people read it, I guess because mostly white people read comics.) Then the Chicanos and other ethnic readers started trickling in.

F.L.A.: You guys took a break from *Love and Rockets*. Why?

J.H.: Burnout. Our comic worlds had become so big and broad that they were just spilling over the sides, and it started to drive us crazy. We needed a break. Not a break like I'm not gonna draw today, but just a break from what we were writing. The only way we could think of doing that for a while was just doing our own separate comics. We just needed some tiny shift in what we were doing. And it just felt new again.

F.L.A.: You returned with *Penny Century*.

J.H.: This included the same cast as *Love and Rockets* plus a few new characters. It was the same world, but everyone was older, and some now lived different lives. I also gave it a new format. I went to comic size. In the grand scheme of things, there wasn't much of a change, but it sure felt like it.

Now we're doing *Love and Rockets*, Volume 2—the tenth issue. I'm wrapping up a Maggie story that I'm going to put in the collection.

Everybody's older and has gone different ways; some characters are re-uniting from the early days. They're all supposed to be responsible adults now, but some can't handle it. Some are alienated from their old worlds—kind of like me. I know what growing old is like for me, so I draw on my experiences.

F.L.A.: Reading comics can be a form of escape. Is writing and inking also an escape?

J.H.: My escape is to be able to sit alone in my studio and create. I'm escaping, but I'm also confronting my world at the same time. Years ago Gilbert had this great quote where he said, "*Love and Rockets* is our love letter to the world." It's our way of reaching the world. Some people have to stand on a street corner and scream, but this is our way.

F.L.A.: It's pretty rare to make a living as an author, much less a Chicano comic book artist.

J.H.: I'm really lucky that I've been able to partially support myself and my family doing exactly what I want to do. It's never made me a millionaire, but I've never had to interrupt it with something else. I have had to take contract work to help support my family. I can't live on macaroni and cheese like I used to. I don't need a mansion, but I do want a comfortable enough living where I can be free to do my work.

F.L.A.: Your mom passed down to Los Bros her love of comics. Will there be a new generation of Hernandez comic book artists?

J.H.: I have a five-year-old daughter that likes to draw unicorns and all that stuff, but I haven't intruded on her art style or anything. I've encouraged her to draw, but I haven't encouraged any of my know-how because to me there's nothing better than a kid's imagination. I don't want to spoil that. I want her to go bonkers her way. When she's older, she can start learning more technical ways to express herself artistically. I remember how much fun I had as a kid not going by the rules. I don't want to spoil that.

Writings by the Author
Books

Los Bros Hernandez. *Love and Rockets*. Stamford, Conn.: Fantagraphics Books, 1982–1996.

———. *Music for Mechanics: The Complete Love and Rockets, Book 1*. Westlake Village, CA: Fantagraphics Books, 1985.

———. *Chelo's Burden: The Complete Love and Rockets, Book 2*. Westlake Village, CA: Fantagraphics Books, 1986.

———. *Las Mujeres Perdidas: The Complete Love and Rockets, Book 3*. Seattle: Fantagraphics Books, 1987.

———. *Tears from Heaven: The Complete Love and Rockets, Book 4*. Seattle: Fantagraphics Books, 1988.

———. *House of Raging Women: The Complete Love and Rockets, Book 5*. Seattle: Fantagraphics Books, 1988.

———. *Duck Feet: The Complete Love and Rockets, Book 6*. Seattle: Fantagraphics Books, 1989.

———. *The Death of Speedy: The Complete Love and Rockets, Book 7*. Seattle: Fantagraphics Books, 2001.

———. *Flies on the Ceiling: The Complete Love and Rockets, Book 9*. Seattle: Fantagraphics Books, 1991.

———. *Wigwam Bam: The Complete Love and Rockets, Book 11*. Seattle: Fantagraphics Books, 1994.

———. *Chester Square: The Complete Love and Rockets, Book 13*. Seattle: Fantagraphics Books, 1996.

———. *Hernandez Satyricon: The Complete Love and Rockets, Book 15*. Seattle: Fantagraphics Books, 1997.

Hernandez, Gilbert. *Palomar: The Heartbreak Soup Stories*. Seattle: Fantagraphics Books, 2003.

Hernandez, Jaime. *Whoa, Nellie!* Seattle: Fantagraphics Books, 1999.

———. *Locas in Love. The Complete Love and Rockets, Book 18*. Seattle: Fantagraphics Books, 2000.

———. *Dicks and Deedees: The Complete Love and Rockets, Book 20*. Seattle: Fantagraphics Books, 2003.

———. *Locas: A Love and Rockets Book*. Seattle: Fantagraphics Books, 2004.

Further Readings
Critical Studies

Cocks, Jay. "The Passing of Pow! and Blam! Comics Grow Up, Get Ambitious and Turn into Graphic Novels." *Time* 131, no. 4 (January 25, 1988): 65–67.

Hatfield, Charles. "Heartbreak Soup: The Interdependency of Theme and Form." *Inks: Cartoon and Comic Art Studies* 4, no. 2 (1997): 2–17.

Scott, Darieck. "Love, Rockets, Race, and Sex." *The Americas Review: A Review of Hispanic Literature and Art of the USA* 22, nos. 3–4 (1994): 73–106.

Reviews

Arnold, Andrew D. "Graphic Sketches of Latino Life." *Time* 157, no. 7 (February 19, 2001): 64.

Markee, Patrick. Rev. of *Love and Rockets Collection, Vols. 1–15. The Nation* 266, no. 18 (May 18, 1998): 25–28.

Reid, Calvin. *Publishers Weekly* 248, no. 11 (March 12, 2001): 35.

Rev. of *Flies on the Ceiling: The Complete Love and Rockets, Vol. 9. Publishers Weekly* 238, no. 50 (November 15, 1991): 68.

Wicherath, Tanya. *Curve* 13, no. 2 (April 2003): 12.

Juan Felipe Herrera

Juan Felipe Herrera was born in 1948 in a small farming town in California. Raised by parents who migrated from Chihuahua, Mexico, Herrera defied his farmworker destiny when, as an adolescent, he discovered a passion for music and a love of poetry. His long hours reading and writing at the library as a teenager gained him entrance to the University of California, Los Angeles, in 1968. At college, Herrera found himself drawn to the writings of such Latin American authors as Miguel de Asturias, Mario Vargas Llosa, Alejo Carpentier, Gabriel García Márquez, Elena Garro, Rosario Castellanos, and Juan Rulfo. He also discovered a deep affinity with the activist poetry of Abelardo Delgado, Rodolfo "Corky" Gonzalez, and the poet known as Alurista; these poets expressed more directly his sociopolitical concerns regarding his own experiences growing up Chicano in California.

Once Herrera finished his degree, he moved to San Diego, where he continued to work on his craft as a poet and dramatist. After several years of trying his hand at drama and working for Teatro Tolteca and Teatro Zapata, Herrera turned completely to poetry. In 1974 Herrera published his first collection, *Rebozos of Love,* which experimented with form (a lack of pagination, for example) to more fluidly contain a series of poems that gravitated around themes of deracination. Throughout the 1970s, Herrera continued to write poetry that combined the experimental play he had learned from Latin American writers with the sociopolitical edge he'd picked up from *raza* poets like Alurista.

Herrera's interest in resuscitating a pre-Columbian voice in his poetry led him back to the university, where he studied anthropology. After receiving his M.A. from Stanford in 1980, he returned to publishing poetry full-time. In 1983, he published a collection of dark, surrealistic poems, *Exiles of Desire*, which textured the violent experiences of urban Chicano life.

By the end of the 1980s, Herrera's poetry had earned him a place at the prestigious University of Iowa Writers' Workshop. During his stint at Iowa, Herrera found a balance between a hard-hitting sociopolitical voice and one that celebrated play and hope. Soon after receiving his M.F.A. from Iowa, he published a collection of bittersweet poems, *Memoirs of an Exile's Notebook of the Future* (1993), which was soon followed by *The Roots of a Thousand Embraces* (1994) and *Night Train to Tuxtla* (1994). During the rest of the decade, Herrera published many collections of poetry that experimented with form but always focused on the Chicano experience. For example, he used a hip-hop style of verse in *Border-Crosser with a Lamborghini Dream* (1999):

Lissen
to the whistle of night bats—
oye como va,
in the engines, in the Chevys
& armed Impalas, the Toyota gangsta'
monsters, surf of new world colony definitions
& quasar & culture prostars going blam.
("Punk half panther," 2)

During this period Herrera also became an award-winning author of bilingual children's books. In *CrashBoomLove* (1999) he employed the free verse form he uses in some of his poetry to breathe life into the autobiographically inspired character César García, a Chicano teen who struggles to survive everyday encounters with racism in Fowlerville.

Juan Felipe Herrera is a Chicano poet and author of bilingual young adult fiction who employs a variety of poetic styles and techniques to richly texture the Chicano/a experience.

Frederick Luis Aldama: Why don't we start with your latest work, *Notebooks of a Chile Verde Smuggler*. Why do you mix poetry with prose and photographs with sketches in this book?

Juan Felipe Herrera: My mother always used to carry this old album around wherever we moved. It was a big, red, plastic-covered album with soft, black, felt-like mounting paper that she kept adding pictures to. Along with showing me the photos, she'd tell me stories. And then sometimes a photo would be missing, and I didn't know where it was anymore. It'd get lost. I conceived of *Notebooks of a Chile Verde Smuggler* as an album of sorts, but one where the photographs—that record of time—wouldn't get lost. Like the album, I conceived the book as a composite of story and image. The photos I decided to use have deep meaning for me—many came from my mother's album—and the poems I wrote became like snapshots of the stories I'd heard. Together, they conjure up a collage of memories, like that of my uncle driving around San Diego with a red pickup truck stuffed with silkscreens and paintings. My uncle—the existential prophet/artist and story catcher—was one of my earliest role models. This book is like opening the tap to let out all those stories that have been floating around in my head since childhood.

F.L.A.: In *Notebooks,* you talk at one point about your father telling stories on the porch and your mother's love of poetry.

J.F.H.: My parents were always telling me stories. And, being the only child, not only was I the only one to drink in their stories, but hearing their stories made me more attentive to my everyday surroundings. At an early age, I became a detailed observer of my world.

F.L.A.: *Notebooks* is filled with a playful spirit, whereas in your earlier poetry there's more a sense of pain.

J.F.H.: I write, then put my pen down, forget about writing, and observe my surroundings. So this would make sense because when I first began to publish poetry in the early 1970s, there was a lot going on in the world that was filled with the pain of social and political protest. I was writing poetry during the time of the Brown Power movement. I even shared an apartment in San Diego on 12th and Broadway with the big poet of the Chicano movement, Alurista, who kicked that whole thing off. Of course, I was still at the starting block as a writer, but I knew which direction I wanted to go: straight into the pit of fire where I could feel that deep, violent brutality that filled my world.

It was also an ecstatic period for me. I'd just come back from Mexico. I did the whole journey from L.A. to Chiapas to Vera Cruz, then back.

It was a deeply moving journey. So while there's pain in *Rebozos of Love,* there's also a sense of ecstasy; there's that ecstasy that comes from playing with and breaking up language and form—particularly the haiku—and finding new ways to express our existence.

F.L.A.: Why the haiku?

J.F.H.: I was caught up in the aesthetics of *el movimiento,* but I was also reading Zen Buddhism, Nietzsche, Krishnamurti, Ginsberg, Ferlinghetti, and Boris Pasternak. And during my visit to Mexico City, I was taken by the rhythm and sound of blues poetry. The whole idea behind *Rebozos* was to have a continuous book with no titles and no page numbers, no commas, no periods—just to let it go.

F.L.A.: Your poetry is characterized by a very visual-verbal style and mode. You seem to want to *exhibit* reality rather than tell your reader of reality.

J.F.H.: You're right: I've always been interested in capturing reality via a visual-lingual register. That's why I use so many graphics and handwritten stuff in my work. After *Rebozos,* I wrote *Akrílica;* that was a no-holds-barred, visual-lingual book. I conceived of it as a series of documentary-like scenes and picture galleries filled with images that cut and destroy: splinters, scalpels, bayonets, dead bodies. It was inspired by García Lorca's poetry: those ink drawings—little hyphens and wiry figures and floating heads—cascading down his pages of poetry; and the texture of his books with their burgundy leather covers, nice red ribbons, and see-through, waxy, onion-skin pages. It was his sense of giving visual texture to his poetry that just grabbed me.

F.L.A.: Even though *Akrílica* was the next collection you wrote, it wasn't published till after you published *Exiles* in 1983. Why is that?

J.F.H.: I started writing *Akrílica* in 1977 while I was living in San Diego. After four years of working on *Akrílica,* I was finally done. Then I just hung onto it for a while. I wasn't thinking of sending books out to publish at that time. I was just writing. Then I met with the editor of the *Santa Cruz Express,* also a poet, who was editing the *Alcatraz Anthology*—a 400-page collection of great poetry. He read my poetry and wanted to have it translated to publish as a bilingual book. So Alcatraz Editions finally translated it as a bilingual book in 1989.

F.L.A.: Lorca, the French symbolists, and the Latin American poets have all been strong influences?

J.F.H.: I've always been drawn to the more experimental, obtuse, and baroque poetry—the kind that creates a sense of ritual out of language. This was the poetry that really moved me and provided that springboard for me to dive into deep wells of feeling. But the influences weren't always so formal. In my early work I was influenced by The Band, Vanilla Fudge, Jimi Hendrix, and Bob Dylan, who all worked from a paisley palette and created kaleidoscopic and prismatic lyrical forms.

F.L.A.: The poetry in *Exiles of Desire* feels as if it were composed to be performed.

J.F.H.: In many ways, *Exiles* was a liberation from *Akrílica*. I wrote these poems during the period when Central America was blowing up—literally and in the media—and people were being massacred and displaced en masse. So I decided to lay it down the way I really wanted to lay it down—to ask, what is this saying about humanity? I wanted to get at the marrow of life in my poetry. I wanted to capture what it was like to be an exile—and exile of desire—both within and outside of your country of origin. To also capture this sense of being exiled from history, the self, and desire. To capture that sense of being violently split apart. To capture our attempt to bring these fractured pieces back together again. *Exiles* was meant to perform a kind of surgery, to delve into that sickened body of society, extract it, and make it visible, then begin a process of healing.

F.L.A.: In one of your next collections, *The Roots of a Thousand Embraces*, you perform a kind of poetic reconstructive surgery on Frida Kahlo.

J.F.H.: I was first drawn to her paintings to try to understand why she was so popular in the early to mid-1980s. What was it about her that spoke to so many women of color? I figured out that it was that sense of her being a broken figure, who prevailed against the odds, that attracted people. I wanted to go deeper in my poetry. I wanted to let myself go, picking up the symbols, metaphors, and themes in her paintings, and only then to let my pen flow freely. I wanted to enter into a more metaphysical realm of imagining Frida Kahlo. So the book is structured more like a series of dialogues that attempt to engage in a discussion [about] our state of being. I used Frida as the language to create this dialogue and to express this sense of being, choosing not to use a romantic language. I also wanted to use a different kind of poetic language: one based on a slave/master dialectic that ultimately leads through labyrinths of paradoxes to a sense of empowerment and synthesis. Unfortunately, the book never had much of a distribution run, sitting in a little corner somewhere overshadowed by my other work.

F.L.A.: Can you talk a little about *Mayan Drift*?

J.F.H.: I had an urgent need to write this. I returned from a year-long journey across Mexico and into Chiapas in search of an old friend, K'ayum, that I first met during my visit in 1970. When I began to write of the journey, all these stories began to take over the pages. I wrote 750 pages in three months. Afterwards, I went back over the writing to make sure I got things right in terms of history and anthropological research. Once it was finished, I chopped 250 pages off and sent it out to the agent, Susan Bergholz, in New York. She told me it was filled with too much purple prose. So I trimmed it down more and changed its narrative voice, excising the syrupy voice and putting in more of these little poetic riffs to break up the reading pace. The published version is a little more concise and straightforward than my original manuscript, but you still get the sense of the narrative stretching out into poetic forms.

F.L.A.: There's much ethnography in *Mayan Drift*. Did you ever consider it an academic, scholarly project?

J.F.H.: Not exactly. I just wrote, wrote, and wrote; then it was done. Afterwards, I realized I had quite a substantial amount of information collected and written about, so I sent it to my former advisor at Stanford, Renalto Rosaldo, to see if he might consider it as a draft for that dissertation I never wrote. He never replied. I mean, I had started the Ph.D. years and years earlier, so I called it even. I bumped into him later on at a memorial service for Yolanda Lopez. At the time he was chair of the Anthropology Department, and he said, "You still want to do that Ph.D.?" And I didn't really hear him. I was just kind of stunned. I was interested, but then I just didn't follow up with him on it.

F.L.A.: You return again to Chiapas in *Thunderweavers*, which you published in 2000, this time focusing specifically on the women.

J.F.H.: It was written to pay homage to those Mayan villagers in Chiapas that were ambushed and killed in 1997 by paramilitary. I had kept some photographs of some of the women in the village who had opened their houses to me back in 1970. My idea was to return the photographs twenty-four years later. They were nowhere to be found when I returned to their village, Acteal. They weren't those massacred in 1997, but that violent event sparked it all up again for me. I love the people and place; they're very deep inside of me. So I decided to write something. Then I began to organize the material into four sections told in the voices of four different women. I thought I'd let each narrator take the narrative in her own direction. I also wanted to give each one room to narrate, giving each fifteen scenes.

Thunderweavers was a breeze to write. I had a set number of scenes, and I had four women narrators, and I had an idea of where it was going to end. I also knew that I had more of a direct poetic style that would be very readable. The only thing I didn't know was whether these four women narrators would, after their own individual explorations, come together or not at the end. I did know that these women's stories and lives were intimately linked to the stories of my mother's, my aunts' lives, and my grandmothers' lives, and that's how, at least on an abstract level, they would all tie together.

F.L.A.: Stepping back in time a couple of years and in a dramatic shift in locale, let's talk about your post–Rodney King L.A. book, *Love after the Riots*, published in 1994. Why, for example, restrict it to a twelve-hour time span?

J.F.H.: That was both a visceral response to the injustices that led to those riots and inspired by Fellini's *La Dolce Vita*, which played in the background while I wrote the book. From start to finish, I wrote the book during the same time it took for the movie to unravel. That was a challenge. Of course, there were misspellings and everything and no line breaks. It was just solid poetry. Then I went back and trimmed it down to give it shape. I used short lines to reflect short moments of time; I chopped up the images and language to let its colors fly. Then I created characters who fell into tangles of love within all this chaos. In a way, the book became like the wires and chalky smell of the stone after you break up a statue.

When I was finished, I sent it to Curbstone Press. I ended up giving it away; it wasn't until after I signed and returned the contract that I realized I wasn't going to receive any royalties. I had been pretty distracted with writing *Night Train to Tuxtla* 'round the clock.

F.L.A.: Before talking about *Night Train*, can we discuss your earlier publication with University of Arizona Press, *Border-Crosser with a Lamborghini Dream*, which you published in 1994?

J.F.H.: My idea was to create a wetback alphabet. I remember I wanted to write a book called *Wetback Alphabet*. I finally gave up on this conceit, thinking it was too easy, but there's still a poem in *Border-Crosser* titled "This is the Z" because I had the idea of writing a poem for each letter of the alphabet. Once I got started, though, I began to write poems in this really jagged, hard-hitting, and rhythmical language—almost like bebop. Mixed in with the language was this sense of danger in the language; you could smell, hear, see something dangerous as you read the poems. I liked doing this book because I got into a new rhythm—a danger lyric—where I wouldn't hold back at all.

F.L.A: Why the title, *Border-Crosser*?

J.F.H.: Well, it's an important subject for all of us. You know, if you take away the neon lights and the bells and whistles from the book, you have a collection of poems that gives readers a direct glimpse at the cruelty and harsh reality that brown people—Chicanos and undocumented Mexican workers—experience everyday. "Border-crosser" because this type of brutal exploitation crosses borders: it's international. It's global.

F.L.A.: Is that why you include a poem that mentions the Ukraine?

J.F.H.: Yes, Ukraine—Poland even. You know, Chicano poets are very much like the Polish poets of the Second World War, who had that real kind of existential, no-holds-barred, stark poetic voice.

F.L.A.: *Lotería Cards and Fortune Poems* also deals with borders?

J.F.H.: I loved writing that book. It was like caviar, man. That was like sitting in the middle of the street with a portable table that you put up with your best friends, and you put some pasta in the middle of the table with some sardines and a pack of Lucky Strikes, no filters, and a couple of bottles of wine. And you let the cars go by, the people walk by. They're kind of looking at you, but you're having such a grand time. You're wearing a light green Italian shirt. You don't have to go to work. The wind's blowing by. And you're sitting back, enjoying the sun. So that's what that book was for me. I just wrote it like butter on bread.

Elaine Katzenberger from City Lights Books called me up one day and asked if I'd be interested in writing some short-lined poetry that would match up with Artemio Rodríguez's art. So, I said, "Sure, send it my way." After I received the lithographs, I realized that I wasn't going to write couplets, thinking somebody else can do that. Instead, I just ran with it. I got so into it, that instead of writing for twenty or so of the prints as they'd originally asked, I wrote on all eighty—all in a week or a week and a half. Then they sent me some more. In less than a month I sent them back over a hundred poems. They go, "Oh, this is different. We love it. We're going to do all one hundred." So I said, "Okay."

I loved writing on those images. I was able to put a lot of things together I never would have been able to otherwise. Nothing was forced. Nothing was artificial for me. Working with art, you know? And I just loved working with this kind of Fellini, macabre, clowny, European, Mexican art. There isn't one piece of poetry in *Lotería Cards* that I don't like. It all just kinda matched me inside, you know?

F.L.A.: Artemio Rodríguez's prints and your poetic themes really bring together everyday issues that face Mexicanos and the Chicanos.

J.F.H.: Rodríguez gave me a lot of room to respond creatively to his Day of the Dead figures, astral projections, and whatnot. More than anything, his art just hit on all those areas that I hadn't written about but wanted to. It was like it he found that musical key—like a D diminished or an augmented ninth with a lot of luscious chords—that I'd always wanted to sing in but hadn't had a chance to. I wrote very short pieces that are very quick to be able to move, like the turning of handlebars or the steering wheels: jerk it right, then left, and then jerk it right, and then jerk it left, jerk it right, jerk it left. I'm not going to take too long going in either direction. That's what that was. I loved it. Absolutely.

F.L.A.: Okay, now let's talk about *Night Train to Tuxtla*. It didn't seem to have much of a life.

J.F.H.: In short: nostalgia does not pay. That book got stopped after four months. It came out, and I got sued for a million dollars. I had to drop it fast, so it ended up never really leaving the warehouse, where it was shredded.

I figured, as a writer you can write and say anything about your life as long as you're not telling a lie; I figured, you could just say what you've got to say. Unfortunately, one of the people that appears in one of the first stories of this semi-autobiographical work heard me read this section at a poetry reading; it was from the section titled, "Let Your Mind Get Sidetracked by Your Wheedle," where I talk about the relationship I had back in the early '70s in L.A. that didn't turn out too good. Right after, I was handed the legal suit. And, when it came down to it, I knew I'd have to spend about sixty thousand dollars to defend the suit. I didn't have the money, and the University of Arizona didn't want to go that route. So they had to throw the book out.

It's a shame because *Night Train* was all the experimental writing I had done while at the Iowa writers' program in 1988–1990. It was also very dangerous writing because I didn't stop to examine, reflect, or edit the material. It's always dangerous to go back into the past. When I received the book in print, it had a death skull/mask on the cover. I jumped back as a chill ran down my spine. It looked good and strong, but little did I know that that chill I felt was a premonition of bad things to come. Somehow, I was casting out all these astral lines, and sure enough, I reeled in the monster.

F.L.A.: You produced enough poetry to fill a book at the Iowa creative writing program, so the program must have worked for you on some level. Were there other ways in which it didn't?

J.F.H.: At first I didn't know what people were talking about, you know, and I couldn't really relate to a lot of the poetry that was being read. I didn't really know their referencing, say, of John Berryman and other Anglo poets. And I didn't know much about Marianne Moore and Elizabeth Bishop. I was reading Neruda, Lorca, Ginsberg, and other crazy cats.

And at first I was resistant. I wanted to honor my Chicano street identity; I kept thinking, any of the poets in the Mission in San Francisco could easily be here with me, but the system wouldn't allow it or something. I had a chip on my shoulder. As time went on, I really learned to enjoy the experience. After all, I could just sit down and write—and get a degree. There were also writers who helped open my eyes to new ways of seeing poetry.

I wasn't exactly familiar with workshop culture and etiquette, but I was happy because I was writing like crazy. Not to mention that the summer just before the program started, I decided to write as many poems as possible so that when I went to the workshop, I wouldn't have any pressure on me. So I wrote a whole stack of poetry.

F.L.A.: How do you see your role as a Chicano writer shaped within a world governed by institutions?

J.F.H.: It's a yin-yang world. You know, the whole idea about wanting to publish, wanting to write, wanting to say something, is very real and good.

At the same time, we don't really need to say anything or write anything or publish anything. You know? I attended the Fifth Chicano Festival in Mexico City in 1974. I was on a bus miles from Tula, the Toltec warrior site, and I was sitting with a whole bunch of Bay Area *pachuco* poets. I was looking out the window, and there was this beautiful land, man. It was green; it was alive. Then one of the poets I was sitting next to said, "Man, I wish I could write a poem about that." And I remember replying, "No, there's no need to write a poem. That is what it is. There's no need to add anything on." So that's what the yin-yang was—that dual force where one is being pulled to say what we've got to say, given our sociopolitical conditions, looking at our communities globally, and speaking out, speaking for those that are suffering. And then the other force has to do with our writing—that's always extra.

The moment that we live in now is fractured; we feel lost, and this can be good because it forces us to look at ourselves and recognize that we're just writers. This doesn't mean that we have to get caught up in the business of writing and the corporate representation of self and other. But it's not just Chicanos anymore; it's not just Latinos anymore because there's no such thing, because we're all intersecting in this multiply fracturing world. Forty or so years ago, yes, it was good enough to take on one point of view to write against the system. But today, it's not good enough. It's not good enough for me to just carve out my little niche and raise my little flag; it's about inhabiting as many different perspectives as possible.

To be a writer is to write and to look at what we're writing about and how we're writing it, what we're saying and how we're saying it. This is how writing can make an impact.

F.L.A.: You are a writer who chose the more marginalized and less secure path of becoming a poet as opposed to a novelist.

J.F.H.: I'd love to give the novel a shot at some point. Right now, though, I'm really excited about writing for young people. I really want to contribute to these young lives. The children's books that I've written actually read more like narrative than poetry and have plots that build suspense. So I've come close to the novel-writing process and know that it's very different from writing poetry. When I write poetry, it feels like I've got twenty eyeballs all flying around observing and re-creating; when I write narrative, my eyes focus and move from one point to another point.

All writing for me is the act of working with words to create new worlds in the middle of a storm. That's what writing's all about.

Writings by the Author
Poetry

Rebozos of Love / We Have Woven / Sudor de Pueblos / On Our Back. San Diego: Toltecas en Aztlán, 1974.

Exiles of Desire. Fresno: Lalo Press Publications, 1983; reprinted, Houston: Arte Público, 1985.

Akrílika. Santa Cruz: Alcatraz Editions, 1989.

The Roots of a Thousand Embraces: Dialogues. San Francisco: Manic D Press, 1994.

Love after the Riots. Willimantic, CT: Curbstone Press, 1996.

Border-Crosser with a Lamborghini Dream. Tucson: University of Arizona Press, 1999.

Lotería Cards and Fortune Poems: A Book of Lives. San Francisco: City Lights Books, 1999.

Thunderweavers / Tejedoras de rayos. Tucson: University of Arizona Press, 2000.

Giraffe on Fire. Tucson: University of Arizona Press, 2001.

Notebooks of a Chile Verde Smuggler. Tucson: University of Arizona Press, 2002.

Children's Literature

Calling the Doves: El canto de las palomas. Illustrated by Elly Simmons. San Francisco: Children's Book Press, 1995.

Laughing Out Loud, I Fly: A carcajadas yo vuelo. Illustrated by Karen Barbour. New York: HarperCollins, 1998.

CrashBoomLove. Albuquerque: University of New Mexico Press, 1999.

The Upside Down Boy: El niño de cabeza. Illustrated by Elizabeth Gomez. San Francisco: Children's Book Press, 2000.

Grandpa and Me at the Flea / Los meros meros remateros. San Francisco: Children's Book Press, 2002.

Welcome to Salsaland! New York: Hyperion, 2002.

Other

Memorias of an Exile's Notebook of the Future. Santa Monica: Santa Monica College Press, 1993.

Night Train to Tuxtla. Tucson: University of Arizona Press, 1994.

187 Reasons Why Mexicanos Can't Cross the Border. Fresno, CA: Borderwolf Press, 1995.

Mayan Drifter: Chicano Poet in the Lowlands of America. Philadelphia: Temple University Press, 1997.

Further Readings
Critical Studies

Cavallari, Héctor Mario. "La muerte y el deseo: Notas sobre la poesía de Juan Felipe Herrera." *Palabra* 4–5 (1983): 97–106.

Flores, Lauro H. "Auto-referencialidad y subversión: Observaciones (con)textuales en torno a la poesía de Juan Felipe Herrera." *Crítica* 2 (1990): 172–181.

———. "Juan Felipe Herrera." *Dictionary of Literary Biography,* vol. 122, *Chicano Writers,* pp. 137–145. Detroit: Gale Group, 1992.

Foster, Sesshu. "From Logan to the Mission: Riding North through Chicano Literary History with Juan Felipe Herrera." *The Americas Review* 17, nos. 3–4 (1989): 68–87.

Rodríguez, Andrés. "Contemporary Chicano Poetry: The Work of Michael Sierra, Juan Felipe Herrera, and Luis J. Rodríguez." *Bilingual Review / Revista Bilingüe* 21, no. 3 (1996): 203–218.

Reviews

Luis-Brown, David. Rev. of *Love after the Riots. The Americas Review* 25 (1999): 245–248.

Nash, Susan Smith. Rev. of *Giraffe on Fire. World Literature Today* 76, no. 1 (2002): 162–164.

———. Rev. of *Mayan Drifter: Chicano Poet in the Lowlands of America. World Literature Today* 72, no. 4 (1998): 846.

Olszewski, Lawrence. Rev. of *Notebooks of a Chile Verde Smuggler. Library Journal* 127, no. 13 (August 2002): 101.

Sanchez, Greg. Rev. of *Night Train to Tuxtla. World Literature Today* 69, no. 3 (1995): 589.

Valle, Emilio del. Rev. of *Thunderweavers/Tejedoras de rayos. Mesoamérica* 22, no. 1 (2001): 227–229.

Wall, Catherine E. Rev. of *Lotería Cards and Fortune Poems: A Book of Lives. World Literature Today* 75, no. 1 (2001): 120.

Welton, Ann. Rev. of *Grandma and Me at the Flea/Los meros meros remateros. School Library Journal* 48, no. 6 (2002): 128.

Interviews

Binder, Wolfgang. "Juan Felipe Herrera." In *Partial Autobiographies: Interviews with Twenty Chicano Poets,* edited by Wolfgang Binder, pp. 95–108. Erlangen, Germany: Verlag Palm and Enke Erlangen, 1985.

Gonzalez, Ray. "Poetry Marauder: An Interview with Juan Felipe Herrera." *Bloomsbury Review* 20, no. 1 (2000): 19–20.

Richard Montoya (of Culture Clash)

ichard Montoya is one of the three performance artists who make
up Culture Clash; the other two are Herbert Siguenza and Ric Salinas. Richard was born in San Diego on August 16, 1969, and raised
in the Sacramento area of California. (Richard is the son of poet José
Montoya, known for his art and political activism during *el movimiento*
of the late 1960s and early 1970s.) Ric Salinas was born in El Salvador on
May 31, 1960, and migrated north to California with his family at a young
age. He grew up in San Francisco's Mission District and later went on to
study broadcasting and communication at San Francisco State University.
Herbert Siguenza, also of Salvadoran heritage, was born on January 26,
1959, and he, too, was raised in the San Francisco Mission District. After
studying visual art at the California College of Arts and Crafts, Siguenza
turned his part-time acting in community theater to a full-time commitment to dramatic performance. All three members gained their dramatic art experience working largely with community theater and with
the first-wave dramatist Luis Valdez and his Teatro Campesino.

The trio came together in 1984 when Rene Yañez asked them to perform
a comedy show for the Cinco de Mayo celebration at the Galleria de la Raza
in San Francisco's Mission District. In 1988 the trio wrote and produced
their first play, *The Mission,* which, unlike their earlier cabaret-style work,
contained a coherent narrative. With their inventive collaborative process,
docudrama interview technique, and name, Culture Clash, they soon took
audiences by storm. These second-wave Chicano theater artists stirred up
audiences as they rioted across the country with such productions as *Bowl*

of Beings (1992), *S.O.S.-Comedy for These Urgent Times* (1992), *Carpa Clash* (1993), *Radio Mambo* (1995), *Bordertown* (1998), a musical adaptation of Aristophanes' *The Birds* (1998), *Nuyorican Stories* (1999), *Mission Magic Mystery Tour* (2000), *Anthems* (2002), and *Chavez Ravine* (2003). While their satirical *rasquache* theater (a Chicano aesthetic that recomposes all that society discards) and urban excavation technique remain focused on the multiform experiences that Latinos and other ethnic minorities face every day in the United States, it does so by touching on universal themes of estrangement within a consumer culture as well as a grandly affirming sense of life. Their work has been recognized by numerous awards, including the Latino Spirit Award and Los Angeles Hispanic Media Award, as well as by institutions such as the Rockefeller Foundation. Culture Clash continues to touch audiences nationally and internationally, both on stage and through television (especially Fox and PBS) and film.

Frederick Luis Aldama: Twenty years of Culture Clash: has a lot changed in your performances?

Richard Montoya: When Culture Clash started in 1984, we were responding to the lack of urban Chicano performances. There had been Valdez's rural farmworker plays, and they had their place, but being urban Chicanos, we wanted to speak to that something else that was going on in the streets of the Mission District, Miami, and New York. José Antonio Burciaga brought Chicano satire—and others like Margo Gómez and Monica Palacios brought queer issues—into Latino/a theater, opening up an explosive space for Culture Clash.

When we started out in an art gallery in San Francisco's Mission District, the emphasis was really performance art/comedy. But Rene Yañez, who was the curator of Galería de la Raza, had been known for performances with Asco (Spanish for "nausea")—an East L.A. performance group that included Harry Gamboa Jr., Willie Herron, Patssi Valdez, and Gonk. Fresh on the heels of that, in '84, Culture Clash was really born.

Even though the stand-up comedy world was thriving, it really was performance art that we were doing from the beginning. I look at our shows today, and there's some of that aesthetic that's still involved in the work. It's performance-driven. It's not so much theater spectacle or even structured in the way of Eurocentric theater; it's a series of performance monologues. This part is still in our current performances.

Our work is constantly evolving. About eight years ago, with *Radio Mambo,* our interview-based work, the life of Culture Clash truly changed, and we went from what was really a cabaret comedy–type situation to full-scale investigations of different regions of the country. And with the production of our play *Chavez Ravine,* that was based partly on interviews and the history of what happened in the city of L.A. in the '40s, '50s, and '60s, I think our work saw yet another transformation. So our work as playwrights and in theater puts us a long way from being a comedy troupe, yet that comic *rasquache* spirit is still very much present. When we look at that Cinco de Mayo '84, and then Cinco de Mayo '04 coming up, we see that presence of the satirical, political, hysterical, lyrical, and now historical.

I believe that we've paid a price for this mixing up of different forms in the academic and Latino playwright world. We're never really included. I think it's because of our roots in comedy. There's a bias against comedy; that's why when the conferences take place, we're never invited to the table. That *crítica* is really by people that really haven't seen *Chavez Ravine* or our interest in darker themes and our taking on the political stuff: land rights, patriotism, what it is to be an American, the war on Communism, the witch hunts, McCarthyism, and the beginnings of a Chicano movement that came out of places like *Chavez Ravine,* and how that might affect us today in present-day Los Angeles. And *Culture Clash in AmeriCCa*—that was just as Yale Repertory Theater looks at the war and post-9/11, and the situations we find ourselves in as olive-skinned people negotiating the country, all while skewering Bush. And the next pieces out of Culture Clash will be highly charged political plays, and not so much sketches or characters or that sort of thing.

The satire and the *política* have been consistently in our work, but we have found other themes and issues to work with. We're secure enough to know that we've explored it; we're comfortable with our skin, and so we're exploring other issues like gender and race outside of the Chicano question. Chicanismo is still present, but as artists we've had to explore other issues. I think of our latest production, *Culture Clash in AmeriCCa,* and its characters as well as all the site-specific work that we've done—*Bordertown, Nuyorican Stories,* and *Radio Mambo*—in San Francisco and Miami as well as the Muslim characters that appear in the D.C.-set *Anthems.* It's the Jewish question; it's the transgender worker with HIV that's trying to save people in San Francisco's Mission District. While there's something Chicano in there, there's also something that's plugged into a larger worldview. We're questioning the madness that's there.

There's too much going on out there in America, and we're trying to gather it as fast as we can and report it back to our ever-growing and -changing audience. This is why we say that the Spanish classics will have to wait for now. We're not going to stage Federico García Lorca just yet. We're not going to do classic Shakespeare stuff just yet.

F.L.A.: The contract's changed?

R.M.: Just as our work is shifting, so is the contract shifting. The old style of Culture Clash yucking it up has shifted to a process of reverse-anthropological, urban excavation. We've become very busy and commissioned artists and mid-career artists and becoming playwrights in the process. And that's a long way from the performance stand-up comedy roots of '84. Yet some things have remained constant, and some things have changed, and that has given the group more life, quite frankly. Gomez-Peña told us once that we were not doing *folklórico* dance so that you might feel our culture, or that you might taste our food. No, we're investigating the other side of the spectrum because, frankly, I need to know more about the dominant culture than they need to know about me.

And so for us that's where the reversal has taken place. We're not explaining ourselves anymore. We're actually trying to find out more about the Anglo ex-Marine that chooses to live in Tijuana, hanging out with exiles. It's really our work of the last five years that we can call *underdog.* Its focus is on those people that aren't really thought of as being at the table and participating in this conversation. Underneath that conversation that takes place among the culture makers and the powers that be, you'll find some pretty amazing stories. So we've been doing our detective work, trying to uncover and discover those underdog stories from all realms of life.

F.L.A.: What about audiences: differences yesterday to today and region to region?

R.M.: Today's audience is not that Mission District audience of 1984. That audience was pretty uptight; they weren't looking for comedy (some pervert doing Julio Iglesias) and weren't into our politically incorrect stand-up material.

In the production of *Chavez Ravine* at the Mark Taper Forum, we were real pleased with the cross-representation; we had an audience filled with elected officials, *cholos/cholas,* as well as old Chavez Ravine residents, the old political guard, and the old Jewish activist guard that started out on the east side of L.A.; we also had their children and grandchildren (nearly 10,000 kids saw the play for free). Of course, performing in different parts of the country like Lawrence, Kansas, or Syracuse, or Tempe, Arizona, or New York, or Washington D.C., you just don't get this kind of Latino representation in the audience. Sometimes there's a couple, but mostly just the three of us on stage performing, so you're sometimes talking to an audience that are listening to three Latino men articulate to them some issues for the very first time.

F.L.A.: You guys are doing site-specific theater now. Does this mean that Culture Clash has found that place of material stability?

R.M.: For the last twelve years, we've been living off our work. It's difficult, but we've managed to make a dignified wage doing it. We basically live off the commissions that we get and the royalties of our work. We're a busy group. We ought to be a busy group.

The question is, how are we going to transfer some of these things to film and television? We're not trying to do sitcom work. We've walked away from that many, many times. We always reinvent and find ourselves on the stage, even if it's a sixty-seater on Santa Monica Boulevard, or if it's the Mark Taper Forum. But film is something interesting to us because it becomes populist. When we did our thirty shows for Fox, it wasn't just that we were trying to be TV stars; it's because it's populist. Every kid in the housing project had a little TV to watch Culture Clash. We were very political on that show. The greatest model now would be Tony Kushner and *Angels in America:* beautiful way of transferring his stage work into epic television. HBO's not in every household, but a lot more people will have seen that in one night than in twenty years of performing it on stage. And so as a model that's a good one, and that's the kind of work that we all should be doing.

We are also diversifying. Guys can step out of the group for a moment to do a piece like Cantinflas [Mexican comedic actor] or travel to New York and do spoken word poetry.

F.L.A.: The process for your docu-style theatre: you amass a bunch of material, and then you sculpt it into something that becomes powerful and engaging for an audience?

R.M.: Well, *Chavez Ravine* is a great example. There was a dressing room that was just for the boxes of information that we found. And buried in that one ton of boxes of information somewhere is the play. One thing that has helped us a great deal in the last couple of years is working with dramaturges, like José Luis Valenzuela, Lisa Peterson, Tony Taccone, and others, that have really helped us in the shaping process. These folks have helped Culture Clash get in a room and shape a piece; they're like midwives helping us decipher and shape experiences and information in an often painful birthing process.

My dad, poet José Montoya, calls it a butcher shop because we will rearrange a Miguel Piñero poem if we have to. And the world's full of writers and actors that think they can improve upon a Shakespeare sonnet. We all have that in us, but sometimes a good director and a dramaturge can even protect your own writing from you: the good directors and good dramaturges reminding us that we were sitting on a gold mine and helping us unearth the powerful voices in the interviews: the three African American cons inside the Dade County prison, the Cuban exiles, the Jewish guy, the Haitian guy. The process is painful. It's long. There's never really a shortcut to it. But you're exactly right: it's a sculpting process.

The advantage of being a performance trio is that we can quickly put stuff on its feet and see if it works, or see if it doesn't work. And so directors come along really wanting to participate and to observe the Culture Clash process. And that's really a fun part of it, just getting up off that table and working something out on its feet, then going back to the table. So it's helpful to be the writer as well as the performer.

There's a price that we've paid for that because we're not categorized as playwrights; we're considered instead actor/performers. Who cares? The work is good, or the work is not good. And there's a lot of mediocre work being directed by a lot of mediocre directors. I want to see one reach inside of me and grab me. I see rag-tag *teatros* all the time do something powerful and beautiful. I'm not talking that everyone has to be at the Lincoln Center or the Mark Taper Forum. In our aesthetic and political agenda we aim for excellence. We make no apologies about that. That's something that comes from a great Mexican director, José Luis Valenzuela [Latino Theater Company], who instilled this sense of excellence in us long ago. It has to be part of us. That's why our shows aren't necessarily pretty. I mean, we can have one backdrop, one suitcase full of costumes, and three chairs. Two chairs, three guys, and a backdrop. I mean, I'm not talking about hydraulics and Broadway and that shit. I'm talking about the power of the performance aesthetic, and what the text is saying.

F.L.A.: Satire, flashbacks, gritty realism, the fantastical, and more appear in your performances. How is this part of the sculpting process?

R.M.: Someone once described it as a kind of a postmodern grab bag of styles and genres that are, like, heaped on a pile in a junkyard. We feel free to grab from any genre and not to be so strict about trying to emulate a Eurocentric style. I mean we are cinematic. We are satirical. It goes back to those José Guadalupe Posada prints from the turn of the century, the *calaveras* (skeletons). I mean there was such a genius in that kind of satire. Underneath it all, we're all bones: rich or poor man, we're all the same in death.

We grab from every style that we need: flashback or flash-forward, magic realism or lyricism, spoken word, dance, Method acting styles. That's the part that is *rasquache*—that sense of survival in and through collage-performance art. That's why we can put on a show in a cafeteria at De Paul University, at the Kennedy Center the next day, or at a United Farmworkers rally and engage and get any kind of audience thinking critically.

F.L.A.: You mentioned plays that grab you.

R.M.: Yeah, we need to raise the bar like August Wilson does when he gives himself permission to write a nine-cycle play. We'd better start having our Naomi Wallaces, our August Wilsons, our Tony Kushners. We need such a Holy Trinity. I'm eager to place a Chicano or Chicana writer up there. I know a lot of us feel we should be up there. I don't see it. I haven't seen it. We're getting close, but we're not quite there.

F.L.A.: Why Aristophanes and the decision to do *The Birds*?

R.M.: David Ems, the South Coast [Repertory Theater's] artistic director, shrewdly said, "How can I place these guys with a classic piece of theater that would be an introduction into his subscriber-based regional theater?" In Aristophanes we found all the satire and all the political comments we could ever hope to make. Aristophanes was making them 2,500 years ago in taking on the Greek authorities.

F.L.A.: Personal memory is history in *Bordertown, Chavez Ravine,* and *Nuyorican Stories?*

R.M.: Absolutely, because before the time of Culture Clash there were Chicano poets like Dad and José Antonio Burciaga standing on street corners with Nuyorican poets like Piñero, Pietri, and Algarín. This first generation was doing poetry, creating life-and-death poetry in innovative ways that need to be remembered. We wanted to capture this moment along with all its voices and lives. Today, only a few of the Nuyorican poets are left, like Pedro Pietri; others, like Algarín, aren't well. In the shaping of *Nuyorican Stories,* we met with Algarín and "El Reverendo" Pietri. They gave their blessing, passing on their word and telling us to carry it forward as the sons and daughters of this important cultural moment.

F.L.A.: In *Bordertown* you have different historical moments and different settings.

R.M.: When you go out to interview people for these site-specific pieces, you never know what era or what story they're going to talk to you about. So when we talked to my dad about his experiences as a sailor living in San Diego in a 1950s Tijuana/San Diego, it was right at the end of the zoot suit era. The story of the '70s came about with the evolution of Chicano Park and the collective memory of a community that took over a piece of land and took it over from the cops, from the Feds, and said, "Enough toxic dump sites in the barrio. We're building a park here, where kids can play."

When looking for the worthiness for the stage, the "sea legs" of a stage piece, there are so many goddamn stories out there that haven't even been told. My dad's family coming from New Mexico to California during Steinbeck's Depression is only one of them. We need a Chicano version of that journey and experience—a Chicano *Grapes of Wrath.*

F.L.A.: There's certainly a lot more being written and produced than in the past: Octavio Solis, Migdalia Cruz, Cherríe Moraga.

R.M.: Cherríe's probably the fiercest playwright around right now. I've gone to seventy-seat theaters and seen her work. But she should be at bigger forums, like the Taper. That audience needs to see her work because you'll find in the audience the Chicano muralist Judy Baca, Rudy Acuna, and *raza* by the tons who like to dress to the nines, as well as those white westsiders. There's an audience there eager to participate in this conversation. We found that with *Chavez Ravine:* an audience that didn't hold back one bit. I mean, it wasn't easy for the city to watch, but it still sold out for nearly two months.

F.L.A.: There are those like Luis Alfaro who are working from inside the establishment to help open up venues like the Mark Taper to help build a critical mass (relatively speaking) of Chicano/Latino playwrights?

R.M.: Luis as a performer, performance artist, and a playwright deserves a lot of respect. We certainly give him that. He has worked tirelessly to make in-roads within the institutions. His work with Diane Rodriguez at the Taper's Latino Theater Initiative has been helpful. They're the ones that initiated the conversation with us about *Chavez Ravine.*

Sometimes these institutions can't reach you, though. They're competitive. That doesn't always make for building of a community. The Labyrinth Theater Company in New York is a good model because even though they select what they might produce or not, they keep their door open for retreats and writing workshops. No red carpet—you just come and you throw down. I think what happens in L.A. is that if you're in good favor, you're in, and if not, you're out all together.

Let's make sure we're developing a community of artists, and not just surrounding ourselves with the people we think would be cool to work with; there needs to be more of a real mix of working artists and working actors. Ultimately, though, forums like the Taper in Los Angeles are like rocket launchers. You blast off, then the booster falls away, and then it's all up to you. Your shit has to hold together on its own; it has to be really tight.

Writings by the Author
Performance/Drama

Montoya, Richard, Ricardo Salinas, and Herbert Siguenza. *Culture Clash: Life, Death, and Revolutionary Comedy.* New York: Theatre Communications Group, 1998.

————. *Culture Clash in AmeriCCa: Four Plays.* New York: Theatre Communications Group, 2003.

Further Readings
Critical Studies

Glenn, Antonia Grace. "Comedy for These Urgent Times: Culture Clash as Chroniclers in America." *Theatre Forum* 20 (2002): 62–68.

Kondo, Dorinne. "(Re)Visions of Race: Contemporary Race Theory and the Cultural Politics of Racial Crossover in Documentary Theatre." *Theatre Journal* 52, no. 1 (2000): 81–107.

Monaghan, Constance. "Mambo Combo." *American Theatre* 15, no. 3 (1998): 10–14.

Pat Mora

Born in 1942, Pat Mora grew up in El Paso hearing the stories told by her grandmother, her mother, and her Aunt Lobo. This storytelling matrilineage planted the seeds that would later blossom as Mora found her voice as a poet, memoirist, and children's book author.

Though Mora's upbringing allowed her to develop an ear especially attuned to the rhythms of storytelling, it was not until years later, after studying to become a teacher and earning a B.A. (1963) and then an M.A. (1967) from the University of Texas at El Paso, that she decided to commit herself fully to writing. In the 1970s, Mora began writing bicultural, Chicana-themed poetry that caught the first wave of contemporary Chicano poetry and appeared in such journals as *Americas Review*. By the 1980s, Mora's poetry had caught the eye of Arte Público's editor, Nicolas Kanellos, who published her first two collections, *Chants* (1984) and *Borders* (1986). In the poem "Mi Madre" from *Chants*, Mora infuses life into a seemingly uninhabitable desertscape as she reimagines it to be a place of nurturing: "she: the desert / She: strong mother." Both collections' poems are steeped in a Chicana feminism that glows with a powerfully radiant aura of land and matrilineage, where grandmothers and *curanderas* act as wise and strong role models who guide new generations of Chicanas through the minefields of a patriarchal society.

Through the 1980s and into the 1990s, Mora continued to develop her voice as a Chicana borderland poet, inventing a complex array of southwestern landscapes that tangle with the lives of her Chicana poet-narrators and figures. After the publication of *Communion* (1991), Mora's presence as a major Chicana poet was firmly established. In 1993 she published her collection of essays entitled *Nepantla,* in which she expresses a deep pride in her Chicana cultural identity (language, cultural symbols, and spiritual belief systems), which is essential for survival, she writes, in "our era of international technological and economic interdependence." In the poem "The Border: A Glare of Truth," Mora defines the origin of her being as poet-curandera:

> That desert—its
> firmness, resilience, and fierceness, its whispered chants and
> tempestuous dance, its wisdom and majesty—shaped us as geography
> always shapes its inhabitants. The desert persists in me, both inspiring
> and compelling me to sing about her and her people, their roots and
> blooms and thorns.
> *(10)*

In other poems in the collection, Mora again employs the imagery of land and matrilineal healing, but expands it to include the experiences of women in such places as Cuba and India. In *Agua Santa* (1995), her woman-of-color, feminist poetics again shines through powerfully. For example, her poem "The Loving Strip" begins: "Not for men alone do we remove our clothes, / slowly unbutton ourselves and stare / at flesh soft as the underside of petals"(3).

As Mora's poetry continued to flow, so did other forms of expression. In 1997 she published her memoir, *House of Houses,* in which she interweaves fact and fiction, past and present, memory and imagination, to render visible the experience of those inhabiting two worlds (U.S. and Mexican) along the Rio Grande between El Paso and Santa Fe.

It was also during this great creative period in the 1990s that Mora began to write her award-winning children's books. As she expresses in *Nepantla,* "My investment is in the future. I suppose that is one of the many reasons why I write children's books." In her first Chicano children's book, *A Birthday Basket for Tía* (1992), Mora turns from her traditional focus on women to paint beautifully the intergenerational relationship between a boy and his grandfather. Giving texture to the complexities of Chicano family life in children's narrative form is one way in which Mora invests in the future. Another way is by revitalizing Amerindian myth. For example, in her bilingual children's book *The Race of Toad and Deer* (1995), she revises the Anglo-European story of the tortoise and hare that privileges individuality and turns it toward an Amerindian collective sensibility and worldview.

Frederick Luis Aldama: You're a writer and a teacher?

Pat Mora: I've taught at all levels, briefly teaching in elementary and middle schools, then two years in high school, and many years of teaching evening classes at community college; I also taught part-time at the University of Texas, El Paso. But it's been years since I was a teacher in a classroom. Now when I teach, it tends to be summer writing workshops—sometimes teacher workshops. It was in the mid-1980s that I realized that I needed to stop grading papers. Either I was going to take the path of the Ph.D. or invest my time in creative writing. I had three children and didn't want to move around a lot, so I chose the creative writing route—with some workshop teaching on the side.

F.L.A.: Do you have a particular method for conducting your writing workshops?

P.M.: Recently, I taught two writing workshops up in Taos and one for the University of Minnesota. Because those that take my workshops tend to have varying levels of experience, I try to create a climate that allows people to take risks. In any given workshop, I might have academics displaying linguistic pyrotechnics along with people who have regular jobs—some corporate—but just really love poetry or fiction. I usually have students bring a work by a writer they admire and have them discuss why the writing dazzles them—something that's brimming with language. It's a way of getting them to open up and think critically about writing, because it leads naturally to an overflow of energy and excitement about writing and tends to open the door for them to experiment. Bringing work we love, we take risks we might not otherwise. This helps foster a learning environment where each participant is interested in supporting the others in their writing. Cultivating communication and helping them find energy and excitement in writing is central.

F.L.A.: Clearly, communication and energy are important elements in your work, both in form and content.

P.M.: I think it goes back to that notion of communion, you know? And I'm very interested in spiritual writers who deal with this concept of communion. It's particularly relevant now when we seem to constantly be on the brink of fracturing as a planet. How can I communicate with you in a way that does create a communion of trust? I would say that's another thing that's very important to me, that I want the reader to feel that he or she can trust the page. As a writer, I am trying to be honest with my reader.

In our everyday relationships, we, too, need to create communion with another human being. We tend to carry so many layers of protection—from the most obvious, like our clothes, to the less tangible aspects, like our ego—but we need to get beyond or through these layers. Poetry can go all the way in and open up the possibility of creating that deep heart-to-heart connection. As a writer, I'm after the heart. I think we all need to soften our hearts, and I think that poetry can help us accomplish this.

F.L.A.: Was there a moment in your life when you decided that poetry would be your primary genre?

P.M.: There are two ways to answer. First, Arte Público took an immediate interest in my poetry, and because success breeds success, I continued. Second, poetry is a form that I've always loved: its music, its spareness, its power—the way it can strike like lightning. When I think about some of the books that I loved reading growing up, I think about this very traditional poetry collection that was in my house. All those rhyming poems collected in the anthology have stayed with me through the years. It's inexplicable, but poetry just knocks me off my feet.

When I think back to my initial luck with publishing, I'm grateful and frustrated. Frustrated because I think about the publishing world's closing its doors to young, talented Chicano writers today; that world has not opened up in ways that we would like to believe. And so there's a part of me that always aches for the young writer because I know what a challenge is ahead and how much persistence is going to be required to persevere through all the hard knocks. I still struggle.

F.L.A.: Who are some poets that have knocked you off your feet?

P.M.: Whenever I flip open any of Pablo Neruda's collections, I'm dazzled by his incredible willingness to let the imagination take flight. Then there's García Lorca's poetry—that moves me like a deep song. In terms of contemporary poets, Mary Oliver's poetry—and her writing on poetry—is very, very important to me: her fascination with that space between syllables that has the power to build symphonic sounds and images. And when I get discouraged, I always think of Lucille Clifton—a woman of color who has been steadfast in her work and in her style. She's my beacon in many ways.

F.L.A.: You published your first collection, *Chants,* in 1984 with, as you mentioned, Arte Público. That's largely focused on storytelling as a way to preserve community.

P.M.: I think the fascination in storytellers has a very personal link in my life, which is that I have written a lot about an aunt of mine called Lobo, one of my mythic women, who was a great storyteller. I grew up listening to her stories before going to sleep, and so her music became a part of me. When *Chants* was published, I had an image, and I think it was in an Amado Peña painting in my office at the University of Texas. And it showed two Native American figures with a pot between them. And I felt that my aunt had passed on the clay through her storytelling: that she passed on the love of storytelling.

F.L.A.: In your third collection, *Communion,* you shift your gaze to those complex areas where race and gender cross borders, and your language shifts back and forth between English and Spanish, as in the poem "Legal Alien."

P.M.: "Legal Alien" crosses all sorts of borders: it's bilingual and bicultural; it's one of the poems that people are especially drawn to. But, to be honest, I'm never sure how much an author knows about what he or she is doing consciously. I like to remain somewhat unaware. It goes back to that notion that visual artists like de Kooning and writers like Borges have written about: that you want to create in such a way that you allow for the unexpected to come through. I think that ideally poetry is such an internal meditation that what comes up should be uncontrolled—as Frost talked about ice on the hot stove. You're following; you're not leading it.

F.L.A.: In your more, say, feminist collection, *Agua Santa / Holy Water,* where you include the poem "Dear Frida," you seem to move away from the more regional-themed poetry of *Chants.*

P.M.: I'm sometimes uncomfortable with the term "regionalism," because I think that it can be a way of denigrating writing: somehow the implication is that to write about a Mexican village isn't as meaningful as to write about Frida. However, both poems were written at different times of my life; for example, the Frida poem was inspired by a trip to Mexico City, when her paintings triggered something deep in me; the poetry in *Chants,* during many other different moments in my life. But I'm not sure there's such a neat progression from one collection to the next. At the end of my life, perhaps my work will look something like a series of concentric circles. Labyrinths and expanding rings fascinate me. So if it turns out that there is movement in my work, this would make me happy. It's certainly not something that I am conscious of now or during the moment that I'm writing.

F.L.A.: Did you conceive of *Chants* and *Communion* as complete books, or were they collections made up of previously written material?

P.M.: Yes, these were collections, as were *Borders* and *Agua Santa.* I've recently completed a manuscript for a book of odes, and that book, like *Aunt Carmen's Book of Practical Saints,* was conceived of as a whole.

I think with age, and after writing the very structured memoir, *House of Houses,* I have become more interested in envisioning a structure for my work, thinking of my work in terms of putting together a house, for example. To one degree or another, you always have to wrestle with structure and ask yourself how you're going to organize your material to convey certain meaning and imagery most effectively. In a book like *Aunt Carmen's Book of Practical Saints,* I wanted to create different mood shifts and sharp contrasts so as not to tire the reader. And you take risks within these structures, hoping that it will energize your work. Recently I read a poem in the *New Yorker* by Czeslaw Milosz. Here's a poet near the end of his life that has reached a peak of writing power that is stunning. So, to some extent we are training like athletes to reach just such a peak.

F.L.A.: You seem to use photographs in *Aunt Carmen's Book of Practical Saints* to break up the pacing and provide sharp contrasts.

P.M.: I'm very interested in the actual appearance of books. In the collection *Nepantla,* I wanted some visuals, so I have little lizards moving through the book. And in *Aunt Carmen,* I wanted to include folk art. I was amazed that Beacon agreed to it, as it's very expensive. Living here in New Mexico, I've been very fascinated and moved by the *santero* tradition—the ritual of carving and giving shape to saints out of blocks of wood. This affected the way I thought about the poem on the page. Just as these *santeros* here carve new shapes out of traditional images, so, too, does the poet reimagine and craft poetic shapes on the page. When the book was published, because it's so beautifully designed, I felt if I never did anything else, it would be okay.

F.L.A.: You shift from poetry to prose with *House of Houses*.

P.M.: It was not only a shift in form, but was also a complete surprise. I never expected to write something like this. At first, working in prose felt like I had walked into a spider web, and I couldn't figure my way out. On the other hand, getting back to your earlier question about communication, I am intensely interested in it. And I am well aware that not everyone will read poetry. So prose allowed me another opportunity to communicate. And I had dear friends who would say to me, "Have you ever thought about writing in paragraphs? You know, they usually go all the way across the page." In part, *House,* like *Nepantla,* was an exercise in trying another way of reaching people.

I also learned a lot from writing *House.* It's hard for me to be excited about plot. The writer Pam Houston once said at a writing conference, "Plots are for dead people." Whenever I've read, I've always been more interested in characters and the use of language than with plot. I would say the joy of writing *House* was the pleasure of spending time with people from throughout my life and their voices.

F.L.A.: Do you think the prose writing that fills out the pages of *House of Houses* helped get you more of a mainstream recognition?

P.M.: Well, it did get very good reviews that helped with its publicity—and to circulate my name; after all, we live in a star-obsessed society where name recognition is vital.

F.L.A.: You also write children's books.

P.M.: When my children were growing up, I would say to myself, "This would make a good children's book"—just as other things in my life would trigger ideas about a poem or an essay. My interest also came out of an impulse to write stories that validated Latino culture. It wasn't easy breaking into this market. I received a lot of rejections—and still receive them, now that I'm published. This fact always surprises people who think that after your first successful publication, it's easy to publish more. It continues to be an unending struggle—even a relentless struggle. It's even harder for writers of color because the children's book marketplace doesn't want to really deal with stories that complicate our cultural and linguistic landscapes. Editors often have a definition of what makes a good story, and not all of us agree on this definition.

The first children's book that I had accepted for publication was *Tomás and the Library Lady,* but it took eight years before it came out from Knopf. (The first one that was actually published was *A Birthday Basket for Tía* with Macmillan in 1992.) Every book has its stories, including *Tomás and the Library Lady.* The second talented illustrator lived in London, but ended up having some problems. The publisher waited for years for her; then finally she just couldn't finish the book. It was a big decision to start over because any time you start over, you're going to wait at least two years. Children's book publishing is very complex and time consuming because of the collaborative aspect; the illustrator may be busy with other projects and so on.

F.L.A.: *Tomás and the Library Lady* is inspired by the Chicano author Tomás Rivera?

P.M.: I didn't know him well, but I had the good fortune of meeting him. He's such an important figure for Chicano/a writers—his journey from being a migrant worker to becoming a successful writer and an educational leader—that I wanted to pay a sort of homage to him. It's also a story that celebrates the power of storytelling and the pleasure of literacy that far too many young people are missing in their lives.

F.L.A.: In your children's book *The Race of Toad and Deer,* you give the traditional toad and hare story a Mayan mythical dimension.

P.M.: What I loved about the Mayan version—and what I tell teachers and students, of course—is that it is the difference between winning as an individual and winning as a team. It was one of the aspects that most drew me to that story. I had asked this gentleman from Guatemala, Don Fernando, if he could tell me some stories that he had heard when he was a little boy. He then sent me a tape with stories, and this was one of the stories. I loved that notion, you know, of a collective success.

F.L.A.: You edited the different writing by Latina writers that went into the children's book *Love to Mamá?*

P.M.: When the publishers, Lee and Low Books, proposed that I edit this collection, I wasn't sure at first. I didn't know that I wanted to edit. The same press had done a book on African American dads. With my mother still alive (she's 86), I thought, well, you know, wouldn't it be a wonderful gift for me to give her. Once we decided to do it, it was very important to me that it be as diverse as possible. People always think of diversity as meaning that they're going to include one Latina writer. But I was interested in a book of Latina writers from all different backgrounds, like rural and urban, and who wrote poetry that might challenge students and readers. I wanted poems about home and poems about different countries of origin. I wanted poems that had traditional rhyme and those that were experimental. I wanted a collection that would show the richness that we Latina writers offer.

So many of the poems submitted were about grandmothers that I told the publisher that half the poems should be about our *abuelitas*. Making the selections was not easy. There were over three hundred submissions, and we only had room for thirteen or so. It taught me a lot about the process, including rejections, because there would be poems that I liked a lot, but I would think, well, we have to have a poem about school, or we have to have a poem that reflects the inner city, because a lot of our children are there, and I want them to see themselves on the page. Only twelve or thirteen was very, very difficult.

F.L.A.: Is the publishing scene improving for Latino/Chicano literature?

P.M.: If we talk about children's books for a minute, the statistics do not show any real expansion; that includes books by and/or about Latinos or Chicanos. Only 2 percent of the children's books published today are by or about Latinos—and the percentage is dropping. So though there can be lot of hype about a few multicultural books, as a whole, there hasn't been much of a change. I'm not pessimistic. But I'm not seeing the change that I would like to see. I'm not seeing, for example, Latina and Latino editors. There are a few. We need more of them. But we also need Latinos as marketing directors, and we need them as art directors.

We have a lot to contribute. We also need to be very committed to literacy. I believe that we have to grow our own audience and that we need to work with parents; that's probably where I spend a lot of my personal energy. We also need to be vocal with our bookstores. We need to protest, write letters to our libraries, and so on. The change will not take place without a struggle.

F.L.A.: Do you see your role as a Chicana writer as part of this struggle?

P.M.: Part of my role is to write the best books I can: to query myself internally and to take risks. Because of the privilege of being published, and it is a privilege, I feel that I do need to speak out. Not just to harangue, because that's not usually very effective, but to be inventive about how to engage people in protecting and embracing the power of language. When I think of the role of the farmworkers, when I think about school integration, when I think about work that's done in housing, and when I think about work that's done in health or in the environmental movement, the role of literature and literacy is part of that work. It's part of that whole, part of our wanting to and needing to be part of a legacy. We want our words and the lives of our grandparents and our history to be recorded and to be read and to be validated and to be rethought and to be rewritten eventually by people who will come through, generations down the road.

Right now I'm working on some essays that explore how to bridge the gap between educators and students; there is an unnecessary cultural and racial gap. Anywhere in the world, people perceive other groups as different. Of course, we are more similar than different, so by learning how to tap into our humanity, I think we can embrace this difference. Literature allows for this possibility. It humanizes, and I think we all long for that. I don't propose solutions, but rather approaches that, I hope, could be helpful for tapping into this deeply humane spirit of ours.

Writings by the Author
Poetry

Chants. Houston: Arte Público, 1984.
Borders. Houston: Arte Público, 1986.
Communion. Houston: Arte Público, 1991.
Agua Santa / Holy Water. Boston: Beacon Press, 1995.
Aunt Carmen's Book of Practical Saints. Boston: Beacon Press, 1997.

Essay/Memoir

Nepantla: Essays from the Land in the Middle. Albuquerque: University of New Mexico Press, 1993.
House of Houses. Boston: Beacon, 1997.

Children's Literature

A Birthday Basket for Tía. Illustrated by Cecily Lang. New York: Macmillan, 1992.

Agua, Agua, Agua: An Aesop's Fable Retold. Illustrated by José Ortega. Tucson: Good Year Books, 1994.

The Desert Is My Mother / El desierto es mi madre. Illustrated by Daniel Lechón. Houston: Piñata Books, 1994.

Listen to the Desert / Oye al desierto. Illustrated by Francisco S. Mora. New York: Clarion, 1994.

Pablo's Tree. Illustrated by Cecily Lang. New York: Macmillan, 1994.

Confetti (poems). Illustrated by Enrique Sanchez. New York: Lee and Low Books, 1995.

The Race of Toad and Deer. Illustrated by Maya Itzna Brooks. Orchard Books, 1995.

With Charles Ramirez Berg. *The Gift of the Poinsettia / El regalo de la flor de nochebuena.* Illustrated by Daniel Lechón. Houston: Piñata Books, 1995.

Uno, dos, tres / One, Two, Three. Illustrated by Barbara Lavallee. New York: Clarion, 1996.

Tomás and the Library Lady. Illustrated by Raul Colón. New York: Knopf, 1997.

Delicious Hulabaloo / Pachanga deliciosa. Illustrated by Francisco X. Mora. Translated by Alba Nora Martinez and Pat Mora. Houston: Piñata Books, 1998.

This Big Sky. New York: Scholastic, 1998.

The Rainbow Tulip. Illustrated by Elizabeth Sayles. New York: Viking, 1999.

My Own True Name. Houston: Piñata Books, 2000.

The Night the Moon Fell: A Maya Myth / La noche que se cayó la luna: Mito Maya. Translated by Domi. Vancouver: Douglas and McIntyre, 2000.

The Bakery Lady / La señora de la panadería. Illustrated by Pablo Torrecilla. Translated by Gabriela Baeza Ventura. Houston: Arte Público, 2001.

Love to Mamá: A Tribute to Mothers. Illustrated by Paula S. Barragán M. New York: Lee and Low Books, 2001.

A Library for Juana: The World of Sor Juana Inés. Illustrated by Beatriz Vidal. New York: Knopf, 2002.

Maria Paints the Hills. Illustrated by Maria Hesch. Santa Fe: Museum of New Mexico Press, 2002.

Further Readings
Critical Studies

Fast, Robin Riley. "Nature and Creative Power: Pat Mora and Patricia Hampl." *San Jose Studies* 15, no. 2 (1989): 29–40.

Fox, Linda C. "From *Chants* to *Borders* to *Communion:* Pat Mora's Poetic Journey to Nepantla." *Bilingual Review/ Revista Bilingüe* 21, no. 3 (1996): 219–230.

Kanellos, Nicolás. "Pat Mora." *Dictionary of Literary Biography,* Vol. 209, *Chicano Writers,* pp. 160–163. Detroit: Gale Group, 1999.

Murphy, Patrick D. "Grandmother Borderland: Placing Identity and Ethnicity." *ISLE: Interdisciplinary Studies in Literature and Environment* 1, no. 1 (1993): 35–41.

Passman, Kristina. "Demeter, Kore, and the Birth of the Self: The Quest for Identity in the Poetry of Alma Villanueva, Pat Mora, and Cherríe Moraga." *Monographic Review* 6 (1990): 35–41.

Rebolledo, Tey Diana. "Tradition and Mythology: Signatures of Landscape in Chicana Literature." In *The Desert Is No Lady: Southwestern Landscapes in Women's Writing and Art,* edited by Vera Norwood and Janice Monk, pp. 96–124. New Haven, CT: Yale University Press, 1987.

Rebolledo, Tey Diana, and Eliana S. Rivero. "Introduction." In *Infinite Divisions: An Anthology of Chicana Literature,* edited by Tey Diana Rebolledo and Eliana S. Rivero. Tucson: University of Arizona Press, 1993.

Rocard, Marcienne. "Du bon usage de la différence: Borders de Pat Mora." *Annales du Centre de Reserches sur l'Amérique Anglophone* 18 (1993): 279–288.

Shuru, Xochitl Estrada. "The Poetics of Hysteria in Chicana Writing: Sandra Cisneros, Margarita Cota-Cardenas, Pat Mora, and Bernice Zamora." Ph.D. Dissertation, University of New Mexico, 2000.

Spencer, Laura Gutiérrez. "The Desert Blooms: Flowered Songs by Pat Mora." *Bilingual Review / Revista Bilingüe* 20, no. 1 (1995): 28–36.

Reviews

Ayres, Annie. Rev. of *Pablo's Tree. Booklist* 91, no. 5 (November 1, 1994): 507.

Beram, Nell D. Rev. of *Love to Mamá: A Tribute to Mothers. The Horn Book Magazine* 77, no. 4 (July 2001): 468.

Engberg, Gillian. Rev. of *The Race of Toad and Deer. Booklist* 98, no. 8 (December 15, 2001): 735.

Gonzalez, Lucia M. Rev. of *Tomás and the Library Lady. School Library Journal* 47, no. 9 (September 2001): 27.

Italiano, Graciela. Rev. of *Listen to the Desert / Oye al desierto. School Library Journal* 40, no. 10 (October 1994): 112(1).

Knoth, Maeve Visser. Rev. of *A Birthday Basket for Tía. The Horn Book Magazine* 69, no. 1 (1993): 76.

Milligan, Bryce. Rev. of *Communion. National Catholic Reporter* 27, no. 28 (May 10, 1991): 24.

Pinto, L. L. Rev. of *Nepantla: Essays from the Land in the Middle*. *CHOICE: Current Reviews for Academic Libraries* 31, no. 1 (September 1993): 122.

Welton, Ann. Rev. of *The Bakery Lady / La señora de la panadería*. *School Library Journal* 48, no. 1 (2002): 130.

————. Rev. of *The Night the Moon Fell*. *School Library Journal* 46, no. 11 (2000): 45.

Interviews

Alarcón, Norma. "Interview with Pat Mora." *Third Woman* 3, nos. 1–2 (1986): 121–126.

Dick, Bruce Allen. "Pat Mora." In *A Poet's Truth: Conversations with Latino/Latina Poets,* pp. 92–105. Tucson: University of Arizona Press, 2003.

Ikas, Karin Rosa. "Pat Mora." In *Chicana Ways: Conversations with Ten Chicana Writers*. Reno: University of Nevada Press, 2001.

Leonard, Frances, and Ramona Cearley, eds. "Pat Mora." In *Conversations with Texas Writers,* pp. 249–257. Austin: University of Texas Press, 2005.

Cherríe Moraga

herríe Moraga was born in Whittier, California, in 1952. She grew up in the San Gabriel Valley, learning from an early age to negotiate her bicultural experiences and biracial identity. Although her Anglo (British/Irish/French) father was present when she was growing up, it was her Chicana mother's family—especially her fiercely feminist grandmother from Sonora, Mexico—who mostly raised Moraga.

From an early age, Moraga was drawn to literature and creative writing. However, with few job options available that would provide her the time to write, Moraga decided to become a schoolteacher. After completing her B.A. at Immaculate Heart College in Hollywood in 1974, she discovered quickly that teaching high school English was not for her; it simply didn't give her enough time to develop her poetic voice. After her first out lesbian poetry appeared to a receptive audience in 1975, she decided that she might be able to make a living as a writer. She knew, however, that she would need more formal training, so she enrolled in the creative writing M.A. track at San Francisco State University. This step proved the beginning of an intensely productive—and experimental—period for Moraga; it was also the period when she discovered her passion for drama. To further her goal to become a playwright and poet, she moved to New York City, where in 1981 she co-founded the Kitchen Table/Women of Color Press. Kitchen Table provided Moraga and other women of color a much-needed venue for their creative voices to be heard. (They published, for example, the trailblazing *Cuentos: Stories by Latinas,* which brought together the stories of Nuyorican, Cuban, and Chicana writers living in the United States.) During this period

Moraga also co-edited and helped publish the field-defining anthology *This Bridge Called My Back* (1981). This book voiced issues and concerns of Chicanas and Latinas long ignored by the Anglo-feminist and Chicano movements. In a poem entitled "For the Color of My Mother," which appears in the collection, Moraga opines: "I am a white girl gone brown to the blood color of my mother / speaking for her / as it should be / dark women come to me / sitting in circles / I pass through their hands / the head of my mother / painted in clay colors." Though "a white girl," Moraga identifies with and speaks for her "brown" mother long silenced within a racist and sexist world.

Such themes and poetic spirit come to inform her work as a playwright. In 1984 Moraga produced her first play, *Giving Up the Ghost: Teatro in Two Acts*, which appeared to critical acclaim first in Minnesota and then in San Francisco. Chicana lesbian characters appeared on stage—a first for Chicano *teatro*—and their experiences and revelations formed a critique of patriarchal oppression. In the early 1990s, Moraga continued to develop and complicate her voice as a playwright, producing plays such as *Shadow of a Man* (1990), *Heroes and Saints* (1992), and *Watsonville: Some Place Not Here* (1996), which gave texture to the trials and tribulations of Chicanos/as living in farmworking communities. Moraga began to explore pre-Columbian mythology in *Heart of the Earth* (1994), which gives a lesbian/*mestiza* twist to the Popul Vuh. Moraga has continued to experiment with theatrical—and poetic—forms to texture the many intersections between world mythologies as tools for empowerment for straight and lesbian women of color. Moraga's powerfully dramatic and poetic explorations of biracial, bicultural, queer identity and experience have led to national recognition as a preeminent artist and added a significant queer presence to Chicano/a letters today.

Frederick Luis Aldama: Let's begin with your recent foreword to *Colonize This*. Does this resonate at all with *This Bridge Called My Back*, which appeared over two decades ago and was recently reissued?

Cherríe Moraga: They didn't know it, but both publishers asked me to write forewords at about the same time. I had to look at *This Bridge Called My Back* twenty years later, as an older woman, and write a foreword to a book about young women-of-color writers who are about the age I was when *This Bridge* first came out.

In many ways, *Colonize This* reflects just how radically diverse the United States has become; it's no longer just the "four food groups," as we used to identify ourselves: Native American, Asian American, Latina, and Black. Yet these young women are still speaking to issues that we were concerned with back in 1981: U.S. imperialist policy abroad in places like the Middle East, and oppression and violence towards women at home—even reacting to the dominance of an Anglo-biased feminism in college. You would have thought that we had made some progress and that these young women wouldn't have the same struggles. So when I sat down to write the new introduction to *The Bridge* and the forward to *Colonize This,* I realized just how little we'd actually changed in the world. The world's still a mess. It's become more hostile and alienating for women of color and queer people. I had more faith in my politics of resistance as a woman of color back in 1981. Today, with the worldwide presence of poverty, I'm not only more pessimistic, but my critique is much more stringent. More than at any other time, we need to build coalitions of women of color if we are to survive—if the planet is to survive.

F.L.A.: Given that we live in such a bleak world, how do you conceive of yourself as poet and playwright?

C.M.: My plays are always the writing of the wound. I can write the wound, or I can put my finger to the wound, and that's where healing takes place. You don't fix something by being happy-go-lucky. You don't fix something through sitcoms. You don't fix something through romantic comedies. You fix and heal by writing the wound—the hard spot. I write the wound with the hope that in that aperture I might help create a better place for us to live.

I'm not sure anymore about real, fundamental change, but as a writer I feel like I need to always be writing at the edge, where I can show others how everything in our world tells us to forget: to forget that we're Chicano, of Amerindian descent, with long ancestral ties to the land. Whether through my writing, my teaching, or my political organizing, I look to the past and to the land to help raise the consciousness of the people. That's why my plays aren't always directed critically at an Anglo mainstream. I mix social realism with mythology in many of them to make visible how many Chicanos/as have internalized the violence of colonialism and deny their ancestral roots.

F.L.A.: In one of your other more recent plays, *Hungry Woman,* you deliberately foreground the mythological dimension, but it's Greek and not Mayan.

C.M.: Medea and *la llorona* are the same myth. Growing up, I heard so many versions of *la llorona,* but they all depicted her as weak, hypersexualized, and destructive. And stories of Medea are similarly negative. The legend of infanticide at the hand of a mother is a universal fear in patriarchal cultures. In my revision, Medea and *la llorona* are both products of patriarchal systems of oppression. I wanted to take these negative depictions of women and turn them into images of empowerment; I wanted them to become meaningful icons for Chicanas and creative ways to critique histories of conquest and colonization. This was especially important for me as a lesbian Chicana. Like *la llorona* and Medea, I've lived as an exile. In order to come out, I had to be willing to be considered a criminal. Even though feminism and the gay movement told me different, there was always a part of me that internalized society's criminalizing of lesbians. That's why I was attracted to these characters who were exiled from their lands because they were too much woman for their worlds.

F.L.A.: Can you talk to me about your beginnings as a writer?

C.M.: I began writing in 1977 because there was nothing to read that affirmed my existence as a lesbian Chicana. I was really a first-generation Chicana lesbian writer with an urgent need to write about all these issues of racism, sexism, and homophobia. Looking back at the writer that I was then, I'm filled with compassion. Here was this young woman whose writing is laden with a desire to state a truth about her sexuality but not lose control. Here's this young woman writing against a wall of existence. I mean, just putting the words lesbian and Chicana together back then, I thought the page was going to blow up on me or something.

F.L.A.: Can you talk about your development as a playwright?

C.M.: My first play, *Giving Up the Ghost,* was staged in 1984. I had already published my autobiographical prose poems, *Loving in the War Years,* and had edited a collection of short stories, *Cuentos: Stories by Latinas,* for Kitchen Table Press. *Giving Up the Ghost* really marked a transition in my writing because for the first time I really started writing fiction. Even though it was drama, it was fiction because it wasn't really me. In a way, the writing of *Loving in the War Years* had relieved me of my own story.

I had cleared room for new characters to enter me and start talking and breathing. Fortunately, I was able to workshop a lot of this writing while I was living in New York and working at the Latino Theater Lab at the Hispanic American Arts Center. That's when I began to really understand its form: how to write engaging scenes and dialogue and how to use the space of the stage.

F.L.A.: Why the lack of props in your plays and performances?

C.M.: More than a technique of dramatic minimalism, this has to with material constraints. For example, rather than go for a hugely elaborate set in a play like *The Hungry Woman* that lends itself to this, given the economic constraints of trying to produce work in this country as a Chicana lesbian, I opted for a play that required minimal stage production. It has always been the case that there are few opportunities for regional theaters with big budgets to produce your work: either the interest just isn't there, or when it is, they don't want to spend the big production money on your work. I've always kept this in mind, focusing more on character than props and action. That's why language and character are fundamentally the most important aspects of theatre for me. Even if you never see the work staged, from the two-dimensional written page, I try to write in such a way that the reader can visualize and imagine three dimensions. The poetry of the language should hold the audience, regardless of props.

F.L.A.: In *Giving Up the Ghost* and later in *Shadow of a Man* you complicate the image of the Chicano family.

C.M.: *Ghost* was very queer; and though *Shadow of a Man* was more about a traditional family, it had a lot of queer subtexts. I wrote the more family-centered *Shadow* because I was concerned that audiences might think that queers don't have families, or that we're not concerned with family. So I wrote the family play—that family where gayness is all over the place subtextually and that we as gay people have come from.

F.L.A.: How do you see your work in relation to mainstream and Chicano *teatro?*

C.M.: I'm always in conversation with Chicano theater. You see this in particular with *Heroes and Saints,* where I decided to write about social issues. So I wrote the story of the plight of Chicano farmworkers in California—my family history—but without compromising my feminism. The play was critical of environmental racism and labor exploitation and it was critical of our community: the oppression of the Catholic Church and the homophobia within the community. I mean all of this is part of the Chicano experience, but not all of it appeared in Chicano *teatro*. My plays are very much in conversation with Chicano *teatro* because they're about Chicanos and not the Anglo mainstream. This doesn't mean that the plays are exclusive. I feel like they can learn much more about who we are if we don't try to translate or universalize our experiences for them. I feel like Anglo Americans and whoever else that might be outside the experience of being Chicano might learn a great deal from our plays if we insist on being who we are and not providing some kind of watered-down, cultural translation.

As far as the mainstream, most Euro-American theater critics say I try to pack too many issues into my plays. Well, you know, walk a day in my life. Walk in my shoes for one minute, and you'll see that all those issues exist in our families every minute of the day.

F.L.A.: A decade after you published your first collection of out prose-poetry, *Giving up the Ghost*, you published a second collection, *The Last Generation* (1993). Why the manifesto-like call to form a "Queer Aztlán"?

C.M.: In all my work generally, I blur the line between theory and practice. My vision of Queer Aztlán, with the insistence that gay people have a place in our Chicano tribe, is a radical reconceptualization of who we are as *familia*—as a Chicano people. In all my work I ask, How do we reconstruct family? How do we critique what didn't work in our families and make it so it works? How do we not betray each other, abandon each other, lose each other to every kind of form of genocide possible, such as the assimilation process? With varying degrees of failure and success, this has been my lifelong goal as a writer-activist.

I have my own family now: my partner and my little boy, Rafael. This has given me the opportunity to put into practice these things that I preach. You see this in *Waiting in the Wings: Portrait of a Queer Motherhood*—a kind of testimony to the ways in which I'm try to shape a Queer Aztlán.

F.L.A.: Why so critical of the queer family in *Waiting in the Wings*?

C.M.: I was very conscious of figuring out a way to tell the truth expected of autobiography and still fictionalize to make it more *real*. I was very tied to the idea of writing a rather sentimental narrative that followed the thread of the child's development. When I got to the end of the book, though,

I decided to break up this overly romanticized vision of the queer nuclear family. I wanted to show the less romantic side of queer family life, adding ambiguity—will the family stay together?—to emphasize just how powerfully racism and homophobia in society can destructively work their way into queer family life.

F.L.A.: Why publish your plays so consistently with West End Press?

C.M.: The editor at West End Press, John Crawford, is an incredible man whose political commitments are right on. He's like an old-school communist. He was publishing radical feminist playwrights and poets long before it was fashionable. They publish and distribute my work, and my work attracts other writers. I feel like that investment has been mutual.

Generally, too, because I've done a lot of mixed-genre books—poems and essays and all that—there hasn't been that much mainstream interest in my work. While queer authors and colored authors are published by some of the bigger houses, queer colored writers are almost never published by these houses. The few times I've attempted to go that route, I've turned back to those presses that have never hassled me and that make sure my work stays in print. Of course, I don't make lots of money from these presses, but I figure it's the quality of the production and the lasting power that best serve me in the end.

I think I might try New York with a novel; that's the only thing that New York knows how to handle.

F.L.A.: Theatre venues like Brava in San Francisco have also supported your work as well as allowed you to hold workshops for new Chicano and Latino playwrights.

C.M.: There are many talented writers coming up, but with the exception of a few sort-of breakthrough plays, like Ricardo Bracho's *Sweetest Hangover,* there's not much support for progressive Chicano *teatro.* There are virtually no Chicano theaters that are consistently presenting new works. Teatro Campesino only does old Valdez work, and the few Chicano theaters around the country are for the most part not even premiering any new work. There is plenty of Latino performance art being produced, but it's generally much cheaper. Guillermo Gomez-Peña is the exception. His performances are over the top, and he gets support, but that's largely due to his being heterosexual and the one that all the *gringos* know about. That doesn't say anything bad about him. It is a fact that there is simply no support for progressive, full-length playwrights. Take Migdalia Cruz, who is, hands down, one of the best playwrights in this country. Her plays are so nontraditional that she doesn't get the attention or the level of production she deserves. Latinas just don't get produced the way the men do.

Writings by the Author
Plays

Giving Up the Ghost: Teatro in Two Acts. Los Angeles: West End Press, 1986; revised edition, Albuquerque: West End Press, 1994.
Heroes and Saints and Other Plays. Albuquerque: West End Press, 1994.
The Hungry Woman: A Mexican Medea / Heart of the Earth: A Popul Vuh Story. [Two plays.] Albuquerque: West End Press, 2001.
Watsonville: Some Place Not Here/Circle in the Dirt: El Pueblo de East Palo Alto. [Two plays.] Albuquerque: University of New Mexico Press, 2002.

Other

With Gloria Anzaldúa, eds. *This Bridge Called My Back: Writings by Radical Women of Color.* San Francisco: Persephone Press, 1981.
Loving in the War Years: Lo que nunca pasó por sus labios. Boston: South End Press, 1983; revised edition, Boston: South End Press, 2000.
With Alma Gomez and Mariana Romo-Carmona, eds. *Cuentos: Stories by Latinas.* New York: Kitchen Table/Women of Color Press, 1983.
With Norma Alarcón and Ana Castillo, eds. *The Sexuality of Latinas.* Berkeley: Third Woman Press, 1991.
The Last Generation: Poetry and Prose. Boston: South End Press, 1993.
Waiting in the Wings: Portrait of a Queer Motherhood. Ithaca: Firebrand Books, 1997.
Foreword. In *Colonize This! Young Women of Color on Today's Feminism,* edited by Daisy Hernández and Bushra Rehman, pp. 11–16. New York: Seal Press, 2002.

Further Readings
Critical Studies

Alarcón, Norma. "Making 'Familia' from Scratch: Split Subjectivities in the Work of Helena María Viramontes and Cherríe Moraga." *Americas Review* 15, nos. 3–4 (1987): 147–159.
De la Peña, Terri. "Of Cursors and Kitchen Tables: Portrait of Lesbian Writer Cherríe Moraga." *off our backs* 24, no. 6 (1994): 10.

DeRose, David J. "Cherríe Moraga: Mapping Aztlán." *American Theatre* 13, no. 8 (1996): 76–79.

Espinosa, Dionne. "Cherríe Moraga, *Loving in the War Years: Lo que nunca pasó por sus labios.*" In *Reading U.S. Latina Writers: Remapping American Literature,* edited by Alvina E. Quintana, pp. 151–162. New York: Palgrave Macmillan, 2003.

Gonzalez, Deena J. "Chicana Identity Matters." *Aztlán* 22, no. 2 (1997): 123–139.

Lewis, Andrea. "The Next Stage: She's Looking for a Bold New Theater of Color." *Mother Jones* 6, no. 1 (1991): 15.

Lopez, Tiffany Ana. "On the Other Side of the Rainbow." *American Theatre* 18, no. 2 (2001): 70.

Mayorga, Irma. "Cherríe Moraga." *Dictionary of Literary Biography,* Vol. 249, *Chicano Writers,* pp. 245–267. Detroit: Gale Group, 1992.

Morales, Ed. "Shadowing Valdez: Luis Valdez's Role in Current Chicano Theater and Film." *American Theatre* 9, no. 7 (1992): 14–120.

Moya, Paula. "Postmodernism, 'Realism,' and the Politics of Identity: Cherríe Moraga and Chicana Feminism." In *Reclaiming Identity: Realist Theory and the Predicament of Postmodernism,* edited by Paula Moya and Michael Hames-García, pp. 67–101. Berkeley: University of California Press, 2000.

Muñoz, Willy O. "La decentralización del hombre en 'Shadow of a Man' de Cherríe Moraga." *Symposium* 52, no. 3 (1998): 165–176.

Romero, Lora. "'When Something Goes Queer': Familiarity, Formalism, and Minority Intellectuals in the 1980s." *The Yale Journal of Criticism* 6, no. 1 (1993): 121–142.

Rosenberg, Lou. "The House of Difference: Gender, Culture, and the Subject-in-Process on the American Stage." *Journal of Homosexuality* 26, nos. 2–3 (1993): 97–113.

Saldívar, Ramón. "The Dialects of Subjectivity: Gender and Difference in Isabella Ríos, Sandra Cisneros, and Cherríe Moraga." In *Chicano Narrative: The Dialects of Difference,* pp. 171–203. Madison: University of Wisconsin Press, 1990.

Sandoval, Trino. "Lesbians of Aztlán: Chicana Lesbian Fictions." In *Chicano/Latino Homoerotic Identities,* edited by David William Foster, pp. 47–58. New York: Garland Publishing, 1999.

Szadziuk, Maria. "Culture As Transition: Becoming a Woman in Bi-ethnic Space." *Mosaic* 32, no. 3 (1999): 110.

Wiley, Catherine. "Teatro Chicano and the Seduction of Nostalgia." *MELUS* 23, no. 1 (1998): 99.

Worthen, W. B. "Staging America: The Subject of History in Chicano/a Theatre." *Theatre Journal* 9, no. 2 (1997): 101–122.

Yarbro-Bejarano, Yvonne. *The Wounded Heart: Writing on Cherríe Moraga.* Austin: University of Texas Press, 2001.

Reviews

"Against Apartheid: Poetry Reading at the University of California, Berkeley."
Feminist Studies 14, no. 3 (1988): 417–446.

Frances, Melodie. Rev. of *Waiting in the Wings: Portrait of a Queer Motherhood.*
Library Journal 123, no. 1 (1998): 110.

Frouman-Smith, Erica. Rev. of *Esta puente, mi espalda: Voces de mujeres tercer-
mundistas en los Estados Unidos. The Americas Review* 19, no. 1 (1991): 117–119.

Gutiérrez, Mariela. Rev. of *The Last Generation. Canadian Journal of Latin American
and Caribbean Studies* 21 (1996): 151–152.

Huerta, Jorge, and Raquel Aguilú de Murphy. Rev. of *Giving Up the Ghost. The
Americas Review* 15, no. 2 (1987): 104–107.

Wiley, Catherine. Rev. of *Shadow of a Man. Theatre Journal* 47, no. 3 (1995): 412–415.

Interviews

DeRose, David. "Cherríe Moraga: Mapping Aztlán." *American Theatre* 13, no. 8
(1996): 76–79.

Ikas, Karin Rosa. "Cherríe Moraga." In *Chicana Ways: Conversations with Ten Chicana Writers,* pp. 152–172. Las Vegas: University of Nevada Press, 2002.

Kevane, Bridget, and Juanita Heredia. "City of Desire." In *Latina Self-Portraits: Interviews with Contemporary Women Writers,* pp. 97–108. Albuquerque: University
of New Mexico Press, 2000.

Lehoczky, Etelka. "Loving in the War Years: Author and Activist Cherríe Moraga."
The Advocate, January 30, 2001, p. 67.

Alejandro Morales

On October 14, 1944, Alejandro Morales was born in Montebello, California. Raised by first-generation Mexican émigrés from Guanajuato, Morales spent his childhood and teenage years in East Los Angeles. With unusual drive and scholarly aptitude, Morales made it out of East L.A., earning a B.A. in English from California State University, Los Angeles, and an M.A. shortly thereafter (1973). With his passion aflame for writing and thinking critically about the world through literature, Morales pursued graduate studies in English literature at Rutgers University in New Jersey. In 1975, he received his Ph.D. and also published his first novel, *Caras viejas y vino nuevo*. Published in Spanish and by a Mexico City press, this experimental novel used fragmented form and a street slang style to texture the lives of two teenage boys, Mateo and Julian, trying to survive life in the *barrio*. More controversially, the novel also portrays their homosocial relationship. While the novel ruffled feathers, it also received great critical acclaim. Soon after, Morales published *La verdad sin voz* (1979), which follows the lives of an idealistic Anglo character, Dr. Logan, and a Chicano, Professor Morenito. Both encounter various obstacles: the former struggling to fit in as an outsider working in a rural Mexican *barrio,* and the latter trying to work within a racist urban university. In 1982 Morales published a series of stories that interweave in surprising ways to create the dynastic novel *Reto en el paraíso* (*Defiance in paradise*). Here, we encounter four generations of a wealthy Hispanic *californio* family, the Coronels, and their painful transition from landowner class to the ranks of the landless. Morales next published a historical novel, *The Brick People* (1988), which plays with fact and fiction in its reframing of the factual events that surrounded various people's experiences working at the Simons Brick Factory, which was in the neighborhood where Morales grew up. In 1992, Morales published *The Rag Doll Plagues,* which uses a Chinese-box narrative structure—stories within stories—to follow characters in three historical periods as they struggle with different incurable diseases. In his 2001 novel, *Waiting to Happen: Volume 1. The Heterotopian Trilogy,* Morales experiments even more radically with storytelling form—intermixing poetry, essay, and epistle—in his texturing of racially hybrid characters that inhabit multiculturally layered spaces in Mexico City and Los Angeles. Morales's novels and essays, which speak to the many different experiences of Chicanos/as north and south of the border, continue to influence Chicano/a and mainstream writers alike.

Frederick Luis Aldama: You began publishing your work four decades ago, first in Spanish with a Mexico City press, then in English with independent and university presses. Can you speak about this experience?

Alejandro Morales: I published my first two novels, *Caras viejas y vino nuevo* and *La verdad sin voz,* with Joaquin Mortiz in Mexico City; that went very well until they were bought out by Planeta. I had given Planeta a manuscript (a collection of short stories) that they liked, but because it's such a huge company, their marketing people didn't think they could fit it into their list the year that I had submitted the work. So I just hung on to that piece. Hopefully, I'll get it published somewhere else. But basically I've always been working with the small, independent, and/or university press. They've been very good to me. Editors like Gary Keller at Bilingual Review [Press] and Nicolas Kanellos at Arte Público have always been very straightforward and honest; Arte Público still has in print *The Brick People* and *The Rag Doll Plagues.*

    I've never worked with an agent. This is not to say that I will never work with one. I've always worked independently. Some people say I should probably get an agent; I think it's hard to work with agents, and also probably hard to work with the big companies. I've never really had an opportunity to do so, but I think that the big companies would ask you to change your books or to make them palatable for a public that they want to get to.

I'm the type of person who believes that writers have to write. And I'm trying to produce a lot more work now. I have several projects at different stages of development. I work on about two or three projects at a time. I'm really now more excited about my work. I look at my age—I'm going to be 60. I wonder, well, how many good years do I have left? I'm working against time.

F.L.A.: What about audience?

A.M.: I'm getting more attention in Europe. In Italy they translated *The Rag Doll Plagues,* for example. In fact, I'm sending them a manuscript, a collection of three long stories. I might write a book that, hopefully, will be published here in the States and then translated and become popular in Europe, for example, or somewhere else. And my work attracts more scholarly attention. Scholars have written wonderful articles about my books. I've been invited to conferences; a couple years ago I was invited to Potsdam, Germany, to attend a symposium dedicated to my work.

Of course, working with smaller presses means that I'm not going to get the distribution that the big companies offer. I'm lucky to get distributed once in a while in Barnes and Noble; usually they have to order my books. I am getting read by the general public even if not as widely as I'd like. My readership is expanding. Readers are discovering my work: what I'm doing now and what I've done in the past. This is a good sign.

F.L.A.: You first wrote your books in Spanish; when did you switch to English, and how was this transition for you?

A.M.: *The Brick People* was the first book I wrote in English. Writing in English wasn't harder; I just did it. Whether in English or Spanish, I just write. For example, I have three long stories (some might call novels) that might even get published in Spanish; and I'm writing now also a lot of what I call travel poems, two or three of which are in Spanish.

F.L.A.: Does the type of story you want to tell determine the language you write in?

A.M.: While I feel a greater desire to write in Spanish, it's the subject that tells me whether it will be in English or in Spanish. Writing in Spanish is becoming more and more important, too, as the Latino demographics shift. The Spanish reading public is growing out there, and I want to reach them with my writing.

F.L.A.: Your books have constantly challenged narrative technique and genre.

A.M.: To me that's very important. I don't ever want to be in *la moda* [in style]. I always want to push the envelope and to try to expand the way I tell stories and convey the subject matter. I'm constantly exploring new ways of telling new subject matter. Now, for example, I use poems in my work. In the past I hadn't done that. I just wrote a book that's in the hands of an editor right now, titled *The Captain of All These Men of Death,* that deals with the history of the treatment of tuberculosis from Hippocrates to the discovery of the antibiotic streptomycin. At different points of the book I tell the stories of Hippocrates, Jimena, Mara De Battagli, Marcel Triguer, characters who have something to do with the history and treatment of tuberculosis. These stories are part of the story of a tuberculant by the name of Ramirez who spends four years (1945 to 1949) at Olive View Sanitarium in Sylmar, California. I tell this story of TB from his point of view, painting the picture of this disease within the Latino community at the time.

Currently, Latinos, disease, medicine, and community are important themes to me. I'm attempting to write a trilogy about disease and the Latino community. The next book would be on the introduction of syphilis into California during the eighteenth century, during the time of the founding of the missions in California: the soldiers and priests' arriving and the subsequent devastation of the indigenous peoples. The third book will probably be on HIV and AIDS and the Latino community.

I'm always expanding possibilities for Chicano writing, trying to see where else we can go and discover other paths we can follow.

F.L.A.: Important literary (or other) influences on your own work?

A.M.: I read a lot, and not necessarily always novels. For the tuberculosis book I read articles from medical journals, book-length studies, historical documents, and other writings on tuberculosis. I'm always looking for descriptions and better ways of saying what I have to say. I'm interested in biographical novels, largely because my novels have a lot of history and real people in them. One such author that I admire is Irving Stone. Not only his book on Van Gogh, *Lust for Life,* but also his research notes in Van Gogh's letters to his brother, *Dear Theo,* are great reading.

Because I teach at the university, I read a lot of theoretical pieces. A theorist I like is Michel Foucault and his book *Discipline and Punish,* for example. I also read historians like Elizabeth Haas, George J. Sánchez, Vicki L. Ruiz, Gilbert G. Gonzalez, and Douglas Monroy, particularly Monroy's description in *Thrown among Strangers* of Native American people in the eighteenth and nineteenth centuries. Such authors create images in my mind.

I read a variety of texts and authors. I enjoy so many U.S. Latino authors like Graciela Limón, Ben Sáenz, Achy Obejas, Esmeralda Santiago, Luis Rodriguez, John Rechy, Denise Chávez, Alfredo Véa Jr., and Alicia Gaspar de Alba, to name a few narrative writers. And I enjoy reading poets. Their use of language captures the essence of images and sounds—an impulse I share. I also read essays, like Richard Rodriguez's book of essays, *Brown*, or Mike Davis's *Magical Urbanism* and *City of Quartz*. I am a fan of Leslie Marmon Silko, Toni Morrison, Reinaldo Arenas, and Carmen Boullosa. This is the kind of reading I do. It isn't always just literature. It can be many, many different kinds of books and themes.

F.L.A.: Some of your books have been identified as psychological dramas and/or magical realist. Do you conceive of your novels as, say, magical realist, or is this a category others like marketers and/or critics apply?

A.M.: I think there's something of the fantastic. Some people have identified the last part of *Rag Doll Plagues* as science fiction or as magical realism. And others have identified two major plots in *The Brick People:* a realist plot and a magical/fantastic plot. I do think that using the fantastic to represent parts of Latino culture is important. The book on tuberculosis, for example, uses elements of the fantastic to describe people who are sick as well as the people doing the experiments on them. In the Chicano community, some people considered the sick as victims cursed by *brujos* (witches) because they didn't know what was happening to them. This situation is an example of the fantastic that is very real and very much with us today. *Waiting to Happen* is another one of my novels that deals with the fantastic, expressed in religious, mystical, sacred themes. In the fantastic resides another part of our reality—a different kind of truth that's with us.

F.L.A.: Many of your novels focus on the diseased and deteriorating body, but there's also a strong sense of the new and creative body.

A.M.: It's part of the way I see things. It's not exactly apocalyptical, but I think the two major energies of apocalypse are present: the energy of destruction and that of creation. They go hand in hand. If you look at history, we reach great heights at specific moments, and then, boom, something happens and we fall back down. The history of Mexico can be described as a series of social utopias that fall into destruction, but from where appears the energy of creation moving forward again to rebuild another utopia like Aztlán, the borderlands, or what Foucault calls a *heterotopia*. You know, all of this is very present with us and will continue to impact us in the future.

F.L.A.: Technically, you challenge yourself as a writer constantly. You play with form and content as well as space. In a phrase from *The Brick People*, your narrator describes the figure of the mandala: "the center and four ovals interrelated in this continuous, unwinding, infinite spiral of energy, time and space." Perhaps you can speak to your play with space and time in your work?

A.M.: In *The Brick People* there's past history and present history simultaneously. One can't escape from either time. It's also future. We're constantly negotiating space and time. Movement in time and space is also important. As people move, they constantly have to renegotiate spaces as well as identities. In *Waiting to Happen: Volume 1. The Heterotopian Trilogy*, the protagonist, J. I. Cruz, renegotiates spaces in Mexico—spaces that nobody would think to inhabit, but that exist (tunnels and in-between leaning walls, for example). There's a scene when she goes to an ancient convent, where people dig out, then live in, these tombs. J. I. Cruz lives in a heterotopia: all the borderland spaces between Mexico City and Los Angeles. To me the borderlands are expanding further and further and further up north into Alaska, New York, into Washington, D.C.—throughout the United States. The United States is almost a complete borderland existence now.

Space, time, movement, borderlands are themes that I'm fascinated with and will definitely continue to work with in my fiction. Literature written by Latinos and other ethnic writers is about creating new knowledge for a new space, the space of the future. In this sense, they're prophetic works that deal with what's happening now but also that point toward the future.

F.L.A.: From *The Brick People* to *Waiting to Happen*, different forms of family and community play a central role your work.

A.M.: In most of my work the characters are not necessarily by themselves. They might be in one way, but in another way they are very much connected to family; they're trying to find family. In *Waiting to Happen,* J. I. Cruz creates a new, much bigger family; all of humankind becomes her family. She has this sacred power that allows her to gather these people: her mom and dad, the two girls that she adopts, and so on. Maybe I'm saying that the family is the family of humankind—of humanity.

F.L.A.: *Waiting to Happen* is a departure from your earlier novels, where you focus more on male characters.

A.M.: *Waiting to Happen* is the first part of the heterotopian trilogy (the second volume that I've finished is tentatively titled *The Place in the White Heron*) that focuses on a woman protagonist. But I don't know why that should necessarily surprise anybody. I mean I've had women characters in the past. In her book *Plotting Women,* Jean Franco discusses *"las ilusas"* of Mexico, which fascinated me. J. I. Cruz is this *ilusa*: this woman who falls out of grace from the different institutions, such as the Church or the family or her husband. In eighteenth-century Mexico or seventeenth-century Mexico these women used mechanisms from the Church; they would scream and tear their body and clothes, and fall into a ecstatic trance in public. Some people began to follow them because they believed that they had a direct connection with God. They also believed that some *ilusas* could perform miracles. What J. I. Cruz does is nothing new, yet she is a powerful modern-day *ilusa*. The *ilusa* is an identity, a being, that has been with us as part of a tradition in Mexico.

Mexico is one country that has fallen in love with all its fantastic women. These fantastic women are present today; people both in Mexico and in the United States still believe and pay homage to them.

F.L.A.: There's a certain eroticism in your fiction. Can you speak about this impulse?

A.M.: You can feel its presence in my first book, where it is both heterosexual as well as homosexual. I think you'll find it throughout all my writing, sometimes in very strong graphic detail and sometimes very subtly. For example, in *The Rag Doll Plagues,* it's underneath the surface in the first part, that's about bodies dying from horrible diseases, yet the book is also a love story. In the second part you have someone dying of AIDS, but it also has a strong love story. In the third part, it's more underneath the surface. In my more recent books, I have tried to explore love relationships without having to be as graphic as in my first novels. I'm doing that now with the book I'm writing (I don't have a title for it yet) about the magnificent and beautiful bridges in Los Angeles; it's about the Latino community and the building of Los Angeles, and at the same time it is a love story.

F.L.A.: When writing, how aware are you of using different narrative techniques to represent characters and so on?

A.M.: I write feeling past the characters, the space that I'm trying to create, the place, the emotions. That's what I write. Sometimes I write very descriptive stuff—even very technical, as with the book I'm writing now about the L.A. bridges. Then there are times when the language just flows because it comes out of the emotions (anger or happiness) that arise from contact between people.

In the next books that come out, you'll see long sections in Spanish. I'm not going to hold back on that. I moved away from writing in Spanish, but now I'm just not holding back. If my characters speak Spanish, they will speak Spanish. Or if the narrator of this section is telling the story of this character in Spanish, that's the way it's going be. This might pose a publication problem, but I've gotten to the point where I can't worry about that. The story has to be written, and the characters have to express themselves in the language that I feel is appropriate.

F.L.A.: We're seeing a lot of Chicano/a writers moving into the mainstream. As a Chicano author, do you think we've reached a stage where one can write about whatever one wants to and get published, or are there still constraints?

A.M.: I think we're getting to that point where Chicano writers can write about absolutely anything they want to write about. This isn't to say that we can do this and get published by the big presses. There continue to be certain consequences in writing for the big presses. They're looking for very specific material that they can sell. So writers who write about themes that they're not looking for won't get published. That's why the smaller presses continue to be very important.

We should never hold back as writers, and we should never tell writers what to write about. Writers should be free to follow whatever route they select. I write constantly facing the Aleph.

Writings by the Author
Novels

Caras viejas y vino nuevo. Mexico City: Joaquin Mortiz, 1975. Translated by Max
Martinez as *Old Faces and New Wine*. San Diego: Maize Press, 1981. Translated by
Francisco A. Lomeli as *Barrio on the Edge*. Tempe, AZ: Bilingual Press / Editorial
Bilingüe, 1997.
La verdad sin voz. Mexico City: Joaquin Mortiz, 1979. Translated by Judith
Ginsberg as *Death of an Anglo*. Tempe, AZ: Bilingual Press / Editorial Bilingüe,
1988.
Reto en el paraíso. Tempe, AZ: Bilingual Press / Editorial Bilingüe, 1982.
The Brick People. Houston: Arte Público, 1988.
The Rag Doll Plagues. Houston: Art Público, 1992.
Waiting to Happen: Volume 1. The Heterotopian Trilogy. San Jose: Chusma
House, 2001.

Other

"Golden Glass." In *Hispanics in the United States: An Anthology of Creative Literature*, edited by Francisco Jiménez and Gary D. Keller, vol. 2, pp. 70–72. Tempe,
AZ: Bilingual Press / Editorial Bilingüe, 1982.
"La Chingada." In *Five Poets of Aztlán*, edited by Santiago Daydí-Tolson,
pp. 140–163. Tempe, AZ: Bilingual Press / Editorial Bilingüe, 1985.

Further Readings
Critical Studies

Akers, John C. "Fragmentation in the Chicano Novel: Literary Technique and
Cultural Identity." *Revista Chicano-Riqueña* 13, nos. 3–4 (1985): 124–127.
Batiste, Victor N. "A Kaleidoscope on Many Levels: A Review Article of *Reto en el
paraíso*." *Revista Chicano-Riqueña* 13 (1985): 91–94.
Ginsberg, Judith. "*La verdad sin voz*: Elegy and Reparation." *Americas Review* 14
(1986): 78–83.
Gurpegui, Jose Antonio. "Alejandro Morales: Fiction Past, Present, Future Perfect."
Bilingual Review / La Revista Bilingüe 20, no. 3 (September–December 1995):
1–114.
———. "Implicaciones existenciales del uso del español en las novelas de Alejandro
Morales." *Bilingual Review / La Revista Bilingüe* 20, no. 3 (1995): 43–51.
———. "Interview with Alejandro Morales." *Bilingual Review / La Revista Bilingüe*
20, no. 3 (1995): 5–13.

Gurpegui, Jose Antonio, and Karen Van Hooft. "Bibliography of Works by and about Alejandro Morales." *Bilingual Review / La Revista Bilingüe* 20, no. 3 (1995): 109–114.

Gutierrez-Jones, Carl. "Resisting Cultural Dependency: The Manipulation of Surveillance and Paranoia in Alejandro Morales' *The Brick People*." *The Americas Review: A Review of Hispanic Literature and Art of the USA* 22, nos. 1–2 (1994): 230–243.

Leal, Luis. "Historia y ficción en la narrativa de Alejandro Morales." *Bilingual Review / La Revista Bilingüe* 20, no. 3 (1995): 31–42.

Martín-Rodríguez, Manuel M. "The Global Border: Transnationalism and Cultural Hybridism in Alejandro Morales's *The Rag Doll Plagues*. *Bilingual Review / La Revista Bilingüe* 21 (1996): 86–98.

Rodriguez del Pino, Salvador. *La novela chicana escrita en español: Cinco autores comprometidos*. Tempe, AZ: Bilingual Press/Editorial Bilingüe, 1982.

Rosales, Jesus. "El cronotopo del encuentro en *Reto en el paraíso* de Alejandro Morales." *Bilingual Review / La Revista Bilingüe* 20, no. 3 (1995): 61–75.

———. *La narrativa de Alejandro Morales: Encuentro, historia y compromiso social.* New York: Peter Lang, 1999.

Somoza, Oscar U. "Choque e interacción en *La verdad sin voz* de Alejandro Morales," in *Contemporary Chicano Fiction: A Critical Survey,* edited by Vernon Lattin, pp. 299–305. Binghamton, NY: Bilingual Press / Editorial Bilingüe, 1986.

Villalobos, José Pablo. "Border Real, Border Metaphor: Altering Boundaries in Miguel Mendez and Alejandro Morales." *Arizona Journal of Hispanic Cultural Studies* 4 (2000): 131–140.

Michael Nava

Michael Nava was born in 1954 in Stockton, California. His family soon moved to a *barrio* in Sacramento in search of employment and a better life. A precocious and sensitive child, Nava spent more and more time reading in the library as he grew older to escape his stepfather's violent hand, which shot sharply through the air of a one-room, breeze-block home in the *barrio*. Nava survived with the help of teachers and books; there was no place for him in this dysfunctional, patriarchal household—especially once he reached puberty and identified as gay. After winning a scholarship, Nava made tracks for Colorado College, where he earned a B.A. in English. After traveling to Spain and Argentina (during the 1970s and the great tragedy of the *desaparecidos,* or "Disappeared"), Nava returned home with the intent of studying law. In 1981, with a J.D. from Stanford under his belt—and a couple of poetry prizes—Nava began to practice as a prosecutor in Los Angeles. By night, however, he continued to hone his craft as a novelist of detective fiction.

In 1986, Michael Nava published his first mystery novel, *The Little Death,* breathing life into the first gay Chicano lawyer-cum-detective, Henry Rios. Nava hasn't stopped to look back since, churning out seven more award-winning novels that fully contour Rios's life as he solves grisly murders and crimes against the disenfranchised, has affairs of the heart, and struggles with the constant loss of friends and lovers to AIDS. Rios encounters a world filled with bigotry that rears its ugly head when it comes to queers and Chicanos/as: a world that outlaws those who are darker of hue, the working class, and people with a different sexuality, often paralyzing them with fear to the point of tragic consequences. In *Goldenboy* (1988), for example, the police unjustly pin a murder rap on Nava's gay teenager character when he is the victim of a hate crime. In *Burning Plain* (1997), Rios awakes from an earthquake only to find himself file-deep in a murder case that involves a "straight" judge and his ex-lover, a gay porn star. In Nava's latest and last mystery-suspense installment, *Rag and Bone* (2001), Henry Rios recovers from a heart attack, stumbles into a love affair, and reconnects with a new generation of the Rios tribe. The erstwhile loner-detective Rios connects with his long-estranged lesbian sister's orphaned daughter and her precocious son. Nava's opus is more than a Dashiell Hammett mystery story. His heartfelt characterization and lucid prose style probe prejudice that affects all of those who inhabit social margins, including Latino immigrants, the urban brown and white underclass, victims of domestic abuse, and alcoholics. As Rios solves crimes, Nava celebrates the triumph of defying the odds while not losing sight of the goal to foster deep human empathy and understanding.

Although Nava has written the last of the Henry Rios novels, he continues to write poetry and in other narrative fictional genres. Michael Nava's recognition as a groundbreaking Chicano author of richly textured, gay-themed novels has won him many awards, including the Lammy Award and an award from the Lambda Literary Foundation.

Frederick Luis Aldama: When did you know that you would become a lawyer or a writer or both?

Michael Nava: Well, in college I was studying poetry. I was going to be a poet. So, yes, I knew I'd be a writer. I just didn't think I'd end up being this kind of writer. As for being a lawyer, I wanted to be a lawyer from the time I was nine years old.

F.L.A.: Was there something that happened at this time that made you decide this?

M.N.: My grandfather was a great fan of Perry Mason, so I used to watch Perry Mason with him. You know, my whole generation, the baby boomer lawyers, were all mesmerized by Perry Mason. Also, I was smitten with Abraham Lincoln from a young age. He was a very literate and eloquent lawyer. I was so taken with Lincoln that I even memorized the Gettysburg Address. So although I didn't actually know what a lawyer was, growing up in a working-class Latino family, the images of such figures that surrounded me impressed me deeply.

F.L.A.: Where did you grow up?

M.N.: Sacramento. I lived in a neighborhood called Gardenland, in north Sacramento—the *barrio*. I've written an essay about this, called "Gardenland, Sacramento, California," in John Preston's book *Hometown*.

F.L.A.: How did you manage to make it out of Sacramento?

M.N.: Well, I was smart. I did well in school. I came from a tragically unhappy family. And I knew I was a fag when I was twelve years old, so I figured out early there was really no place for me in my family or in my community, and I would have to leave. It was just a matter of how I was going to do it. I knew education would be my ticket out.

F.L.A.: Were there any role models or mentors in your community?

M.N.: No Latino ones. When I was nine years old, teachers would take me under their wing; they saw that I had exceptional ability. There wasn't much to help foster my intellectual growth at home, but there was at school, where I found much nurturing by my teachers until I graduated from high school. Without them, I wouldn't have made it out of the oppressive conditions of the *barrio*.

F.L.A.: How much autobiographical fact is in your latest novel, *Rag and Bone*?

M.N.: I don't like saying it's autobiographical because with fiction you're always transforming and reinventing reality. However, I can say that in the portrait of Vickie and her son Angelito, there are some direct traces to my relationship to my mother when I was a child. In fact, my middle name is Angel, and my mother's name is Vickie.

F.L.A.: Why characterize Angelito as "invulnerable," and someone who overcomes the odds with the help of Henry Rios?

M.N.: Well, there was no Henry in my childhood, unfortunately. Perhaps the writing of Angelito was a form of reenacting an idealization of my childhood—the way I would like to have had a mentor like Rios in my life as a child.

F.L.A.: Various forms of disease—social, physical, and psychological—show up in your novels. Can you speak about this?

M.N.: Well, I have a friend who tells me that I turn everything into a problem as a writer. I guess it's just the way I see the world. It's a matter of temperament. And I see the world as filled with people who have irreconcilable or contradictory desires. This creates a lot of tension—and disease is a symptom of such tension.

F.L.A.: Often your characters are put in positions where they cannot act, which leads to tragedy. And your novels often normalize gay sexuality. Are these issues that you think about when you write?

M.N.: Well, the thing about writing a series of books over a sixteen-year period is that I've changed my own attitudes. To some extent, they reflect the moment in which they were written. So, for example, a book like *The Hidden Law,* that I wrote around the early 1990s, when the activism of Act Up and Queer Nation was in the air, clearly reflects some of this queer activist attitude.

I would say, generally, my position in the books about homosexuality has been twofold. On the one hand, I want to indict the mainstream for its homophobia, its twisting and distorting of the lives of homosexual people in ways that are completely gratuitous and very ugly. On the other hand, I've also indicted the gay male subculture for its own pathology, especially in *The Burning Plain.* There were all those African American writers in the 1940s, like Richard Wright and James Baldwin, who went to Paris because they could wake up and write about something other than race. And I think my goal would be a world where I could wake up and not have to think about being homosexual. So in this sense I don't know that I "normalize" the gay experience. Gay people should not be prevented from doing anything straight people do, including marrying if that's what they want to do, or being Republicans. But I don't necessarily think that those are desirable outcomes for all of us. I would like a world in which you could be who you are, basically, wherever that journey takes you, without the distorting effects of social hatred or self-hatred.

F.L.A.: In *The Burning Plain* you bring a sense of spiritualism to the novel. I think of the moment when the character Josh Mandell comes back from the dead as a spirit and visits Henry. Can you talk about your sense of spiritualism here?

M.N.: Well, I think that may just be a desperate hope that there is a plane of consciousness which is less difficult than this one. So *The Burning Plain* uses the spiritual framework of Buddhism: it's about the continual creation of karma and rebirth. However, spirituality is very fluid; for example, when I wrote that novel, perhaps I thought this might be one way for us to heal the hurt caused in the world by a homophobic society. However, today I've returned to Catholicism as that belief system that might help us find compassion and a better way of relating to our fellow man.

F.L.A.: Family is central to your novels. Why the contrast between the biological and the self-constructed family in a novel like *Rag and Bone*?

M.N.: Because of my own personal experience of really having to leave my family in order to quite literally survive, it's a very difficult subject. In *Rag and Bone*, it's complicated by other issues: the classic difference between those of us from working-class families who get educated and those who remain behind, which in some ways is a far more significant difference than, you know, homosexuality. I mean, working-class Mexicans can accommodate homosexuality of a certain kind, but when class enters the picture, it becomes much more complicated.

On the one hand, I think Henry Rios's ambivalence toward family results from his rejection of the notion that biology is destiny, and that just because you're biologically related to a set of people doesn't mean that you have some moral responsibility to them. On the other hand, he does embrace his nephew, in part, because he sees himself in the boy, and he even comes to see in Vickie, with whom he has a much more difficult relationship, a kind of deeper familial resemblance. He recognizes that, like him, she's a survivor—a *family* trait. I'm not done thinking about family yet, but I have come around in my own life from feeling completely alienated from my family to being very curious about what connects me to them beyond the mere accident of biology.

F.L.A.: Why make many of your characters' romances interracial (Jewish and Chicano)?

M.N.: Well, writing a novel is like dreaming for me. You can't account for everything that comes out. I mean, all the characters and events come out of you, but you don't always have a conscious grasp of everything that pours out into the narrative. I think Henry's relationship with Josh—that I emphasized more in the last two books—is really about Rios's need to take care of people; it's about his need almost to expiate some kind of guilt that he's not even aware of himself. I wouldn't say it was really an adult relationship. It was more of a parent-child relationship, and that's why I finally had Josh leave Henry. On the other hand, the relationship Henry Rios has with John is much more of an adult relationship—a relationship between equals. And it is extremely significant that John is Latino and points directly at the subtext of *Rag and Bone:* the power of coming back to your point of cultural origin after you've spent your whole life evading it, and discovering it to be a place of self-empowerment.

F.L.A.: Can you talk about class? There is often tension between working-class and middle-class characters.

M.N.: In *Rag and Bone,* class isn't so much a problem for the character John, although he alludes to it. It is for Rios. For Rios, part of the return is to see past the self he has created and discover who he really is. And he recognizes that there's this class issue between him and John and his niece and his nephew, and it's not their job to work it out. It's *his* job to work it out.

F.L.A.: You blur the boundaries that traditionally divide genres of writing: the so-called lowbrow mystery novel and the so-called highbrow bildungsroman. Maybe you can speak a little bit about your writing—the process and how you conceive of the novel itself?

M.N.: I started writing as a poet, and really until I was in my mid-twenties I only wrote poetry. In fact, when I was in law school, I won this prize from UC Irvine for Chicano poetry. So I came to fiction very late in life for a writer, and when I started to write my first book, I didn't want to write that autobiographical first novel that every young writer writes. There was too much about myself that I hadn't figured out and didn't want to talk about, basically. But I had been reading these mystery novels, and it occurred to me that the hero of American mysteries occupied really the same position in the culture that a gay man did. In other words, in all these Dashiell Hammett and Raymond Chandler and Ross Macdonald novels, the private investigator stands outside the mainstream. He embodies the virtues that the mainstream pretends to admire: he's loyal; he's decent; he's courageous; he's conscientious. However, while the mainstream supposedly admires these qualities, it rarely exhibits them.

This is exactly how I felt psychologically as a gay man living in a mainstream culture that said one thing but did another. I lived in this culture that told me that there was something seriously wrong with me, that I was either sick or sinful. And yet I didn't experience myself that way. I experienced myself as an intelligent, hard-working, decent, compassionate person. So the mystery genre really lent itself to that kind of exploration of the outsider and his relationship to society. And the other layer on that was that Rios is a lawyer; in one of the books, he says that it's the disenfranchised who believe the most in the law because the law is the only thing that protects them. So he has this relationship with the legal system also.

So the murder mystery element came out of this character's direct involvement with the legal system. However, it also provided an occasion for me to ask larger questions. I mean, murder is a very dramatic event. It opens a lot of doors in a novel. So it's useful from that point of view and provided me with a vehicle to explore large social issues in a way I don't think I would have been able to do had I written literary novels. Contemporary literary novels just seem very small to me, for the most part, failing to creatively and interestingly address race and class issues within our justice system. Instead, contemporary novels seem more interested in the banal lives of middle-class people. I'm just not interested in that. So writing a mystery with a loyal protagonist against this background of Los Angeles gave me an opportunity to write about larger things.

F.L.A.: You mention at the end of *Rag and Bone* that this is it for your mystery writing. Is there another genre or something else that you're going to explore?

M.N.: Well, eventually. You know, I've been writing since I was twelve years old, so I assume I'll continue to write because that's just the way I think. But I really want to take a break. Including this nonfiction book I wrote about gay rights, I've published eight books in sixteen years. That's a book every year while practicing law full-time and going through the usual personal crises.

F.L.A.: How do you find the time to write?

M.N.: Well, I don't have a family. That makes a huge difference. And I'm very disciplined. I just do it. And that's what it takes if you're a writer. Lots of people have talent, but if you can't harness it, then nothing's going to happen.

F.L.A.: Do you have a particular routine and a specific process for writing?

M.N.: When I'm writing a book, I write at night and on weekends. I plotted in great detail the first books I wrote. But now I just start with an idea. I write a little synopsis for myself, just so that if I get lost, I can go back to it and see what I intended to do. And then I sit down and start writing. Once you get in the framework of writing a book and you have an idea of what it is, connections will occur to you even when you're not working. I think that ninety percent of the writing gets done when I'm not writing. If I'm in the mind-set of the book, things are getting worked out, kind of at a subconscious level. Sometimes at a conscious level I'll jot notes to myself during the day. And then, when I sit down, it actually flows fairly easily, for the most part. I am thinking about another book now, a historical novel, and I've been doing the research for that off and on for four years. But only now am I at the point where it's starting, you know, to work inside of me.

F.L.A.: In *Rag and Bone* you quote Yeats in the epigraph; in other novels you reference Dante and Borges, even Bertolt Brecht. Clearly, there's a fluid movement in your novels between highbrow and lowbrow aesthetics. What do you make of this?

M.N.: I didn't realize until I started writing them that most people consider mysteries junk, because the mysteries I read were these really good writers. I mean Raymond Chandler, whatever one thinks of his politics, is quite a brilliant writer. Ross Macdonald and Joseph Hanson are wonderful, smart writers. When I first read these books, it didn't occur to me that they were lowbrow literature. It was only after I started publishing my books that I realized the extent to which mysteries are ghettoized and deemed second-class citizens next to literary novels—even though most literary novels are trite.

F.L.A.: How was it trying to break into the publishing marketplace as a writer of Chicano- and gay-focused mystery novels?

M.N.: Well, it was very hard at first. My first book was rejected by fifteen publishers before it was picked up by this small gay publishing house, Alyson. During this period in the mid-1980s I would receive letters that said, basically, "Well, this is well written, but we don't think there's an audience for this book." This was of course a euphemism; the editors invariably didn't think they could sell a book with a gay Chicano protagonist. However, after years of struggling, the times changed, and gay became more fashionable. By the late 1980s and early 1990s, the publishing industry decided there was money to be made from gay and lesbian writers, so they were sweeping us up. Of course, that bubble has now burst.

F.L.A.: Why move from Alyson to Penguin Putnam?

M.N.: It was a question of distribution and money. After the success of my second book, *Goldenboy,* that I published with Alyson, I got my break into the New York scene. In 1990 I sold the third installment, *How Town,* to Harper and Row (which later became HarperCollins), who also bought my fourth novel, *The Hidden Law* (1992). The success of both paved the way to Ballantine, who published both in paperback, and then to Putnam. They published my last three novels.

F.L.A.: What is your sense of the marketplace for the gay mystery novels today?

M.N.: Well, it's a tough market for any queer writing now because the big publishers have basically decided they've overestimated the market. A couple years ago they just started dumping gay and lesbian writers right and left, and I'm one of the few who survived that shakeup.

There are two upsides to the coin, however. One is that there's a rebirth of small publishing, and that's a good thing because the problem with being with a big publisher is that unless you're Tom Clancy, you're pretty much shunted around. Small publishers can really give their books a lot more attention. So that's really a good thing. The other positive recent development is the Internet. The problem with small publishers in the past was that their distribution could not compete with the big publishers because they couldn't get their books into the bookstores. Bookstores require a minimum number of copies published in order to distribute them, which was usually more than the little publisher could afford to publish. But with something like Amazon, this marketing system has radically changed; now small publishers don't have to rely on distributors. Perhaps, too, the more democratic publishing-on-demand process will become more pervasive.

F.L.A.: There's a sense of hopefulness to the endings of *Rag and Bone* and your earlier novels. Can you speak to this hopeful vision? How do you read today's social climate in terms of race and queer politics, and writing?

M.N.: Well, in the short term I'm actually pretty pessimistic. I mean I see a society where people are increasingly alienated from one another and where, instead of being citizens, we see ourselves as consumers that fight for resources—the kind of greed that's here in San Francisco. You know, I think people are just going crazy basically. But I don't think this can last. And I think in the long run, I'm more optimistic. I mean, I think it's wonderful that Latinos became the largest segment of the population in California; that betokens a demographic shift that will have very interesting consequences for people living here.

Writings by the Author
Novels

The Little Death. Alyson Publications, 1986.
Goldenboy. Alyson Publications, 1988.
How Town. New York: Harper and Row, 1990.
The Hidden Law. New York: HarperCollins, 1992.
The Death of Friends. New York: Putnam, 1996.
The Burning Plain. New York: Putnam, 1997.
Rag and Bone. New York: Putnam, 2001.

Other

"Gardenland, Sacramento, California." In *Hometowns: Gay Men Write about Where They Belong,* pp. 21–29. New York: Dutton, 1991.
Ed. *Finale: Short Stories of Mystery and Suspense.* Alyson Publications, 1997.
With Robert Dawidoff. *Created Equal: Why Gay Rights Matter to America.* New York: St. Martin's Press, 2002.

Further Readings
Critical Studies

Hames-García, Michael R. "'Who Are Our Own People?': Challenges for a Theory of Social Identity." In *Reclaiming Identity: Realist Theory and the Predicament of Postmodernism,* edited by Paula Moya and Michael Hames-García, pp. 102–132. Berkeley: University of California Press, 2000.
Herren, Greg. "Michael Nava Is Ending the 'Henry Rios' Series." *Gay and Lesbian Review Worldwide* 8, no. 3 (2001): 42.
Klawitter, George. "Michael Nava." In *Contemporary Gay American Novelists: A Bio-Bibliographical Critical Sourcebook,* edited by Emmanuel S. Nelson, pp. 291–297. Westport, CT: Greenwood Press, 1993.
Lopez, Enrique, Jr. "The Intersection of Ethnicity and Sexuality in the Narrative Fiction of Three Chicano Authors: Oscar Zeta Acosta, Arturo Islas, and Michael Nava." *Dissertation Abstracts International, Section A: The Humanities and Social Sciences* 59, no. 8 (February 1999).
Ortiz, Ricardo L. "Sexuality Degree Zero: Pleasure and Power in the Novels of John Rechy, Arturo Islas, and Michael Nava." In *Critical Essays: Gay and Lesbian Writers of Color,* edited by Emmanuel S. Nelson, pp. 111–126. New York: Haworth, 1993.
Rodriguez, Ralph E. "A Poverty of Relations: On Not 'Making *Familia* from Scratch,'

But Scratching *Familia.*" In *Velvet Barrios: Popular Culture and Chicana/o Sexualities,* edited by Alicia Gaspar de Alba. New York: Palgrave Macmillan, 2003.

Reviews

Callendar, Newgate. Rev. of *The Little Death. New York Times Book Review,* August 10, 1986, p. 23.

Klett, Rex E. Rev. of *Goldenboy. Library Journal* 13, no. 4 (March 1, 1988): 79.

———. Rev. of *Rag and Bone. Library Journal* 126, no. 2 (2002): 127.

Pela, Robert L. Rev. of *The Burning Plain. The Advocate* 756 (March 31, 1998): 74.

Stasio, Marilyn. Rev. of *The Burning Plain. New York Times Book Review* 103 (January 25, 1998): 20.

———. Rev. of *The Death of Friends. New York Times Book Review* 146 (October 27, 1996): 42.

———. Rev. of *Rag and Bone. New York Times Book Review* 106, no. 11 (March 18, 2001): 18.

Interviews

Aldama, Frederick Luis. "Tooth and Nail Survival." *El Andar* 12, no. 3 (Autumn 2001): 19–20.

Whipple, Elizabeth. "Writers Talk about the Literary Life." *Library Journal* 122, no. 10 (June 1, 1997): 18–20.

Daniel Olivas

Daniel A. Olivas was born in Los Angeles on April 8, 1959. Along with his four siblings, Olivas was raised by first-generation Mexican émigré parents with an overwhelming sense of the importance of education. They helped drive Olivas to do well in school and eventually gain entry to Stanford University. Always interested in literature and in the craft of writing, he earned his degree in English literature. However, he shelved this interest to follow a career in law. He received his J.D. from UCLA and now works for the California Department of Justice in land use and environmental enforcement law. However, his passion for writing continued to grow. With his professional career fully afloat, he was able to turn once again to writing. When not working as a lawyer, Olivas spends his time writing short stories, novels, poetry, and children's books. In each of these genres, he constantly challenges storytelling conventions and employs different techniques and subgenres (realism, postmodern metafiction, surrealism, and the fantastical) to explore many different experiences of middle-class Chicano life, as well as interracial love and romance. In his powerful collection of short stories, *Assumption and Other Stories* (2003), Olivas introduces us to a variety of characters and portrays the complex relationships between Jewish and Chicano middle-class characters. In his historical novel, *The Courtship of María Rivera Peña* (2000), he stretches the boundaries of the romance and the historical narrative to texture the twentieth-century growth pains of Mexicanizing Los Angeles. In *Devil Talk: Stories* (2004), he gives a new shape to the Latin American storytelling tradition of the *fantasma*. In his recently published children's book, *Benjamin and the Word,* Olivas both simplifies and complicates racial identity as it intersects with various religions, such as Catholicism and Judaism. Olivas is committed to reaching a wide range of readers, publishing stories in both book form and other media, including newspapers, such as the *Los Angeles Times,* magazines, journals, and the Internet.

Frederick Luis Aldama: You work as a lawyer, and you're an author. How did you come into this way of becoming a writer?

Daniel Olivas: I grew up in a working-class neighborhood near downtown Los Angeles; my father worked for years on a turbine assembly line near Watts, and my mom was a homemaker. They wanted to improve their lives, he to wear a suit and she to teach preschool, so they both went to community college. They did this to make a better life for their five children, whom they intended all to go to college. Needless to say, when I did get to Stanford and majored in English, the goal at the back of my mind was to be able to make a living. But from an early age, when my father pushed James Joyce and other authors on me, I fell in love with the written word.

I was always very creative. In grammar school and high school and in college, I drew cartoons. I was very artistic. But I always liked to write, too. When I was in college, majoring in English, I decided not to take any creative writing classes in college because I thought it would be a frivolous thing to do. I thought that it was important for me to major in something that I could use: perhaps become an English professor, or go into the law, or do something where I knew that I would have a steady paycheck, but also fulfill myself emotionally and intellectually. And creative writing didn't fit into that. That doesn't mean I wasn't being creative. I was art director of Stanford's student humor magazine, *Chaparral,* for a year, and staff artist for a year before that. So I was always writing and drawing and getting involved that way, artistically and creatively. Then I went to law school at UCLA, where I eventually became editor-in-chief of the *Chicano Law Review.* And as a lawyer I do a ton of writing. I specialize in environmental enforcement and land use for the state government.

In the mid-'90s I started to write articles for the legal newspaper, *The Los Angeles Daily Journal.* And those articles became more and more like short stories. They started to develop, with characters who confronted legal issues. And then in the late '90s, my wife suffered the fifth of what would be six miscarriages. I was trying to deal with my wife's grief and my son's grief. But I wasn't dealing with my grief very well at all. And I didn't know what to do. I was struggling with very dark emotions. So I started to write. I decided, well, maybe I should just try to get some words on paper and see what I could do. What came out of that was my first book, a novella, *The Courtship of María Rivera Peña*. That book is loosely based on my paternal grandparents' migration from Mexico to Los Angeles in the 1920s. And the reason why that book turned out to be very cathartic for me and really helped me get on track emotionally was because I dealt with the joys and the great pain that we all encounter in life. You know, alcoholism and cancer and horrible things like that are within probably most families, but also the great joy of loving someone and loving your children and producing something, producing a family that you care about. Those are all the things I was trying to write about. And it helped me—it really helped me tremendously. But once I finished that, and then it got picked up by a small press in Pennsylvania, I couldn't stop writing. So I started doing short stories. And because of my work schedule as a full-time lawyer and a husband and a father, the short form seemed to work very well for me. And I started to write these short stories, and they kind of tumbled out of me, and they started to be published. And so that's how I started writing creatively. I'm going to be 45 in April, so I started very late in life. I started writing professionally as someone who's actually selling and publishing work at the age of 39. So I'm a late bloomer, but I think I'm a better writer because I've experienced so much more than some kid right out of college.

F.L.A.: Were you raised bilingual?

D.O.: My parents raised us bilingually. But when I was three years old, I stopped speaking completely for a full year. I was completely mute. They took me to see doctors, who told my parents to cut all Spanish in the house. My parents were afraid, and with little information to the contrary—this was 1962—they cut all Spanish. So ever since I was very young, I've been struggling with language and the idea of language and also the identity of language.

I grew up in a working-class, Mexican American neighborhood, where most of my friends spoke Spanish as a first language. So I was sort of an oddity when it came to language.

F.L.A.: You first began publishing your stories in magazines and at Internet websites? Was this your way of getting your writing out there and of building a readership?

D.O.: I make my living as an attorney, so when I write fiction, poetry, and essays, there's no pressure that it has to support me. I write because I have to; it comes out of me; it's something that's an organic part of me. Of course, the next step after that very private part of writing is transforming it into something public. Because I don't have an M.F.A., I didn't know anything about marketing. So I went to resources such as *Writer's Market* and *The International Directory of Little Magazines and Small Presses,* which could teach me what the markets were, how to submit work to those markets, and how to get the work out there for people to start reading. I also started subscribing to magazines like *Poets and Writers,* that I began to read voraciously. This is how I taught myself how to submit work.

And one of the wonderful things about the Web is that it has opened up a huge market for writers. One of the most distressing things I found in submitting work to print journals is their timeline: sometimes they take up to a year to respond, and sometimes that would be a rejection. More and more online journals are getting the kind of respect that many print journals have. *Exquisite Corpse* (first a print and now a web journal), where I published one of my stories, is a good example. The other exciting aspect of online publication is that you start getting emails from people who've read your work. Like the story called "Listen to Me," about the undocumented worker, that was published in *Latino LA*: I've gotten several emails from people thanking me for writing it. And one person in particular wrote to me and said, "You wrote about me." And another person wrote to tell me that he read another one of my online stories on his anniversary of sobriety and told me that my story helped keep him dry. This kind of response and engagement makes you realize that, as a writer, words are important. From the very private experience of getting those words and thoughts onto your computer screen, to then having it published, and then having people get back to you, it's really a remarkable feeling. Local book clubs have also expanded my readership and my contact with readers.

F.L.A.: Agents?

D.O.: When I first put this collection together, I had submitted it to several agents. I received beautiful rejections that said, "You're a wonderful writer, but you're unknown, and short story collections are not market-able." Okay. "Will you please write a novel?" Ignoring the fact I'd put a lot of work into this collection. Two agents said, "Would you mind writing a Latino version of *Waiting to Exhale*, i.e., the characters are young, beauti-ful, middle- to upper-middle-class, with movie potential?" People have been making money off of commercial fiction for years, and some would say that *The Dirty Girl Social Club* is exactly this kind of book. God bless all of them. But that kind of book ain't gonna tumble out of me—even though I could write that book, but do I want to? Is that going to be fulfill-ing? Is that going to be why I write? I really have to be inspired to write a story or a book, and it really has to come out of me.

F.L.A.: I read a couple of reviews that were critical. How do you deal with these reviews?

D.O.: I've received some very nice reviews including a rave in the *Los Angeles Times* by the novelist James Sallis. But one review from *Dallas Morning News* was hypercritical—mean-spirited, even. When that review came out, it hurt. It felt as if I had lost a case that I really believed in. The re-viewer had said something like, "I never thought I'd see product place-ment end up in Chicano literature," ignoring the fact that the particular story he was complaining about was about a man dealing with his wife's multiple miscarriages and that the only thing that was solid in his life at that point were these particular products. He didn't get this central part of the story, ignoring the emotional tragedy of that story. My writer friends who saw the review told me that the reviewer seemed to have some kind of ax to grind. But worse things happen in life, I can guarantee that. So you move on and don't let the nasty reviews affect you unless some kind of constructive criticism is being offered.

One of the things I did was to link the bad review to my web page. I included that review along with the great reviews, because that's part of the social discourse of literature.

F.L.A.: Important Latino writers who have influenced your work?

D.O.: When I was at Stanford, back in '77 to '81, the concept of Chicano fiction and poetry wasn't really established yet, so I took classes through the Chicano Fellows Program that crossed disciplines: sociology, an-thropology, and health care. In English, I took courses on authors from William Shakespeare to the poet William Blake, from writers such as

D. H. Lawrence and Somerset Maugham to Hemingway and F. Scott Fitzgerald. *The Great Gatsby* is probably one of the most important influences on my writing. Djuna Barnes's stories and her novella *Nightwood* were quite influential. Later, when all these wonderful Chicano and Chicana writers were being published, I decided to make a list and start reading. One of the things I was trying to do was to see what worked: what part of writing really touched me, in terms of structure and character development.

Reading all this Latino/a fiction not only formed my own M.F.A. program of sorts but inspired me. We can tell stories, create situations, and use language in a way that not only touches our community but can also speak to universals—the universal through the specific and very private. That's what *The Great Gatsby* is, for example. Writers have been doing that, of course, forever. And so that's what I did. I made certain I read a lot, and I wrote a lot.

F.L.A.: Has being a lawyer helped or hindered your creative writing? Do you attend to detail more because of your profession as a lawyer?

D.O.: I think being a lawyer has helped me be a very fast writer and a scrupulous editor of my work.

The attention to detail—yes, I think that's right. When I first started out after law school, I worked for a small plaintiffs' civil rights law firm. There was a wonderful senior lawyer that dedicated himself to doing civil rights for minorities and for women. He said to me, "When you write a brief, don't build a bridge. Paint a picture." Writing the brief that painted the picture was important because that's how you'd get the judge on your side. You've got to tell the story that attends to form, theme, and detail (statutes and cases cited). So storytelling through brief writing was how I was trained.

F.L.A.: Can you talk a little about the writing process?

D.O.: I do approach my writing in this way: when I write, I don't usually think of specifics. What I usually do is I have some kind of story in mind, some sentence I heard on the radio, or something that just triggers something. When I start writing, it's almost as if I'm in a trance. Usually, by the time I sit down at the computer, I have a general plot and characters in my mind, which I've developed during my long commute from my home to my job. So when I write, it's almost like a trance. When I go back to it and start editing, I start figuring out what works and what doesn't. And then I begin to lay in some of the specific details, such as the names of streets, stores, restaurants. If the story took place in the sixties, I get my books on the sixties, and I try to find what would work here.

Sometimes I begin with the actual detail. For example, before the new millennium, the *L.A. Times* published this very funny—darkly funny—story about people who'd preordered tombstones, thinking that they would die within the last century. They had already chiseled in the year of birth, but for the year of death, all that was chiseled was the "19," and then they had left a blank for the last two digits. It turned out, as people were approaching the new millennium, they were still alive and very healthy. And how were they going to fix this? And it turned out that the whole "death care" system started coming up with ways to fix this. There are different ways. You can grind up granite and mix it with epoxy and then fill in the "19" so you can begin again. Or you can put a plaque over it. Or you can resurface the whole thing. And I thought, oh my God, this is an amazing story. So I wrote a short story called "19." It's in *Assumption and Other Stories*. And the main character is a smart, tough grandmother, and she's dealing with the fact that her husband, who's now dead, preordered these tombstones many years before.

F.L.A.: You write in a number of different genres, with their attendant conventions. However, you often play with reader expectation. Can you talk a little bit about this, and maybe also some common ground, such as themes of relationships and intergenerational conflict that come up in your work generally?

D.O.: When I write short stories, it's like being a character actor. For a very short time, you can be something very, very different, and just run with it, and push it to the extreme. And then you're done, and then you move on to the next acting role. For example, when I wrote the story "Rosie"—a film noir–like piece with murder, incest, some really horrible issues—it was after watching (for the fifth time) *Chinatown*. I had watched the film the night before, and Saturday morning I had this fever, and I wanted to write. I ended up writing this really bizarre, *noir*ish story. I couldn't get it published by a journal. I submitted it to so many journals, and no one would touch it. And now people tell me that they really like that story.

I also try to experiment with voice. Several of my stories are in the voices of women. "Res Judicata" is about a woman lawyer who eventually marries a poet, who dies of cancer. Originally that story was reversed, where the man was the lawyer and the woman was the poet, but it wasn't clicking for some reason. So I asked, why not just reverse and see what would happen? What would that do to me? What would that do for me in terms of my inspiration? Once I switched it, then the story really started to come out of me. And it was all first-person, in the woman's voice.

F.L.A.: You experiment with chronology and also place. In "Melancholy Chimes," you have a Chicano professor in Britain.

D.O.: That story is going to be in my second collection, called *Devil Talk*, which will be coming out from Bilingual Press. As I said, in college I didn't take any creative writing. However, when I turned 40, as a present, my wife found this creative writing class being taught at a community college near our house. And I'd been writing for about a year and getting a few things published, and she said, "Here's this class. Why don't you take it?" Okay, so I took it, and that's when I wrote that story. It's in six parts, and it's backward, beginning in Part 6 and moving to Part 1. Each class had us focus on one thing, like dialogue, or whatever it might be. So I wrote each piece for each class.

When I was in college, I studied in England for a quarter. It was just the most remarkable experience, you know, for this little kid from near-downtown L.A. to be living in this place called Cliveden, where the last owners, occupants, were Lord and Lady Astor. As it made a very strong impression on me, I kept a lot of the materials, like brochures and booklets, that I put in a photo album. I was going through these materials, and I thought, I should use this for a story. So I did, and that's where that story comes from. *Twelve Gauge* (a New York online journal) really liked the story and published it.

F.L.A.: Your male characters suffer from a sense of impotence.

D.O.: I was interviewed for a local TV show and was asked if the story where the main character deals with his wife's miscarriages was about the guy going through a midlife crisis. I said, "Well, there's a crisis; yeah, the guy's in midlife, but the real crisis is that this is a man socialized to want to fix things, and he can't." I also reflected my own dealing with a wife who was grieving over multiple miscarriages and feeling like I had no power. I thought, I'm not good as a husband and father because I can't fix this.

I have a third collection of stories titled *Anywhere but L.A.,* where there's a lot less of this impotent feeling; there are also a lot fewer stories involving children. To borrow a phrase from Stuart Dybek, "my fictional children have all grown up." So I think there is an evolution in my writing, and probably with most writers. As writers write, I think most writers are working through things, working through whatever it might be—trauma or just dealing with life. And if they're successful, and if they develop as people, their fiction will begin to reflect that.

F.L.A.: You often give texture to some traumatic event in your stories. I think here of Amna and the grandmother.

D.O.: The world can be a very ugly place. I've known too many people who have been sexually abused as children. It's a horrible part of life. As a parent, in particular, I'm very watchful of anything that might indicate that someone might be hurting my child. As you get older, you hear from your friends stories of children hurt by adults. Even though it's fiction, I really try to write the truth. And sometimes it's very disturbing to people.

F.L.A.: The undocumented worker story is polemical?

D.O.: "Listen to Me" is a very angry piece, and written after this horrible recall election we went through here in California, where undocumented workers and the whole driver's license issue—all that started to come to the fore, and there was a lot of unwarranted anger being expressed towards undocumented workers. So I wrote that piece. I just had to write it. I was so angry with the things I was hearing: people not realizing how important all workers are, and how much of a benefit people get from people who work in the kitchens, people who work in the fields, people who work in the factories, taking jobs that no one else is going to take—just, you know, it got me very angry. So I wrote that piece. Hopefully, it's not too much of a polemic. But if it is, oh well. It's very short. The reader can just move on to my next story.

F.L.A.: You also use a variety of narrative styles: realism and the fantastic, as seen in the story "Bender."

D.O.: "Bender" is a *fantasma.* It's about a Chicano couple, and they have a little visitor who comes by, and this little visitor is basically a creature, and you never really hear what that creature says. I describe what the creature says, but there's a dialogue because the Chicano and this creature have an unpleasant conversation. And the creature is really a metaphor for something that's wrong in that relationship. I wrote the story after reading Aimee Bender's short story collection, *Girl in the Flammable Skirt.* I had a chance to give it to her after it was published in the *Pacific Review.* She was so gracious and said she really liked it. Aimee is such a wonderful writer and certainly one of my primary influences.

Of the twenty-six stories collected in *Devil Talk,* thirteen are *fantasmas.* When I started writing, about a quarter of my stories were *fantasmas.* There's something wonderful about the surreal, about the supernatural, where sometimes you can actually tell more truth by using this form as opposed to writing something that's more realistic.

F.L.A.: You employ a variety of different voices, from Anglo bigots to middle-class Chicanos.

D.O.: One of the issues when Chicanos move into the middle class is, of course, that we're crossing another border. Our grandparents or parents crossed the border from Mexico to the United States and had to struggle with language and usually had to struggle, at least in my family, with economics. When we move into the middle class, our struggles begin to change a bit.

This is a struggle of identity. I feel very, very comfortable about my culture, who I am. But at the same time, I remember going through grammar school and being called the little white boy because I didn't speak Spanish, feeling separate from the culture in that way. Yet then, moving into Stanford, where it was a mostly white population, I remember being told by this young Caucasian lady I started to have a crush on, "I can't date you because you're Chicano." This is a kind of limbo that we find ourselves in as we move up the educational and economic ladder. But all immigrant groups go through this.

In this collection, *Assumption,* I do present two different Chicano communities: one is working-class, which is where I came from, and the other is professional, which is where I'm at right now. I think some critics think that Chicano literature should be all border literature. Border literature is beautiful. There are some wonderful books out there, which I will recommend to anyone. But that's not my story. I'm totally urban, and I'm educated, and I'm professional. And I'm in a mixed marriage, too. My wife is Jewish. So, I think it's fair to lay out the mosaic of experience. I mean, imagine if you did a grid of the types of Latino experiences you could write about. First of all, you have to figure out immigration status: did the writer come from Mexico or some other Latin American country? Is the writer first-generation, second-generation, third-generation? Is the writer descended from people who lived in a part of the Southwest that used to be Northern Mexico? In such a case, there was no immigration experience; they were already there. Then you mix in other categories: gender, education level, religion, sexual orientation. The grid becomes so complex that there's no way anyone can tell me there's only one way Chicano literature should be. So I try to present as much as I can, based on my experiences.

F.L.A.: The place of history in your work, especially your novella, *The Courtship of María Rivera Peña?*

D.O.: When people talk about L.A. literature, sometimes they think Hollywood: movie stars and movie producers and Malibu and swimming pools and all those types of things. So in my novella I wanted to give a historical context that tied in to what I know about L.A. Los Angeles used to be part of Mexico, and we can't forget that. So that's what I was trying to do with the historical markers in that book. I've discovered since, from the L.A. Public Library, that my novella is very rare because there are almost no books that are fiction that deal with the Mexican American community in the '20s and '30s in Los Angeles. I think history plays such an important part in fiction, and in particular, I think, Chicano fiction from L.A. People sometimes think we have no history in L.A. That's through the lens, I think, of the majority. We have a lot of history in the city. And a lot of it is, of course, Mexican American history.

F.L.A.: You also write poetry. How does this differ from your fiction writing?

D.O.: It's more emotional and more immediate. But in many ways the poems are almost like short stories—like flash fiction. A lot of my poetry deals with the metaphor of crossing the border, not only the actual crossing of the geographical border, but also crossing cultural borders.

When my father was still working in the factory, he wrote a novel. He studied, bought books, and read a lot of poetry. He bought all kinds of poetry books. His novel was rejected ten times, and he destroyed it—which is heartbreaking to me. One of the things he did when I started writing and publishing was that he gave me all these how-to-write-poetry books. When I started to read them, I broke out in a sweat because I didn't want to intellectualize the process. So I put those books on the shelf. It's such an organic type of thing, that's really from inspiration. It's really a pure form of language—the purest form probably being the haiku, because of the brevity of it, yet the power of those few words!

F.L.A.: You've written children's books?

D.O.: I wanted to write a story about a mixed-race child, who's Jewish and Chicano, who is dealing with prejudice at school. I submitted it to the *L.A. Times* "Kids' Reading Room" and waited for six months before they sent me a letter agreeing to publish *Benjamin and the Word,* as well as inviting me to be a contract freelancer for them. They've since published several of my stories, including one about Dolores Huerta that's written in the voice of a little girl who's a daughter of a farmworking family. *Benjamin and the Word* is going to be published as a picture book by Arte Público Press. [Published in 2005.]

We need more children's literature for Latinos/as, and for other children to understand our community better. It's so important because the kids need something to connect with. And sometimes that's going to spark kids to read. When I was growing up, there was almost nothing. I mean, yes, I loved books by Dr. Seuss and other books that were around back then in the early sixties and mid-sixties. I don't remember there being any Chicano writers doing kids' books. Maybe they were writing them, but they weren't being published. And now, luckily, we are publishing.

F.L.A.: Is there more or less freedom to play with form and content in Children's literature than in your other writing?

D.O.: For children, you can't have too much ambiguity in the story. So in *Benjamin and the Word* there is a reconciliation between Benjamin and the boy who used that word against him. As they get older, children begin to realize there's not always closure. But when you're writing for the younger audience, there needs to be closure and a sense of teaching a lesson about how to deal with people and how to deal with things that come up.

F.L.A.: You mentioned *Devil Talk* and *Anywhere But L.A.* What are some of your current and future projects?

D.O.: As I mentioned, *Devil Talk* includes the *fantasma,* departing from the style of those collected in *Assumption. Anywhere But L.A.* consists of stories that take place outside of Los Angeles. L.A. is a big city, but I've written a lot about the city, so I thought about locating the stories outside it. Of course, many of the characters are dealing with being transplanted from L.A. to somewhere else. I have a poetry collection called *Crossing the Border,* and I've also written a script based on my novella. And I've been toying with a novel told through the eyes of many different characters that make up the Chicano community in Los Angeles, but haven't put the finger to keyboard on that yet.

F.L.A.: How do you feel about the small press/big press issue as a Chicano writer?

D.O.: The university press and the independent press are really producing some of the more exciting, cutting-edge fiction and poetry. And why? And there's been a lot of coverage about this in *Poets & Writers* and the *L.A. Times,* for example. The smaller presses are able to say, okay, we're not going to make a million bucks off this book, but we believe in this author, we believe in this piece of literature, and we're going to publish it. And we'll stay with this writer. To those small presses, selling twenty thousand copies of a book, that's a best-seller. It's wonderful, fantastic, and that writer's going to have a home.

Then you flip the coin, and you read about some writers who went to very large presses, and their books are now out of print. Their publishers will not publish another book because they couldn't make up the advance. Of course, a small press will not get you the same kind of press coverage. A lot of reviewers will not review you unless published by a larger press. I give a lot of credit to the *L.A. Times.* They tend to review almost an inordinate number of books from university presses. I mean, there are about one hundred thousand books published every year, and the *L.A. Times,* for example, can review only about fifteen hundred books a year. And of those fifteen hundred reviews, many are books from small presses.

I talk with my Latino writer friends who've been published by university presses—you know, "Can we make the leap?" "Don't we need an agent?" Agents won't touch many of us, don't want to take the risk. And with the economy being what it is, it's even worse. I have mixed feelings. I have a wonderful home with Bilingual Press. And Arte Público Press has been fantastic in preparing the drawings and the manuscript for my children's book; I'm very excited about that project.

F.L.A.: What lies in the future for Chicano/a fiction?

D.O.: The future will see the very idea of a Chicano writer disappear. We will just be writers. There was a time when people would say "woman writer." They don't say that anymore. It takes time, but eventually we will reach a point when people will talk about, say, Sandra Cisneros without saying "Chicana writer." Our writing is beginning to enter the mainstream and winning big national awards. So we'll get there. We'll get there. I remember someone asked me at a poetry conference I was invited to, "How do you feel being called a Chicano writer?" And I said, "Well, I feel very proud." But at the same time, I don't want to feel like the books by James Joyce and Ernest Hemingway are in one section, and our books are someplace else. No, we should be mixed in. You know, we should all be there because it's all literature.

Writings by the Author
Short Stories

"Señor Sanchez." In *Nemeton: A Fables Anthology,* edited by Megan Powell, pp. 169–170. Los Angeles: Silver Lake Publishing, 2000.

"The Plumed Serpent of Los Angeles." In *Fantasmas: Supernatural Stories by Mexican American Writers,* edited by Rob Johnson, pp. 123–138. Tempe, AZ: Bilingual Press/Editorial Bilingüe, 2001.

Assumption and Other Stories. Tempe, AZ: Bilingual Press/Editorial Bilingüe, 2003.

Devil Talk: Stories. Tempe, AZ: Bilingual Press/Editorial Bilingüe, 2004.

Novels

The Courtship of María Rivera Peña. Los Angeles: Silver Lake Publishing, 2000.

Children's Literature

Benjamin and the Word. Houston: Arte Público Press/Piñata Books, 2005.

Poetry

"Hidden in Abuelita's Soft Arms." In *Love to Mamá: A Tribute to Mothers,* edited by Pat Mora, pp. 22–23. New York: Lee and Low Books, 2001.

Further Readings
Reviews

Chung, Hyun Joo. "Short Story Anthology Portrays an Evolving Code of Masculinity." *Latino LA,* November 10, 2003 <<http://www.latinola.com/story.php?story=1393>>.

Garcia, Edward H. "The Culture's Hot, but La Raza Is Faceless." Rev. of *Assumption and Other Stories. Dallas Morning News,* November 14, 2003.

González, Rigoberto. "Attorney-Author Puts L.A.'s Diverse Population on Paper." Rev. of *Assumption and Other Stories. El Paso Times,* October 5, 2003: Living Sunday, 2.

Sallis, James. "A Latino Omnibus." Rev. of *Assumption and Other Stories. Los Angeles Times,* November 30, 2003, 12.

Cecile Pineda

I n 1942 Cecile Pineda was born to a Swiss-French mother and a
Mexican father. As a single child growing up in Harlem with largely
absent parents (the father physically and the mother emotionally), she
found solace and warmth in the literature and art books that filled up her
godmother's apartment nearby. It was here that Pineda's love of reading
and writing blossomed.

Having grown up breathing a domestic air filled with Spanish, French,
and English, Pineda was already widely read in world literatures by the time
she entered Barnard College in 1964. After graduating from college and
working as an editor at Harper & Row, Pineda moved to San Francisco,
where she discovered a passion for theatre. Working with dramaturge Paul
Rebillot at San Francisco State University, Pineda quickly found her footing
as a playwright. In the space of the theatre, she felt she could most effectively voice her sociopolitical concerns. Soon after graduating, she founded
a collaborative ensemble company, Theatre of Man. Conceiving of it as a
poet's theater, she developed a theatrical language and archetypal characters
to explore issues of sexism and racism in society. After her funding dried up
in 1981, she turned full-time to the writing of narrative fiction.

Inspired by authors like Kobo Abe, Alain Robbe-Grillet, and Juan Rulfo,
and by the mathematical concept of catastrophe, Pineda set pen to paper
and wrote her first novel, *Face* (1985). Published to great critical acclaim,
Face unfolds as a series of tangled, lucid dreams that follow the disfigured
protagonist, Helio Cara, as he embarks on a journey of self-discovery in Rio
de Janeiro. Following closely on its coattails, Pineda published her lyrical

second novel, *Frieze* (1986). It takes the reader into the story of Gopal, a Javanese sculptor, and his mythically dimensioned journey through fluctuating time-spaces.

As Pineda's first novels didn't gravitate around U.S. ethnic themes, she was largely ignored by mainstream publishers and Chicano/a literary scholars. With this partially in mind, she chose to write a novel that would both play the Latino-ethnic game and critique an East Coast publishing machine that sought only to churn out much of the same. In 1992 Pineda published her novel *The Love Queen of the Amazon,* in which she cleverly exaggerates the genre of magical realism seen in Isabel Allende and Gabriel García Márquez to playfully tell the story of Ana Magdalena Arzate de Figueroa. In a direct parody of such Latin American writers, Pineda invents the character Federico Orgaz y Orgaz, who, as his name suggests, is full of hot air or gas when talking about his great literary achievements. He exclaims on one occasion, "Fabulation! Fabulation is what is needed, the endless and obsessive elaboration of the narrative line to form labyrinthine arabesques, polyhedrons, dodecahedrons of astonishing and dizzying complexity" (58). Following *Love Queen,* Pineda returned to the more abstract and experimental narrative form of her earlier novels, publishing *Redoubt* (2001), *Fishlight: A Dream of Childhood (2002),* and *Bardo99* (2003). Her radically experimental form made it difficult for her to find a publisher. After a five-year struggle, she found San Antonio's Wings Press, which published all three books. Pineda's career, first as a dramatist and then as a writer of narrative fiction, demonstrates a writer who pushes at the borders of genre and theme to take her readers into unpredictable territories.

Frederick Luis Aldama: Your novels all show an unusually keen eye for spatial detail.

Cecile Pineda: This has to do with my training in theater. My theater experience, during the decade of the 1970s and spilling over into the early 1980s, was a wonderful apprenticeship for writing narrative fiction—in all, twelve years working with my own theater ensemble. The rise to power of the "Great Communicator," Ronald Reagan, didn't help. Our funds dried up completely. It became very clear to me that if I stayed in theater, I was going to feel a very hard rain.

I made the transition from working in theater to focusing exclusively on fiction. Not only was my writing shaped by my work in theater, but I'd always been spatially inclined. In fact, I was first drawn to theater because of its relationship to space and to the concept of space. I wanted to draw on my experience as a director, whose first priority is always the development of a mis-en-scène derived from a central, seminal visual image. I think it's Elizabeth Spencer who said, "I can't start writing until I can visualize the whole space." So whether it's the landscape as far as the eye can see or the dwelling within the dwelling, the configuration of a staircase, the height of the risers—spatially, it all has to be very present.

I was also interested in time. I wanted to see if I could write in such a way as to make time stand still. Slowing time down doesn't just happen: you can control time in the way you choose to relay the events of the narrative, and you can also have your characters subjectively experience time. You see me play with time in *Face* and *Frieze* especially. After writing my memoir of childhood, *Fishlight,* I realized that you can also make time stand still with silence. I became very interested in what is not said: to freeze time by representing that which is left out or cannot be said—the silence. *Fishlight* ends with the process of letting out, the gesture (after inhaling) of exhaling.

F.L.A.: You imagine the body—its thresholds of pain and pleasure, its presence and nonpresence—differently in your work?

C.P.: We walk the earth, but what would our consciousness be, I ask, if what we moved through were water or air? What would we then possess? What would we hold onto? What would we have to have to satisfy ourselves? Do you know? I explore these questions in all of my writing. I also ask how the rhythms of breathing, the rhythms of digestion, the rhythms of sex, cloud our thinking or inform it. I think that, ideally, writing should be able to embody the self in all its permutations.

F.L.A.: Can you talk to me about the writing of your second novel, *Frieze*?

C.P.: I worked on *Face* for three years, and then sold it. While *Face* was in press, I began and finished the writing of my second novel, *Frieze*. I didn't have my then-publisher or anyone breathing down my neck, asking me what I was going to write next. It was already done. It must be terrible for a young writer to have no arrows in the quiver but to have that huge pressure to produce a follow-up work.

Frieze came completely by accident. I was tired after writing *Face*. I felt written out. With the money that was left over from my advance from Viking, I traveled around the island of Java, visiting the ninth-century Buddhist pyramid and temple of Borobudur, with its cycle of ornate stone relief panels. *Frieze* started to write itself—every writer's dream; it began on the plane back to the States. I had a beginning and an end by the time I landed, and because beginnings and endings are half of the struggle of writing fiction, I was well on my way to completing my second novel. I had a first draft six months later that I entitled *Frieze*. I sent it to the editor I'd already worked with at Viking. Although I disagreed with some of her editorial suggestions—for example, I refused to delete the first epigraph (which decries arms build-up at the expense of children the world over)—they agreed to publish the book.

F.L.A.: After *Frieze* you wrote a less introspective, less metaphysical novel, *Love Queen of the Amazon*.

C.P.: *Love Queen* was largely a response to the late 1980s boom in Latina and Chicana fiction. Ana Castillo, Sandra Cisneros, Isabel Allende, Julia Alvarez, Cristina Garcia, to name a few, had hit the big time with narrative fictions that successfully crossed over. At the time, I was writing another novel, *Bardo99*—a very depressing narrative. To take a break from *Bardo99* and to bring some laughter into my life, I decided to write a novel that would parody García Márquez and others whose magic realist novels had become so famous.

I had an agent at that time to whom I sent the first chapter. Even though I had promised myself never to sell a book based on an outline, I agreed to write *Love Queen* this way. (I usually write more intuitively and without plot outlines; the less I know where I'm going, the more terrified I become and the better the work turns out.) I continued writing, this time working more closely with an editor at Little, Brown in Boston. I had twelve months to spin straw into gold. They wanted magical realism, so I thought, I'm gonna give you a magical realism that parodies magical realism and include within its framework a harsh political satire. I used parody to poke fun at the convention of magical realism that, to my mind at least, had become overused and boringly predictable.

F.L.A.: Why didn't you continue publishing with Little, Brown?

C.P.: Because after the editor [who bought *Love Queen of the Amazon*] quit to start a coffee house in Brooklyn, the book withered on the vine. It was published, but there was nobody in-house to promote it; there was nobody to propose a promotion budget. It quietly fizzled out and went out of print. Wings Press has resurrected *The Love Queen of the Amazon* in a new, revised edition and published all my new work, *Fishlight*, *Redoubt*, and *Bardo99*, as well as *Face* and *Frieze*, in a uniform edition with cover designs by internationally recognized artist Kathy Vargas.

F.L.A.: Can you tell me a little about books like *Fishlight*?

C.P.: *Fishlight* was catalyzed by very unhappy circumstances. When I had my company, I always urged my actors to take the bad juju and use it to create something. With *Fishlight*, that journey led me to a completely altered state of consciousness—a fever dream. *Fishlight* centers on an event that happened to me when, as a child, I came close to dying. In a way, I had to go to that feverish place before I could find the voice and form to write it. There are no mediating narrative frames; the narrative just exists in and of itself. It's an excursion into the child mind. The following two mononovels, *Bardo99* and *Redoubt*, (mononovels in the sense that each occurs in the mind of one consciousness) expand my excursion into pure consciousness.

F.L.A.: And *Redoubt*?

C.P.: When I began writing *Redoubt*, I had just seen a Moroccan film in French titled *The Citadel*. I was fascinated by the film's extraordinary shots of kids running through dried-up cisterns in their desert village. I've always adored the desert, and this film really fired up my imagination. What would it be like to live, not just in the desert, but in complete isolation? I related to this question personally as someone who—as a Latina, certainly—has felt exiled all her life.

Redoubt is very much my attempt to deal with the question of gender. People are not born masculine or feminine. From a gonadal point of view, yes, we are born man and woman—and we learn to identify as such as we grow up—but I wanted to get at how this social construction of gender affects the shaping of our consciousness.

I started *Redoubt* with six dictionary definitions in two languages (French and English) of the word *redoubt*—hence the novel's organization into six sections. This helped give the material a structure and allowed me better to control a narrative of consciousness that had no sense of containment and that meandered and curled in on itself over and over. As the narrative spirals in and out, several themes begin to emerge. When it was finished, I gave *Redoubt* to my agent, who felt that it was too unconventional for a mainstream publisher. She shopped it around to alternative publishers. (This same agent flat-out refused to send *Fishlight* out to any publisher.) I received rejection after rejection, and like all agents who prefer money to art, she just gave up.

F.L.A.: What about *Bardo99*?

C.P.: I actually began *Bardo99* before writing *The Love Queen of the Amazon*. So *Bardo99* sat unfinished on my writing table for at least ten years. It was difficult to get back to it and finish, not only because I had become interested in other writing projects, but because I was teaching full-time. While both activities support one another—in my mind at least—ultimately teaching does drain you of your energy to write. Good writing, of course, takes a lot of energy. After I finish a writing day, I'm exhausted, and I'm hungry. I devour great quantities of food. Anyway, *Bardo99* languished unfinished for some time. Then I just got a second wind out of nowhere. Although I was still teaching full-time, I decided to take the bull by the horns. It still took some time; I went around and around with the narrative until I became satisfied that I had shaped the material into a narrative that "reads" in the structural (rhythmic) sense. It's a novel which proposes the twentieth century as an actual literary character, one who must pass through a bardo state, that time-out-of-time between death and rebirth where, according to the teachings of Tibetan Buddhism, the spirit encounters its fiercest terrors, followed by its most sublime joys. Even with my revisions, to my agent the book seemed completely unpublishable.

My agent had failed to sell *Redoubt*, was uninterested in *Fishlight*, and knew that she couldn't sell *Bardo99*. It was a real down period for me. I had three books that were out of print: *Face, Frieze,* and *The Love Queen of the Amazon.* Just to keep it alive, I had been mailing Xerox copies out in cardboard boxes to teachers who wanted to teach *Face* and my other novels in their classrooms. I had three new books that weren't finding a publisher. I started to learn about self-publishing through the Internet.

I thought that Internet publishing might finally offer a venue of absolute freedom for creative expression by providing a direct bridge to the reading public. I began the process of digitalizing every single one of my books. In principle, I believed it was a phenomenal concept.

The reality of Internet publishing is completely different. I found that it was an unqualified disaster. I discovered that the people at iUniverse who were digitalizing and then proposing to distribute my books didn't give a fig about the word. The vast number of typos that resulted from their re-scanning my work could have been edited out, but they just weren't interested. Perhaps even worse, they took some liberties in terms of composition and layout. To those like myself who are sensitive even to the smell of a book, I felt such liberties were unacceptable. I found the results extremely disappointing, so I canceled every one of their contracts.

However, my problem with iUniverse did end up opening a door for me. It led me to Bryce Milligan, who had already written an in-depth review of *Face* and *Frieze*—and who runs Wings Press. He said, "Well, Cecile, you don't have to digitalize your books. Wings will publish anything you write." My entire nightmare was over. I no longer had to deal with an incompetent Internet publisher; I no longer had to ship Xeroxes of my novels in cardboard boxes. I found myself suddenly becoming very excited. I didn't have that burden anymore. I could write again.

F.L.A.: Can you speak more about your writing process?

C.P.: Writing is not easy; I'm always trying to keep my nose to the grindstone and my person glued to the chair. To do this, I play games with myself, or I experiment with narrative technique, allowing me to explore challenging new territories—pure consciousness, for example. There's nothing new under the sun, neither archetype nor story. The challenge is really to see if one can write in new and interesting ways, ways that allow one to create new worlds. To me creating a world is the quintessential task confronting a writer. At the same time, one has to keep in mind how the narrative will sustain the reader's interest. I never want readers to have to suffer through my books.

Writing is also about reading. Just as I want to write something that is challenging and that stretches the imagination, so I want to read it. It's the very rare work that engages me.

F.L.A.: I see the South African writer Coetzee and also the Argentinean, Borges, as just a few of your influences.

C.P.: I wouldn't quite put it that way. It is certainly the case that anything seen or read tends to imprint one. I've been reading since I was a kid, mostly stuff that was really inappropriate for a child. I read Beckett's Trilogy when I was 18; his images and deep probing of consciousness have stayed with me ever since. Ultimately, the Trilogy is about breathing. It asks, how do you get to pure consciousness (as opposed to narrative)? It probes the is-ness of being. The third book, *The Unnamable,* is all about writing that which lies beyond anything named. Just think about that as a challenge! I have immense respect for the Swiss writer Max Frisch, particularly *I'm Not Stiller,* and Dürrenmatt's *The Visit.* I would add Kafka, Juan Rulfo, and many, many others, including the poets St. John Perse and Salvador Espriu, who write in French and Catalan, respectively.

F.L.A.: Biographically speaking, your godmother also played a great role in your life.

C.P.: My godmother was wonderful and very French. The first edition of *Frieze* was dedicated to her. She was an intellectual, a language professor, who came to be my main pillar of support during my adolescence. She took care of me. Much later, towards the end of her life, I took care of her. (I have written a short story, "Notes for a Botched Suicide," about this experience of caring for her. It's a short story about departure, which will shortly appear in an anthology published by Longman.) Besides her humanness, she had a huge library—and a very small apartment. So she would be constantly throwing out books, such as Duchartre's *The Italian Comedy.* What I could, I tried to rescue from the dustbin. She introduced me to Nathalie Sarraute, Samuel Beckett, and Ionesco. I had plenty of time to read, and she had plenty of books with which I could spend my time.

F.L.A.: You mentioned that you identify as a woman writing fiction. Do you also identify racially as a writer?

C.P.: First, probably because I identify as a woman and a mother, I feel this terrific burden of caring. There's no God. The idea that God has "His eye on the sparrow" is off the mark. It's my eye on the sparrow. That's my responsibility. Second, I identify politically. My responsibility today is to fight as much as possible to bring basic civil rights to people everywhere, starting with the United States. Third, I identify culturally as Jewish. I was married to a Jewish man (educated by the great ethicist Emanuel Levinas), and most of my close associations while I was growing up were Jewish. Fourth, I identify with my Mexican heritage. Pineda is a Sephardic name, but my father was Mexican through and through.

But, as far as my writing goes, I do not prioritize race as a category for determining one's position in the world of writing. The question of race seems to me to raise the specter of stereotypes. I try to avoid anchoring identity to delimiting categories in my novels because, as I know it, human nature is full of surprises. One of the big impediments connected with being identified as a Latina writer is the pressure to adhere to a provincial framework. I consider that human experience lies beyond race or geography.

F.L.A.: Where is home for you?

C.P.: Where is home? I've been running all my life, but I think that home is in my body. I think that's home. I've traveled all over the world, and everywhere I go, I almost never experience culture shock. I feel at home, perhaps because I feel at home in my body and in my spirit.

F.L.A.: Have your books reached other audiences around the world?

C.P.: At first I traveled to Europe, where I met with my then-agent's Italian, French, and Spanish correspondents to try to encourage the foreign publication of my work. My sense was that it might continue to live if presented to a public that might better know how to read my more experimental narratives. However, it turned out to be a completely futile trip. Finally, it was my most commercial—and least favorite— novel, *The Love Queen of the Amazon,* that was translated into German and Dutch. Perhaps it is not so surprising that these Protestant countries bought the book because, among other transgressions, it's extremely anti-clerical.

Seeing to the publication of my books certainly has been a great challenge. Perhaps the rather conservative book marketplace will change; perhaps not. It's like the political climate of this country today: it's so thick with reactionary politics that we might suddenly see a groundswell of rebellion.

F.L.A.: Do you think the publishing market has become any more receptive to your work today?

C.P.: The publishing world is a disaster, and it's becoming more and more so because fewer and fewer people who know how to read well are making decisions about what will be bought. Some publishers now approach salespeople in chain bookstores to ask if they were to publish a novel with X and Y characters and Z settings, would they push it? Additionally, we have a completely managed press. I don't call it the media; it is a managed press. It's becoming harder and harder to have access to good writing. Publishing has become less and less about the word and more and more about profits. In the U.S. book business, like any other corporate business, the buck is sacred. To me, it's the word that is sacred. If I didn't think it was sacred, I wouldn't be doing what I do.

Writings by the Author
Novels

Face. New York: Viking, 1985; reprint, San Antonio: Wings Press, 2003.
Frieze. New York: Viking, 1986; reprint, San Antonio: Wings Press, 2004.
The Love Queen of the Amazon. Boston: Little, Brown, 1992; revised edition, San Antonio: Wings Press, 2002.
Redoubt. Writers Club Press, 2001; reprint, San Antonio: Wings Press, 2004.
Fishlight: A Dream of Childhood. San Antonio: Wings Press, 2002.
Bardo99. San Antonio: Wings Press, 2003.

Other

"Deracinated: The Writer Re-Invents Her Sources." Berkeley: Third Woman, 1997: 57–70.

Further Readings
Critical Studies

Bloom, Lynn Z. "Autobiographical Inscriptions: Form, Personhood, and the American Woman Writer of Color." *American Literature* 73, no. 2 (2001): 437–438.
Bruce-Novoa, Juan. "Deconstructing the Dominant Patriarchal Text: Cecile Pineda's Narratives." In *Breaking Boundaries: Latina Writings and Critical Readings,* edited by Asunción Horno-Delgado, Eliana Ortega, Nina M. Scott, and Nancy Saporta Sternbach, pp. 72–81. Amherst: University of Massachusetts Press, 1989.

Christian, Karen. "The 'Boom' in U.S. Latina/o Fiction: Performing Magical Realism in *The Love Queen of the Amazon* and *So Far From God.*" In *Show and Tell: Identity as Performance in U.S. Latina/o Fiction,* pp. 121–148. Albuquerque: University of New Mexico Press, 1997.

Christie, John. *Latino Fiction and the Modernist Imagination: Literature of the Borderlands.* New York: Garland, 1998.

———. "Preface: Latina/o Writers of the United States." *LIT: Literature Interpretation Theory* 11, no. 2 (2000): i–vi.

Connor, Anne. "Desenmascarando a Ysarel: The Disfigured Face as Symbol of Identity in Three Latino Texts." *Cincinnati Romance Review* 21 (2002): 148–162.

Gonzalez, Ray Marcial. "The Postmodern Turn in Chicana/o Cultural Studies: Toward a Dialectical Criticism." Ph.D. Dissertation, Stanford University, 2000.

Johnson, David E. "Face Value: An Essay on Cecile Pineda's *Face.*" *Americas Review* 19 (1991): 73–93.

Lomelí, Francisco A. "Cecile Pineda's *Face* and Ralph Ellison's *Invisible Man*: Poetics of Synthesizing an Identity." In *El poder hispano: Actas del V Congreso de Culturas Chicanas de los Estados Unidos,* edited by Alberto Moncala Lorenzo, Carmen Flys Junquera, and José Antonio Gurpegui Palacio, pp. 465–472. Madrid: Universidad de Alcal, Centro de Estudios Norteamericanos, 1994.

Rocard, Marcienne. "Cecile Pineda's *Face:* Reconstructing the Self." Ph.D. Dissertation, University of Toulouse, 1994.

Reviews

Gonzales-Berry, Erlinda. Rev. of *Face. The Americas Review* 5, no. 2 (1987): 107–109.

Heron, Liz. Rev. of *Face. New Statesman* 110 (September 13, 1985): 31.

Hopkinson, Amanda. Rev. of *The Love Queen of the Amazon. New Statesman & Society* 6, no. 239 (February 12, 1993): 47.

Mason, Deborah. Rev. of *Frieze. The New York Times Book Review,* November 23, 1986, p. 24.

Rev. of *Fishlight. Publishers Weekly* 249, no. 4 (January 28, 2002): 271.

Six, Abigail Lee. Rev. of *The Love Queen of the Amazon. TLS: Times Literary Supplement* 4689 (February 12, 1993): 21.

Lourdes Portillo

orn in Chihuahua, Mexico, in 1944, Lourdes Portillo moved with her parents and four siblings to Los Angeles when she was thirteen. Her father worked as a newspaper administrator in Mexico, and Portillo was exposed from an early age to stories. As one of the oldest of her siblings, Portillo soon took on the role of family interpreter in L.A., and she took easily and quickly to storytelling. Inspired by her Los Angeles movie environs, she set her sights on the visual art of telling stories. Having experienced racism and sexism as a Latina, she hoped to tell stories that would be conscious of issues of race and gender. During the late 1960s she pursued an M.F.A. at San Francisco Art Institute and in the 1970s apprenticed with several documentary filmmakers. During this climate of great civil rights activism, Portillo's politics and visual artistry began to galvanize. She was a participating member in the 1970s of the Marxist collective Cine Manifest; in 1976 she established her own company, Xochitl Productions.

Since her first documentary, *After the Earthquake/Después del terremoto* (1979), she has produced and directed nearly a dozen others that together represent her complex vision as visual artist, investigative journalist, and activist. Her many documentaries move back and forth across the U.S.– Mexico border, representing diverse and complex Latin American, Mexican, and Chicano/a experiences and identities. Her award-winning, fact-based storytelling documents human rights struggles both large and small, from archiving the mothers' struggle to get answers from Argentina's government regarding *los desaparecidos,* to the effect of Latina pop star Selena's death on young Tejanas, to affirming the important place of cultural traditions like the Día de los Muertos/Day of the Dead celebrations on both sides of the border.

Frederick Luis Aldama: You've been working on documentary journalism since the late 1970s—from *After the Earthquake* to the more recent *Señorita Extraviada.* Can you speak to changes in your own work, audiences, funding, and so on, during this stretch of time?

Lourdes Portillo: I think that I've been unusually lucky to be able to get funding for my work. It has enabled me to share my vision out in the world. But in the film world, it has become more difficult to find money to do films. It's not as easy as it was, say, in the '80s and '90s. It has become more challenging. And we'll see what happens during this next phase of work because I'm transforming my style once again, so it's going to be more challenging to raise the funds.

I feel that it's a time in my life where I need to go even deeper into the whole notion of creating rather than to continue to focus on the themes that have characterized my work so far. I'm old enough now to begin to reflect on the role of the artist in the greater society. All this filmmaking activism has brought me to this point of self-reflection on the role of the artist in an ever-changing world.

F.L.A.: Given the big juggernaut of mainstream America, how much of a role can a documentary filmmaker interested in questions of race, ethnicity, gender, and sexuality play in society? I'm thinking of Mike Moore's *Fahrenheit 9/11,* which has just gotten huge publicity and which places questions of race and gender very much more in the background. Where do you think your work touches people?

L.P.: The documentary has traditionally been marginalized—especially documentaries that touch on all the subjects that I touch on. There are a lot of people that have been so influenced on seeing the world a certain way that they aren't interested to see other forms of inequality represented on film; they're not interested in my point of view. But there are a whole lot of people who are interested, who are curious, who want to hear and see the other side of the Hollywood-style American dream story.

My work, along with that of other independent filmmakers, has other concerns: to show another side of life not being represented by Hollywood and other conglomerate media. And even now, with a documentary like Michael Moore's *Fahrenheit,* that has become a crossover success, its issues allow it to become commercially viable because he is speaking about the things no one else has addressed. Yes, now it has become a commodity, but we need those sole, independent voices that speak what they perceive as the truth. When I make a film, for me it's a way of being profound. I want depth from a film.

F.L.A.: What drew you to the visual arts and documentary filmmaking? Why not print journalism, poetry, or novels?

L.P.: I think it was just circumstances. When I emigrated from Mexico when I was a teenager, I went with my family to live in Los Angeles, which is like the Detroit for movies. During this period, even though I loved films, I couldn't even dream of making feature-length films. I was an immigrant. I was a kid. We were working class. Nobody was going to give a Chicana—someone that looks like your maid—five million dollars to make a film. Fortunately, I had this opportunity to work on a documentary when I was about twenty-one years old; it was a perfect fit. Later, I moved to San Francisco, which had a much livelier independent art film community. I became very engaged in the Bay Area's art film community. It seemed clear that this was the genre for me.

F.L.A.: What drew you to the art of storytelling and to uncover and share truths?

L.P.: Well, I think my parents were a very big influence on me. I can't say that I had a mentor or that I had anyone that was guiding me, though many people have been very generous with me.

I think that I'm just kind of continuing on the tradition of storytelling and the sense of right and wrong—denouncing injustice—that my father and my mother taught me. The most burning desire inside of me to tell these stories has been the fact that I suffered a lot of racism when I came to this country. I started to get beaten down, and I saw how others were beaten down. I didn't like it. When I arrived, I felt that we were these very special people, but others failed to recognize it. I wanted to tell everyone about it.

F.L.A.: Your films cross lots of borders—geographical, national, linguistic, and psychological. This is obviously a part of the political dimension of the documentaries and the films, but it seems quite an aesthetic aspect as well.

L.P.: What really interests me is art. I've always tried to keep abreast of what is happening with films as art. I never had formal documentary training, but I did get a sort of formal training for art film. So I've always tried to use all the techniques that create a work of art within films that always center on my concerns about injustice in its many expressions. So the aesthetic storytelling aspect and the political themes are embedded within all my films.

To me film is an art, and there's so much to be done with it, not only visually, but narratively. This process of filmmaking happens very slowly because you often have to educate audiences that are very accustomed to seeing film narratives told in a certain way.

F.L.A.: Can you speak to the collaborative process of your filmmaking?

L.P.: Of course, now you can make video by yourself, but filmmaking still requires a crew. And to have a crew means that you have a series of collaborators because all of them manage a skill that you can't be managing at the same time you're directing. Over the course of several years, I've developed very close relationships with different people that have different skills; they're people that really impact what I create. This interrelationship of collaboration in order to create this work is one of the most important aspects of my filmmaking. Curiously enough, a lot of my collaborators are not Chicanos/Latinos, but are North American people that I've developed a relationship with over the course of many years. We've become like an organism that works together. I am the director-producer. I come up with the idea, and they bring other concerns about aesthetics, the message, and the editing, and invaluable personal advice.

So collaboration in filmmaking is very, very important. If you don't have it, and you're trying to make complex films, it's very difficult.

F.L.A.: Your films share many common themes, but also cover a wide range of topics. Where do your ideas for stories come from?

L.P.: Well, they come from, really, my own experiences. For example, the idea for *Las Madres* was inspired by conversations I had with the only other Latina, Susanna Blaustein, who was also at the San Francisco Art Institute studying for our master's. We developed a deep friendship. During our many deep and long conversations, she told me about the Mothers of Plaza de Mayo. Neither of us had any formal training in documentary filmmaking, but we decided to embark on making this film about these brave women.

The Devil Never Sleeps was like an obsession of mine—a family obsession. After my uncle died, there was all this agony and all kinds of gossip. I wanted to get to the bottom of this. The whole thing was so engrossing—better than any documentary I'd seen—so I decided to keep track of everything that was unfolding at the time by creating this documentary story around his life.

Señorita Extraviada came out of a conversation with Renee Tajima-Peña in Los Angeles. She showed me an article about what was happening in Juárez. I became very interested. I was from Chihuahua and had spent some summers in Juárez when I was a kid. But her husband Armando warned me: "Don't go make a film there. There's something really evil behind this."

I care about how young women are viewed in society, how they are taken care of or not taken care of. Motherhood interests me. We see this in my film about Selena. We see this in *Las Madres* in the relationship between the state and the mother, the Church and the mother.

So the list of interests is long, but they generally come from issues that speak to me and that capture my imagination.

F.L.A.: You've mentioned the art of filmmaking several times. People forget that documentary films are more than just putting a camera in a room and letting it roll while life passes by. Of course, you use various techniques of editing, camera movement and angle, musical score, and so on to engage and affect the audience. Is there a fine line between manipulating an audience and reframing reality to engage and make the story interesting?

L.P.: Well, I think that here what happens is that you can do so many things in a documentary to manipulate that could be morally corrupt. But they are obvious a lot of times to the audience. I think that you have to always come back to the idea that you're making a film for an audience, not only to entertain them, but to explain and to move them to action. The root intention of a documentary film is the truth; you want to always be grounded in the truth. You can use many different strategies to demonstrate what you perceive as the truth—to make known your intention to be truthful—and at the same time you want it to be aesthetic. You want it to be pleasurable in some kind of deep human way.

F.L.A.: You constantly challenge yourself with using different techniques in the telling of your stories.

L.P.: Each project has been a challenge for me because I want to flex my muscles with the form. I want to be able to challenge myself and have fun doing what I'm doing.

Because I've kind of run the gamut of documentary, I've been debating about the type of film that I should be making next. I want to work on a narrative film to face an ancient fear of not being able to do a narrative film. But now that I have a foothold in the world of documentary film, I want to try to make a hybrid documentary that encompasses the use of actors and that delves into the whole idea of what it takes to create. That's my journey right now.

F.L.A.: What distinguishes documentary from narrative film?

L.P.: I think the most basic thing is that you can create anything with a narrative film. You can invent anything. Dialogue, situation, all of that stuff—you can create it. In documentary you have to be rooted in the facts, so you have to construct around the truth or what you perceive to be the truth. So you're limited by that. Consequently, you can't script anything. You have to be like a boxer, really quick on your feet. And you have to think quickly to be able to move and keep on weaving the story at the same time that everything is whirling around you. It's much more difficult to do documentary than it is narrative. In narrative you can control almost everything whereas in documentary you can barely keep any control; you are driven by the facts.

F.L.A.: Do you think much has changed for Latino/a filmmakers—documentary or otherwise—today?

L.P.: I haven't seen a lot of documentaries made by Latinos in the U.S.A. Most of the kids going into film school want to be Hollywood filmmakers and directors. That's the big driving force, principally because it does not have the glamour and it's not like you're going to get rich off of making documentaries. You're going to get a lot of satisfaction, you're going to be able to have a voice, and you can move people to action, but you'll never have all the things that Hollywood promises. It's not about that. It's either you have a calling or you don't. It's a religious vocation.

F.L.A.: Have you been able to largely make a living from the documentary?

L.P.: It's hard. It's very difficult—especially because I don't teach all the time. But I can't teach all the time and think and make films. I can't do that for some reason. At the same time that it's very difficult, though, it's also extraordinarily rewarding.

Works by the Author
Documentary Films

After the Earthquake. San Francisco: Xochitl, 1979.

Las Madres: The Mothers of Plaza de Mayo. San Francisco: Xochitl, 1986.

La Ofrenda. San Francisco: Xochitl, 1988.

Columbus on Trial. San Francisco: Xochitl, 1992.

Mirrors of the Heart. San Francisco: Xochitl, 1993.

The Devil Never Sleeps / El Diablo nunca duerme. San Francisco: Xochitl, 1994.

Sometimes My Feet Go Numb. San Francisco: Xochitl, 1997.

Corpus: A Home Movie for Selena. San Francisco: Xochitl, 1999.

Señorita Extraviada: Missing Young Woman. San Francisco: Xochitl, 2001.

Further Readings
Critical Studies

Espinoza, Dionne. "Feminist Visions: Women and Maquiladoras on the U.S.–Mexico Border." Review of *Señorita Extraviada: Missing Young Woman.* *Feminist Collections: A Quarterly of Women's Studies Resources* 25, no. 1 (2003): 18–24.

Fregoso, Rosa Linda, ed. *Lourdes Portillo: The Devil Never Sleeps and Other Films.* Austin: University of Texas Press, 2001.

McBane, Barbara. "Pinning Down the Bad-Luck Butterfly." In *Lourdes Portillo: The Devil Never Sleeps and Other Films,* edited by Rosa Linda Fregoso, pp. 160–185. Austin: University of Texas Press, 2001.

Prieto, Norma Iglesias. "Who Is the Devil, and How or Why Does He or She Sleep? Viewing a Chicana Film in Mexico." In *Lourdes Portillo: The Devil Never Sleeps and Other Films,* edited by Rosa Linda Fregoso, pp. 144–159. Austin: University of Texas Press, 2001.

Thouard, Sylvie. Performances of *The Devil Never Sleeps/El diablo nunca duerme.*

In *Lourdes Portillo: The Devil Never Sleeps and Other Films,* edited by Rosa Linda Fregoso, pp. 119–143. Austin: University of Texas Press, 2001.

Yarbro-Bejarano, Yvonne. "Ironic Framings: A Queer Reading of the Family (Melo)Drama." In *Lourdes Portillo: The Devil Never Sleeps and Other Films,* edited by Rosa Linda Fregoso, pp. 102–118. Austin: University of Texas Press, 2001.

Reviews

Backstein, Karen. Rev. of *Señorita Extraviada. Cineaste* 28, no. 1 (2002).

Gillespie, Marcia. "Women of the Year 2002: Lourdes Portillo." *Ms.* 12, no. 4 (2002): 48–50.

Klawans, Stuart. "Global Rights: The Movies." Review of *Señorita Extraviada: Missing Young Woman. The Nation* 274, no. 24 (June 24, 2002): 34.

Masuoka, Susan N. Rev. of *La Ofrenda. Western Folklore* 53, no. 1 (1994): 92–95.

Pally, Marcia. Rev. of *Las Madres: The Mothers of the Plaza de Mayo. The Nation* 135 (April 26, 1986): 595–597.

Interviews

Newman, Kathleen, and B. Ruby Rich. "Interview with Lourdes Portillo." In *Lourdes Portillo: The Devil Never Sleeps and Other Films,* edited by Rosa Linda Fregoso, pp. 48–73. Austin: University of Texas Press, 2001.

Velasco, Juan. "The Cultural Legacy of Self-consciousness: An Interview with Lourdes Portillo." *Journal of Latinos and Education* 1, no. 4 (2002): 245–253.

Luis J. Rodríguez

Born in El Paso in 1954, Luis Rodríguez found himself swiftly uprooted when his parents decided to move to Watts, Los Angeles, in
search of a better life. By the time Rodríguez was nine, his family
had replanted their roots in the South San Gabriel *barrio*. With few opportunities, Rodríguez found himself running with gangs, which led to
jail time and a sudden wake-up call. He knew that if he didn't turn from
gang life, it would swallow him whole.

Rodríguez's epiphany coincided with the great wave of the *raza* power
movement that was sweeping across L.A., and many of the protest poets he
heard and read gave voice to his experiences. Rodríguez decided to turn to
poetry with the hope that this might provide guidance and a way out of the
chaos of the *barrio*. At eighteen, he became the youngest Chicano to receive
the Quinto Sol Literary Award, earning a check for $250, a trip to Berkeley,
and a sense of purpose. Knowing that he would need formal training as a
writer and also a job to support his craft, in 1972 he enrolled at California
State University, Los Angeles. In the 1980s Rodríguez left Los Angeles and
took a job in Chicago as an editor for a leftist journal. He could finally support himself and have the time to write poetry. Although he soon made a
name as a Chicano poet at poetry slams all across Chicago, he discovered
that publishers were not interested in his work. So he founded Tia Chucha
Press and in 1989 published his first collection of poetry: the gritty, realistic, urban *barrio*–themed *Poems across the Pavement*. He then published a
second collection on *barrio* themes, *The Concrete River*, adding some sections of prose poems and poetry that were critical of the *machismo* within

the community. In his third collection, *Trochemoche: New Poems* (1998), he used the form of the lyric to transform the facts of his own experiences. One stanza of the poem "Notes of a Bald Cricket" reads: "There is a mixology of brews within me; I've tasted them all, still fermenting / as grass-high anxieties. I am rebel's pen, rebel's son, father of revolution in verse" (91).

By the time Rodríguez published *Trochemoche*, he had become a nationally recognized figure as the author of a hotly controversial best-seller. *Always Running: La Vida Loca—Gang Days in L.A.* was first published in 1993 with Curbstone, then picked up by Simon and Schuster as a paperback in 1998. In the book Rodríguez transformed his own experiences of gang activity in the mid-1960s to early 1970s into an unsentimental, gut-wrenching cautionary tale. The book's controversy hit America hard, and many school districts across the country banned the book from libraries and curriculum. After several forays into the essay form, and the writing of a volume of ethnographic scholarship that traced the individual lives of youth gang members, Rodríguez began writing children's books. In *América Is Her Name* (1998), he celebrates the power of poetry as a way for a young immigrant Latina to find a sense of place. In *It Doesn't Have to Be This Way* (1999), he again textures gang violence, this time from the point of view of ten-year-old Monchi. And, three years after Rodríguez returned to California to replant his roots, he published his first collection of short stories, *Republic of East L.A.*, in 2002. In this series of twelve hard-hitting, sharp-cutting stories, he variously portrays the trials and tribulations of a parade of characters struggling to survive in East L.A.: the young and old, the immigrant and the multigenerational Chicano, the Chicano/a gang member and hard-working, law-abiding urban parents.

Luis Rodríguez's profusion of poetry, narrative fiction, ethnography, memoir, and children's stories has led to national recognition. He has received many awards, including the PEN West/Josephine Miles Award, the Carl Sandburg Award, the *New York Times Book Review* Notable Book Award, the Hispanic Heritage Award, and the Americas Award for Children's and Young Adult Literature. He continues to write in all genres and is currently completing a biography on the Native American author John Trudell. He has also taken up the longer narrative fictional form, writing a novel that explores the lives of three generations of a Chicano steelworker family.

Frederick Luis Aldama: Is the writing of the short story—like those collected in *Republic of East L.A.*—a shift for you?

Luis Rodríguez: Although writing short stories isn't exactly new for me—one of the oldest stories collected I wrote twenty-two years ago—it's true that I've spent more time with this genre in the last three to five years. I'd written a lot of poetry and essays, my memoir of course, and, more recently, children's books. Learning to write in all these genres is something I think most writers have done around the world, including Mexico, Latin America, and Europe. But in the United States, people are taken aback when you shift genres. Anyway, with the short story I was faced with the issue of whether I could imagine characters and situations within a short narrative span. To me, every genre has its own dynamic, and in order to switch from one to another you have to understand the dynamic of each one. Of course, the genres can overlap, but you've got to know what is the central dynamic of each one. With fiction, of course, there are all sorts of different storytelling techniques that you can use to open up the imagination. So while there are poetic moments in *Republic of East L.A.,* I had to remind myself to keep focused on point of view and plot.

HarperCollins was very pleased with the short stories that I wrote. It's always a tricky thing with a big publisher because you know they have a lot of books to push. And I think sometimes you can get lost. But big publishers are always good because you get great distribution. The great thing about the Harper imprint, Rayo, is that it's dedicated to Latino writing. They have a really good editor, Rene Alegria. They're dedicated to making sure that Latino literature gets its proper place in the American literary scene. So far, the reviews have been great: from Washington, D.C., papers to California papers. Hopefully, because it has been a good seller, it will open up more doors for my other projects.

F.L.A.: Which one was the story you wrote twenty-two years ago?

L.R.: It's the last story in the book, "Sometimes You Dance with a Watermelon," that won me the UC [University of California] Irvine Best Chicano Fiction prize. After I wrote the story and won the award, though, I didn't do any more fiction. I was more into poetry, and I just wasn't sure at the time if I could write another equally strong story. After the success of *Always Running* in 1993, I gained more confidence and started to write more stories.

F.L.A.: Where do you draw your material from that gives shape to the stories in *Republic*?

L.R.: The stories are based on real people that I knew or in my experiences—but they've been all reimagined. With the exception of two children's books, I had written the essays in *Hearts and Hands,* my memoir, and my poetry—all of which is really nonfiction. So I wanted to take similar subject matter, but let the imagination run wild. For some stories, I'd have a general idea of the plot but would let loose so as to delve deep into the characters and the situations; the characters would then begin to take on a life of their own and take over the story, reshaping the plot and ending. This was a good process, finding that balance between controlling the story and letting the characters find their own way and determine their own ending.

F.L.A.: Your stories give texture to the diverse range of communities and individuals that make up East L.A.

L.R.: East L.A. is a very complicated place. I think the general idea about East L.A. is that it's got a lot of gangs. You get stuck with the drama of these stereotypes that limit people's vision of how others live everyday life. The gang stuff is there, but it's not everything. I wanted to bring out other aspects of life in East L.A., such as the struggles of undocumented peoples, Chicanos who no longer speak Spanish, Chicanas whose voices aren't heard. Without being heavy-handed, I wanted to challenge the stereotypes. And the way to deal with any stereotype is to make your diverse range of characters fuller human beings.

F.L.A.: I was struck by your interesting portrayal of Chicanas in the story "Las Chicas Chuecas."

L.R.: That's an important story because it's about those young women who are really pushed down in life and their struggles to survive. It speaks to this issue of *machismo* in the community that tends to restrict women's behavior; a lot of girls try to address it either by conforming to expectation or completely turning away from it. Some of the girls that negotiate this *machismo* are gang girls. There's the character Liver, who's an extreme gang girl, and others that just hang with the gang, like the sister, Noemi. Violence isn't restricted to just guys; there's a lot of violence and hurt that these young women carry. I've worked with a lot of girls like this and wanted to bring up some of what I learned and picked up from some of these young women because their stories just needed to be told. Sometimes, because of the circumstances, they can't be the ones to tell their stories. I mean they should, but they can't. Either they don't know how to write or they don't have the confidence—all kinds of issues. And I thought, well, I will try my hand and try to tell some of those stories with the voices of these girls.

F.L.A.: There's also love, too, between the young women?

L.R.: There are young women who are lesbians in East L.A., just like there are girls who are not. You've got the whole spectrum of society in this community. I mean, in greater East L.A. there are probably a million people, with every type of person you can imagine. It's been a large Mexican community for a long, long time with a rich history. There were the '60s and '70s with the school walkouts, marches, demonstrations. Now you have more immigrants from all over Latin America adding to its vibrancy. So by capturing and reimagining some of the tensions and complex situations that make up everyday life in East L.A.—like the love, mistrust, and violence in this story about the young women—I wanted to get at some of the underlying issues and concerns that most people probably won't think exist in this community.

F.L.A.: In the story "Finger Dance" you turn to a father-and-son relationship.

L.R.: That story is probably the closest one to my life. It started out first as a poem to my dad, but I realized that I couldn't give shape to my dad in poetry. So I turned to the short story, where fictionalized characters allowed me to get at some truth about my dad. Now, the characters are not my family, but by imagining these characters that reconcile years of silence only in death, I really got at something in my own relationship with my dad. I didn't go to my dad's funeral. He died of cancer. My family was around him, but I did not go because of our terrible relationship. He was a very cold, unemotional person. My struggle was always that my father was there, but he was never really there. So in writing the story, it was like me imagining what I would do or what would happen if I were there next to him at his deathbed. Even though it turned out to be a fictionalized character, I think I exorcised a lot of those bad feelings toward my dad.

F.L.A.: When crafting your short stories, how do you decide point of view, style, and so on?

L.R.: It's a very hard decision. I guess it depends on how complex you want the stories. I think that if you're writing from a first-person voice, you wouldn't want to make it complex. Your narrator can't go into other people's heads; it can't be omniscient, and this will convey a certain feeling to the reader. But really the decision is based on the context of the story: the parameters of the story, where you want to take it, how deep you want to get into it. Some of the stories are a little bit more straightforward, and some of them are more complicated. Ultimately, then, it's how you want to convey the content of the stories that helps direct your decision.

F.L.A.: Who are some of your big influences in terms of short story writing technique?

L.R.: I have read a lot of short stories, but the ones that stand out are by authors like T. C. Boyle; the humor and depth of the Native American writer Sherman Alexie; as well as John Fante and Dagoberto Gilb. Believe it or not, Anton Chekhov also sparked something within me and posed certain challenges for me to think about. All these writers are great, and they have all taught me something. At the same time, I was always trying to figure out my own style, my own way of telling the stories, breaking a little bit of my own ground.

F.L.A.: Let me take us back to the time when you won the Irvine award for the short story "Sometimes You Dance With a Watermelon," but decided to write poetry instead.

L.R.: Around the same time that short story got published, I began to write my first "real" poems; before, when I wrote poetry, I really didn't know what I was doing. This all changed during this period. I took some classes on poetry writing and joined the L.A. Latino Writers Association. I then became very active as a Chicano writer, running the Barrio Writers' Workshop in East L.A.

Although I had written short fiction like "Sometimes You Dance With a Watermelon," it was during this period that I realized that what I had to say could be said more powerfully in poetry. It's like I had to work through and then let go of a lot of personal issues and demons — something that I could do only through poetry. I wasn't ready to open up to the imagination in the way that fiction requires.

After years and years of writing poetry, I finally worked through a lot of those issues and came to terms with my demons. That's why, over the last couple of years, I've started to really hit it off with narrative fiction.

F.L.A.: You published your first collection, *Poems across the Pavement,* in 1989 with Tia Chucha Press?

L.R.: I actually started that press just to publish my book. (Eventually, of course, I ended up publishing a lot of people over the years.) I left East L.A. in '85 and was living in Chicago, working at newspapers and for the radio, when I discovered this poetry scene that was popping up in Chicago: the poetry slams. There was poetry going on every night in venues throughout the city. It was a perfect time for me. By '88 I was really getting out there and known; at first I was kind of embarrassed and afraid because I didn't think they'd pay attention to a Chicano from East L.A. By '89 I had enough poems that I thought I could publish a book. *Poems across the Pavement* ended up having a huge impact in the community. People loved the book. All the poets came to me who wanted to get published. Tia Chucha Press grew as I got more and more involved with the Chicago poetry scene.

F.L.A.: Why create your own publishing venue?

L.R.: I had a hard time getting my poetry published. I didn't quite know why. I went to workshops in Chicago. I went to readings. I read a lot of literary magazines. And I was doing my own poetry, and I even had poets I would exchange with. But I just couldn't seem to get it published. Then the opportunity came for me. I was working at the time for the Archdiocese of Chicago as their typesetter in their publishing department. I ended up typesetting *Poems across the Pavement* with their equipment. When everybody saw the book, they couldn't believe that some poet with no money, with no big publishing house, could make such a high-quality product. This inspired me to start a press to publish other poets who were having a hard time.

F.L.A.: The poems in *Poems across the Pavement* deal with racism and alienation as a young Chicano?

L.R.: I had over a hundred different poems that I could have used: some are coming of age poems; others are poems about drinking too much; some poems are about my first marriage, and others about my second marriage. They're poems of life. And I ended up using only thirteen in *Poems across the Pavement,* each one dealing with different aspects of racism and alienation.

Eventually, after I published the second book of poetry, without knowing it, I was already leaning towards the writing of *Always Running;* some of the poems in *Poems across the Pavement* about my life eventually would be part of the memoir in one form or another. So the poems were the first expressions of whatever it was I was going through, and living, and people I knew. I just wanted to voice that experience—that experience of the urban Chicano working class that wasn't present in mainstream literature.

F.L.A.: Why poetry?

L.R.: Well, for one thing, it's all free verse. Not that I didn't want to write formal verse; I was just absolutely captivated by free verse. The free verse forms would allow me to do the things I wanted to do. But free verse doesn't mean you're free to do whatever you want. You have to follow rules that govern cadence and rhythm, alliteration, metaphor, and assonance. Unlike the lyrical form, that's tighter, free verse allows me longer, looser lines that I can break up based on what I think the rhythm should be. With lyrical poetry, you're stuck with the meter. Of course, free verse is very big in the United States, dating all the way back to Walt Whitman. So it has a legacy and plays an important role in the American poetry tradition.

F.L.A.: In your second collection, *Concrete River,* you include the poems "Always Running" and "The Black Mexican."

L.R.: *Concrete River* was really an expanded version of *Poems across the Pavement,* taking the reader into different areas, like the relationships of love seen in the two poems "The Black Mexican" and "Always Running." One is about a teenager who goes to Tijuana and falls in love with a prostitute, but who wakes up, so to speak, to see that the world isn't quite that romantic a place. "Always Running" is a poem about my first wife. It's really a poem where I exorcised a lot of my own rage. It came out of a moment in my life when I was actually going to try to shoot my first wife.

You know, I'd come from a gang life, and what had happened is, I was prepared to get married because in many ways that was my salvation: get married and have a kid. But life didn't turn out that way. I worked in a steel mill, and I drank too much. It was a very horrible time. And about two and a half years into the relationship, she ran off with my best friend. I was going to kill her then. But I eventually took that kind of craziness and decided to just run. And it was a very good thing, because all that energy and all that pain went into running. And that's why it's "Always

Running," because in many ways running was something that I would always do in the neighborhood anyway. You run away from the cops. You run away from other gangs. You're running from this and that. I think that's really a metaphor for what that whole life was. (Later, I also titled my memoir *Always Running*.)

F.L.A.: In your third collection of poetry, *Trochemoche,* you present the concept of "soul death."

L.R.: *Trochemoche* is a much more mature work than my earlier collections. I reworked many of the poems I'd written and wrote new, more condensed poems to explore my life, the people I knew, the incidents that were important, but from a slightly different angle. *Trochemoche* also has the longest poem I've ever written—seven pages—as well as the shortest poems I've ever written. I also include some lyrical poems.

The soul death concept speaks to how people can be estranged from their own spirit. This was important to me because I saw it so much in my neighborhood. I saw it in my dad. I saw it in the Mexican East L.A. communities as well as in the African American, Puerto Rican, and poor white communities. Soul death happens to the poor and disenfranchised. It destroys your physical, intellectual, and spiritual ability to respond actively to your environment. You end up just walking around this earth without seeing and feeling, as if you're dead. You lose that soul presence—like my dad, who walked the earth and didn't have anything to contribute or give. It happens when your dreams are destroyed. I didn't want to end up that way. I didn't want to end up soul-dead too, so I wrote the poems that make up this collection.

F.L.A.: *Trochemoche* came out in 1998, the same year that you published your first children's book, *América Is Her Name,* which was soon followed by another, *It Doesn't Have To Be This Way.* Can you talk a little about the shift from poetry to writing children's books?

L.R.: Writing children's books was a little harder for me because they have their own particular dynamics. I had to read a lot of children's books as well as read about the writing of children's narrative. *América Is Her Name* and *It Doesn't Have To Be This Way* went through several drafts before I finally got something that I liked.

The real beauty of these books is the artwork. Artists like Carlos Vázquez and Daniel Galvez would take my words and then illustrate them so beautifully. This collaboration with these artists on these first two projects—Carlos from Oaxaca, Mexico, on the first, and Daniel on the second book—was a spectacular experience. *América Is Her Name* is about a young girl from Oaxaca who ends up lost and confused in a *barrio* in Chicago. After being put down at school for being undocumented, she loses her voice, and with it her gift of poetry. The story is really about how she rediscovers that voice. *It Doesn't Have To Be This Way* wasn't published with Curbstone; it was a challenge that Children's Book Press presented me: to write a children's book for Chicano kids thinking of joining gangs. So I thought I would try my hand at telling the story without putting the kids down and by talking up community activism: the role of mentoring to help kids find something that they can do with their own hands, their own hearts, their own art, that can contribute something valid and invigorating and give them a sense of purpose in life.

It Doesn't Have To Be This Way ultimately says: sometimes we get trapped in what we think is the world we have to enter. Some of it might be gangs. Some of it might be drugs. Some of it might be just kind of bad relations between men and women. But all the time, if you use your imagination and if you open up all the doors that you can open, you realize that *it doesn't have to be this way.* You always can go a different way, with another kind of vision.

F.L.A.: In your book of essays, *Hearts and Hands,* you talk about the power of art and creative writing as opening up those doors that offer positive ways of engaging with life.

L.R.: I think that's right. Writing, literature, and art can give youth a sense of purpose. We definitely need to have better social programs to get kids off the streets and out of gangs: role modeling and introducing into the community extracurricular activities, like sports programs and so on. But there have to be other ways to clear space for kids to become actively involved in their communities. And that's what *Hearts and Hands* is about. It asks how we can bring together the teachers, the parents, the scholars, the business people, the poor working guy on the corner, and reimagine and reestablish our community to be a place that will foster positive growth in the new generation. It doesn't require millions of dollars. It requires a shift in your thinking, a shift in your imagination as a community. We can't get rid of gangs outright, so we need to remove those social injustices in our communities that give them a basis for existing.

F.L.A.: Writing seemed to save you from *la vida loca*.

L.R.: *Hearts and Hands* is based on my own experience. When you're traumatized, hurt, lost, trapped, you can either turn to drugs or gangs, or turn to something outside of all this, like religion. For me, it was writing that became my passion—my lifeline. I was going to either become a drug-addicted kid or find meaning in art. Poetry allowed me to see past the hurt and violence and see the real inner, innate beauty that everybody carries. I was going to die. I was going to hurt people. I was really at the bottom. Poetry was what pulled me out of it.

F.L.A.: In 1972, you won the Quinto Sol literary prize for "Barrio Expressions," a series of poetic vignettes. You were eighteen years old. Did winning this award help you realize that writing could be your lifeline?

L.R.: Winning the Quinto Sol was extremely important for me because up to that point I had not won anything related to my art. I was in gangs, where fights were the only thing you lost or won. But the gang was also losing its luster for me. Too many people were dying. Too many things were happening that were destroying that original impulse I had when I joined the gang; that sense of belonging was gone. I felt as if I had become a predator, just hurting people and myself. So winning the award showed me that I could have an outlet like writing that was viable and recognized by other people. I no longer felt like I had to hurt people to be recognized.

F.L.A.: Your big break came in 1993, when you published *Always Running*?

L.R.: *Always Running* was the story I always wanted to write, but I never knew whether I should because I wasn't sure if I wanted to reveal those real sensitive parts of my life. At first, I wasn't quite sure how to write it. I thought to write it as a novel, completely fictionalizing my life. But the narrative kept going back to the autobiographical mode, so I let the novel version go—and the project altogether. That is, until my son came to live with me when I was in Chicago. He was very troubled, so his mother thought it best if I raised him away from L.A. By the time he was 15, we were living in Humboldt Park in Chicago, which has a big Mexican and Puerto Rican gang community; this was a real draw for my son. I didn't want him to go down the same path I had, so I did a lot of soul searching to try to figure out how best to throw him a lifeline. One of the things

I had was my writing, so I returned to the writing of my memoir so I could show him a way out.

I spent eight months putting together all the little bits of writing I had over twenty-some years—clippings, articles—writing down stuff I remembered, reimagining conversations. I didn't have a tape recorder with me when I had all these experiences, so while there is fact, there is also reinvention. The process was very painful because there were events and people I didn't want to remember. I finally finished the book; it ended up being a healing process for me that I had never imagined was possible. And after Curbstone published it, the healing process continued as the book entered into the community. I think it also had an impact on my son's life. It's hard to say because he's been sitting in prison, but I think his life would've turned out much worse if I hadn't written *Always Running*. I suppose, though, he had to go through his own experiences and make his own way here. And, unfortunately, that landed him in prison for many, many years.

I started to speak all over the country, and I did Oprah Winfrey, *Good Morning America,* CNN. I was on NPR. I mean I did a lot of TV, radio, and newspapers. And so the word got out to a lot of people. And over the years the young people and teachers have kept the book alive; for some kids, it's the only book that they can relate to. Of course, in this sense, I hope that one day it will become obsolete because we'll have cured those social ills that lead to gang life. For now, it's still very raw and shows kids like my son a different way of living; it offers an alternative—a lifeline.

F.L.A.: Why did you move *Always Running* from Curbstone to Simon and Schuster?

L.R.: Curbstone went all out with their marketing of the book, probably one of the biggest campaigns done by a small press. And I got all sorts of media attention. By the time Simon and Schuster got it, there was a bidding war. Eight big-time publishers were bidding for the paperback rights to the book. I was amazed because I didn't think people would be that interested in a book that talked about kids in the L.A. *barrio.* But it was good, because it meant that the complexity of these kids' lives was becoming visible in the mainstream. Simon and Schuster put out the best deal in terms of marketing and money, so they ended up publishing it under their imprint, Touchstone Books. They did a good job.

At first, I didn't like the colorful cover, but it's since grown on me. Now people know the book just by the cover, so it worked out. There were censorship battles after Touchstone reprinted the book. It was banned in school districts in Illinois, Michigan, Texas, and California. San Jose was the biggest battle because here you have a community that could really use the book—this wasn't a conservative community like Rockford, Illinois—to get kids out of gangs. A few adults banned it because they thought it would encourage kids to join gangs; some even called it "a manual for murdering kids." But most young people that were reading the book understood that it was critical of gang life. Ironically, it became a bestseller in places like Rockford, Illinois, and in San Jose. The more people tried to ban it, the more interest it generated.

F.L.A.: Why Tia Chucha Press when there are already several small presses that publish Chicano/Latino work, like Cinco Puntos?

L.R.: Cinco Puntos is a press that publishes U.S.–Mexico border writers, and they do fiction as well. Hopefully, Tia Chucha can also expand to include fiction. I'd like to see it happen. But we've expanded our list to include not just Chicanos and African and Jamaican Americans, but also Japanese Americans, Filipino Americans, Native Americans, and Irish Americans. We just decided that we would publish strong, performance-oriented poetry that's not academic necessarily or probably won't find a place in a lot of the poetry places. Either we do it, or somebody else does it. Anyway, we still want to carry that kind of quality, good work from people who don't normally get known or paid attention to. Tia Chucha's vision is to make a place for strong, mature poets; it's also about mentoring and teaching young writers. There are a lot of good Chicano writers out there, and I try to work with these writers to develop their work so it's publishable. We want to make sure that their work gets published.

Tia Chucha's café and art gallery provides a venue for mentoring writers and artists—and also gives kids in the community a place to come and do homework after school. It's also a venue for poetry reading, and a place to workshop art and theatre; we also have a film and open mike night. So there's more than just the press; there's this space where we can bring people together, mentor young kids, and have all the arts represented.

F.L.A.: There's more to building a strong Chicano arts community than just publishing books?

L.R.: Oh, I think so. We've got to create our books. We've got to create our stories. We've got to create our songs. We've got to create our films. We've got to do this to make sure that we're not doing what other people think we should be doing; we're doing the work we should be doing and know we need to do.

It is creating our own arts communities that will help us to expand the imagination of who we are, our relationships, the world we live in. My effort with Tia Chucha press, the art gallery/poetry reading café, and my books is to imagine and not lose sight of the dreams that we should have.

Like I said, a lot of what I see in the world today is this soul death. People just give up on their dreams. They give up on their lives. They give up on their communities. When I returned to L.A. from Chicago in June of 2000, it was kind of bittersweet because, on the one hand, there's family, great energy, great art; on the other, there's a lot of sadness: people addicted, alcoholics on the corner, homeless people. You see people beating up their kids. It's all these terrible things happening, and all these people not realizing their potential, that we have to break through and change. The vitality of art in the community is one of the best ways to help them shake off the soul death once and for all.

Writings by the Author
Poetry

Poems across the Pavement. Chicago, IL: Tia Chucha Press, 1989.
The Concrete River. Willimantic, CT: Curbstone Press, 1991.
Trochemoche: New Poems. Willimantic, CT: Curbstone Press, 1998.
My Nature Is Hunger: New and Selected Poems, 1989-2004. Willimantic, CT: Curbstone Press, 2005.

Children's Literature

América Is Her Name. Illustrated by Carlos Vázquez. Willimantic, CT: Curbstone Press, 1998.
It Doesn't Have to Be This Way: A Barrio Story/No tiene que ser así: Una historia del barrio. Illustrated by Daniel Galvez. San Francisco: Children's Book Press, 1999.

Other

Always Running/La Vida Loca: Gang Days in L.A. Willimantic, CT: Curbstone Press, 1993; reprint, New York: Simon and Schuster, 1998.

Hearts and Hands: Creating Community in Violent Times. New York: Seven Stories Press, 2001.

The Republic of East L.A.: Stories. New York: Rayo/HarperCollins, 2002.

Music of the Mill: A Novel. New York: Rayo/HarperCollins: 2005.

Suggested Readings
Critical Studies

Brown, Monica. "East Side Story: Chicano/a Urban Myth and History." *Gang Nation: Delinquent Citizens in Puerto Rican, Chicano, and Chicana Narratives.* Minneapolis: University of Minnesota Press, 2002: 36–80.

Castillo, Dina G. "Luis Rodríguez." In *Dictionary of Literary Biography.* Vol. 209, *Chicano Writers,* pp. 243–250. Detroit: Thomson Gale, 1999.

Herrera-Sobek, María. "Geography of Despair: The Mean Streets of L.A. of Luis Rodríguez's *Always Running.*" *Latino Studies Journal* 8, no. 2 (1997): 56–68.

Perez, Vincent. "'Running' and Resistance: Nihilism and Cultural Memory in Chicano Urban Narratives." *MELUS* 25, no. 2 (2000): 133–146.

Rodríguez, Audrey. "Contemporary Chicano Poetry." *Bilingual Review,* September–December 1996, pp. 203–207.

Sullivan, Patrick. "Class War: Luis J. Rodríguez Casts a Skeptical Eye on Attempts to Ban His Autobiography." *Sonoma County Independent,* February 4–10, 1999, pp. 21–22.

Yamashita, Brianna. "Latino Author Plants Cultural Roots: Luis Rodríguez Opens Tia Chucha's Cafe Cultural in California." *School Library Journal* 48, no. 4 (2002): 7.

Reviews

Erfurth, Beth. Rev. of *América Is Her Name. Skipping Stones,* May–August 1999, p. 6.

Gallegos, Aaron McCarroll. "A Few of My Favorite Things." Rev. of *The Republic of East L.A. Sojourners* 31, no. 5 (2002): 49.

Nash, Susan Smith. Rev. of *Trochemoche. World Literature Today,* Winter 1999, p. 156.

Olszewski, Lawrence. Rev. of *Trochemoche. Library Journal,* June 15, 1998, p. 82.

Rev. of *Hearts and Hands. Publishers Weekly* 248, no. 45 (November 5, 2001): 58.

Rochman, Hazel. Rev. of *It Doesn't Have To Be This Way*. *Booklist*, August 1999, p. 2059.

Soto, Gary. "The Body Count in the Barrio." *New York Times Book Review*, February 14, 1993, p. 26.

Stavans, Ilan. Rev. of *Always Running*. *Nation* 256, no. 14 (April 12, 1993): 494–498.

Interviews

Cohen, Aaron. "An Interview with Luis J. Rodríguez." *Poets & Writers*, January–February 1995, pp. 50–55.

Dick, Bruce Allen. "Luis J. Rodríguez." In *A Poet's Truth: Conversations with Latino/Latina Poets*, pp. 184–200. Tucson: University of Arizona Press, 2003.

Benjamin Alire Sáenz

Benjamin (Ben) Sáenz was born on August 16, 1954, in a farming community just outside Las Cruces, New Mexico. Sáenz grew up in a family of humble means; to make ends meet and feed their seven children, his mother worked as a cook and his father as a cement finisher. Sáenz grew up without books to read at home, but he was always drawn to the power of words—the words of his parents' stories and later those words he found bound within books in the school library. From an early age, Sáenz instinctively felt that words, either written or spoken, in Spanish or in English, had the power to hold people together and create community. While literature played a central role in his elementary and high school experience, upon graduation Sáenz sought a different avenue to understanding the world: religion. After working for some time as a roofer, an onion picker, and a janitor, Sáenz enrolled in seminary school at the University of Louvain in Belgium. He graduated with a master's degree in theology in 1980 and then joined the Catholic priesthood, where he was to spend the next seven years of his life. During this period, however, his passion for creative writing became more and more of an ache. So in 1988 he left the priesthood and enrolled in the creative writing program at University of Texas at El Paso. While at UTEP, Sáenz was taken under the wing of the late Chicano novelist and professor from Stanford, Arturo Islas. Greatly encouraged by Islas and with a greater confidence in his craft as a storyteller, Sáenz went on to pursue an M.F.A. at the University of Iowa. He went on to a stint at Stanford as a Stegner Fellow, during which time he put together and published his first collection of poetry, *Calendar of Dust* (1991). Sáenz has since written and published critically acclaimed collections of poetry, novels, short stories, and children's books, which gravitate around issues of displacement, class conflict, and the contradictions of family life.

Frederick Luis Aldama: You've been many things, including a priest. Why also a writer?

Ben Sáenz: I've always had this idea of myself as a writer. I've always enjoyed writing nonfiction. It was the only thing that interested me at school; it made me feel like I was a disciplined student. It wasn't until I entered the seminary that I started writing poetry. I wrote and read a lot of poetry (really bad, frankly) during this period, especially Eliot, Pound, and Thomas Merton; he was very important to me. Later, when I was living in Belgium, I discovered Latin American and Spanish poets like Neruda and Lorca.

After I left the priesthood and went back to school, I was either going to get into painting—I always laugh when I tell this story because it's so silly, in some ways—but I either wanted to be a painter or a writer. So I decided to be a writer because I didn't want to be a starving artist.

F.L.A.: That's interesting that you were in Europe when you discovered the Latin Americans.

B.S.: In seminary I was exposed to many theologians and philosophers, even Karl Marx, but not to Latin American writers. In Europe I met people from Latin America who opened this door up for me. At that point in my life, I'd only read one Chicano author, Rudolfo Anaya. I really liked *Bless me, Última,* but didn't love it.

So, when I entered the University of Texas, El Paso, I started taking formal writing classes and formal literature classes. This is when I worked with Arturo Islas; he was a visiting professor at UTEP for a year, and he took me under his wing. He's the one who told me that I should apply for a Stegner [fellowship]. At first, I didn't apply. I didn't think it was for me; I thought I wasn't prepared for it. Eventually, I went to Iowa for a Ph.D., and Islas would badger me about the Stegner. During this period I'd written a novella for my master's thesis, "City of the Conquered" (later published as *Carry Me like Water*), so I finally did apply in fiction and in poetry.

One cold spring Iowa day in 1987, I got a call from Stanford University to inform me that I'd gotten a Stegner.

F.L.A.: Is this when you tried your hand at seriously writing poetry?

B.S.: I was a Stegner fellow for two years and then started the Ph.D. program. I never did finish the degree, but in the four years that I was there, I wrote my first book of poems, *Calendar of Dust.* Denise Levertov is responsible for getting that book published with the Seattle-based Broken Moon Press. I was really lucky and blessed because that book went on to win an American Book Award.

I'm very sentimental about *Calendar of Dust,* not because I necessarily think it's my best book of poems, but because it was my first publication and because Denise took such an interest in it. I think of all those people who helped me publish that book, who are all dead now: Denise Levertov, Arturo Islas, and Antonio Burciaga. While at Stanford, there was a group of us Latino writers that would get together at Burciaga's house; many of the poems that ended up in *Calendar of Dust* came out of this experience.

I also began writing short stories during this period. I would reward myself after finishing my more scholarly work by working on a story. Those stories eventually made up my second book, *Flowers for the Broken* (also with Broken Moon Press), which was published during the time that I was still a Ph.D. student at Stanford.

F.L.A.: You eventually returned to El Paso?

B.S.: After Stanford, there was a position advertised at UTEP. My experiences in the Midwest weren't particularly good, and I didn't just want to end up at any college town. I really wanted to come and live back in El Paso, so I applied. I thought it might be one of my last opportunities to go back and live in the Southwest. Against the advice of some of my mentors at Stanford, I took the job; they probably didn't think it had enough status, but I wasn't interested in that particular kind of discourse. After my experiences at UTEP, I now know that where you teach will not make or break your career.

F.L.A.: It's one thing to want to be a writer and another to be able to support yourself as a writer, either as a teacher of writing or simply in book sales. Did your early success with publishing your work help the transition to the latter?

B.S.: When I look back, I think that I've really been very lucky. My agent sold my first novel, *Carry Me Like Water,* to Hyperion within a month after I finished it. They then sold the paperback rights to HarperCollins, who bought my second novel.

F.L.A.: You've had experiences with big and small presses, like Cinco Puntos.

B.S.: I much prefer working with small presses. It doesn't have the same kind of cachet as the New York trade press, but at least people know what they're doing at the small press. Lots of the New York editors seem to have ADD. They put it out there for a millisecond, like a saturation bombing, and then they move on. With Cinco Puntos, when they published my poetry books, like *Dark and Perfect Angels* and *Elegies in Blue,* they have sold well but over a long stretch of time; they keep printing and pushing them. They remain important because of the press's commitment. My children's book with Cinco Puntos Press is being read within the bilingual Mexican American community and used as an educational tool. It has been out for five years and is in its sixth printing.

When a small press like Cinco Puntos agrees to take on a book, they're committed to keeping it alive and to help it become part of our consciousness. That's not true in New York. Unless you sell at least 100,000 copies, you're history. When you work with a New York house, there are other risks. My editor left Hyperion before I began my book tour, so I was kinda left out there alone. I also think they don't "get" Latinos in New York.

This isn't to say that publishing generally is problem-free. My first agent (a former editor for Northpoint Press) said that publishing and selling a book was like spinning the dreidel. Much can go wrong in the publishing world.

F.L.A.: Clearly, the New York trade presses will ensure that your book gets to a larger audience. Are there other ways to get your work out there?

B.S.: I have many different kinds of publics—I have poetry readers, people who read Chicano literature, people who read novels, schoolteachers, kids—but I believe you have to earn your audience. I believe that if you're going to be a writer in today's cultural marketplace, then you have put yourself out there. I think one of the reasons that I have a readership as widespread as I do is that I make the effort to get out there.

Sometimes we so privilege our identities as writers that we believe that we are entitled to an audience simply because we wrote something. Even if it's good, why should this entitle you to an audience?

And developing an audience comes in many shapes. As a citizen and politicized Mexican American, I reach out to the community: my Chicano community, my border community, my American community. I have a deep relationship with these communities, and this relationship is a two-way street. It's not enough to say, "I'm a writer, so buy my book"; you have to give to the community in other ways. I think that part of writing means that I have to nurture an audience and earn an audience, not only through the quality of my work, but through the quality of my entire relationship with my audience.

F.L.A.: Does nurturing an audience go hand in hand with nurturing a sense of a Chicano/a writing community?

B.S.: Not everybody gets along, but for the most part I think I have good relationships with my peers. I really respect and honor and have a great deal of affection for Luis Rodríguez, Luis Urrea, Denise Chávez, Demetria Martínez, and Norma Cantú; I teach the work of Jimmy Santiago Baca. I've known Denise all my life. We both grew up in Las Cruces. I also respect the work that Ana Castillo has done. I really respect the work that Sandra Cisneros has done. I feel like in many ways we belong to each other, that we're peers in lots of ways. Many of us are early to mid-fifties babies.

F.L.A.: Has this sense of a Chicano writing community of sorts helped open doors for others?

B.S.: I think it has helped open some doors; there are some wonderful Latinos coming through our program at UTEP, like Manny Velez, who's publishing with Calaca Press out of San Diego. There's another young Latina, Olga Garcia, who's a great performance poet living in L.A. While we're here for the younger generation, I still don't think we mentor enough.

F.L.A.: You've written poetry, short stories, and some hefty novels, like *Carry Me Like Water*. You use a variety of different techniques and styles in all of them.

B.S.: With *Carry Me Like Water*, I wanted to write this novel that would be a tribute to my two favorite genres: the Latin American Boom novel and the Victorian novel. If you look at *Carry Me Like Water* from that perspective, you'll see that I'm paying tribute to and making a knot of both, so it necessarily had to be a big book. And, I wanted to write a book that was about borders: national, gender, class, and the border of the body.

It took me about seven years to write *Carry Me Like Water* because I was learning how to write a novel as I was writing. You learn how to write a novel by writing one. And it requires a great deal of commitment. The novel I just finished has taken me a little over three years.

Writing poetry is different. I love writing poetry. I will always consider myself a poet. I'm also finishing up a new book of poems called *Dreaming the End of War*. It's one long poem with different sections—different dreams, if you will. I could never write a novel that explored the border, and male identity, and violence, and our current situation in the world, and nationalism, in the same way that I could in writing this long poem.

Writing children's books also requires you to take on a different voice. No matter what you write, you somehow have to be a ventriloquist. It can't simply just be about you and your voice. It's about all of those voices and languages and grammars that you've been given by the people and the communities around you. They give us language, words, jokes, ideologies, as well as rage and humor. This is also how you access appropriate forms. Sometimes it's the form of the essay, like one I'm writing, "Just Another Mexican," that's about the shooting of Juan Pedrosa here in El Paso by the border patrol. I don't want to write a novel about that. I don't want to write a poem about that. I want to write an essay about what happened here; that seems like the appropriate forum to do that. Writing essays also requires taking on a different voice and using writing strategies that differ from that of the novel, poem, or children's book.

The great privilege of being a writer is to pick a genre that truly, truly best represents that which you feel so strongly needs to be represented.

F.L.A.: You mix genres as well?

B.S.: We are ideological about our aesthetics. So I ask, what is poetry? Well, poetry is many different things. Some people dismiss a prose poem. They dismiss it just out of hand: "That's not a poem." That's an aesthetic ideology. And I reject those kinds of notions: that this is better because it uses postmodern techniques; this is better because it uses formal techniques. So you have those kinds of debates that happen between what they call the New Formalists. Just because one uses postmodernist techniques in one's poetry doesn't de facto make you a good poet.

If you look at *Elegies in Blue,* it has prose poems, it has free verse, and it has blank verse. I thought it was interesting to write a blank verse poem honoring Che Guevara and Castro; I even made the Spanish fit into iambic pentameter. It's interesting and humorous at the same time. You take a traditional English metrics, and then you do something contemporary with it that's transgressive—not in a big way, but in a small way. There's also a lot of blank verse in that book, which nobody's picked up on. I like to stretch myself. Just because I write in blank verse and can do it doesn't make me not Chicano. It also doesn't make me conservative.

I do think that it's important for writers to have a range. You know, if you don't stretch yourself, then what's going to happen to you is that you're going to start parodying yourself. Why does any writer want to parody himself? It's not something I'm interested in. If I don't know how to do something, I should move on and learn how to do something else. We keep our art alive with ideas and by constantly challenging ourselves as craftspeople.

Having good ideas alone doesn't make you a good writer. Nor do you create a poem by breaking up a line. There's more to it than that. And you have to earn the right to call yourself a poet. Writing is a discipline. It's an art. It's a craft. And you have to keep at it.

F.L.A.: You mention at one point in your writing that the city of El Paso is your home.

B.S.: If you use the word in all its ancient meanings, *polis* (city) meant the people. It meant civilization. And for me El Paso means civilization. It is the place that holds me and keeps me. It's where the border isn't a metaphor, but an actual material place, where real people live, breathe, work, and die. This is the place where I am most alive.

F.L.A.: Memory is also important, and I think especially, of course, of *The House of Forgetting:* the title and the dislocation and violence of the body in the story.

B.S.: Memory is such an important part of what really makes us. We live partially in our memories. We're always housing our memories. Memories aren't an escape from the present; they are part of the present. That's why people are scarred, because they just can't get over some things. The scar is so deep that yesterday is today. And to me that's a very real thing. I know it to be true, and I think it's a physical thing because I experience memory in my body. I sometimes feel a physical pain of my father's death in my body. I sometimes feel a physical pain over my niece that was killed 18 years ago. Everything we feel is a bodily thing. It's not transcendent. I'm not a dualist. My mind is in my body. If I didn't have a body, I wouldn't have a mind. So I see it as a physical thing. I'm a big believer in the body.

F.L.A.: In *The House of Forgiving,* Gloria's struggle is also tied to her being cut off from her roots.

B.S.: Gloria can only experience her culture as memory and as loss. She's changed forever because of her forced dislocation. There is really no getting it back. It's like if you didn't grow up speaking Spanish, you didn't grow up speaking Spanish. Her dislocation is an act of colonization. Thomas has changed her history forever. In the end she can burn the dress he gave her, and this is significant. Now the question is, who is she now? Maybe for the first time in her life she has a choice. But that choice that she makes is built on a particular kind of context and a foundation, which Thomas Blacker built. She is in many ways a symbol for me of the Chicano people in America.

F.L.A.: You mentioned earlier that you've been writing a novel for three-plus years?

B.S.: This new novel, titled *In Perfect Light,* is about a boy who loses his parents, but his older brother decides to keep the family together. This act of trying to keep a family together, however, destroys them all because of what befalls them once they move to Juárez. I think it's my bleakest novel, yet it's also hopeful.

There's also the book of poems *Dreaming the End of War,* which brings together my politics with my aesthetics. I think to write a good political poem is a very difficult thing indeed. And I take that challenge very seriously. And I've written a young adult novel for Cinco Puntos. It began as an exercise in writing a short story in the first person, something I hadn't done in my fiction. And as it evolved into a young adult novel, it was a challenge for me to keep its aesthetic and plot unencumbered and uncomplicated. It's got its own kind of sophistication, though.

Writings by the Author
Poetry

Calendar of Dust. Seattle: Broken Moon, 1991.
Dark and Perfect Angels. El Paso: Cinco Puntos, 1995.
Que linda la brisa. With photographs by James Drake, poem by Jimmy Santiago Baca. Seattle: University of Washington Press, 2000.
Elegies in Blue. El Paso: Cinco Puntos, 2002.

Novels

Carry Me Like Water. New York: Hyperion, 1995.
The House of Forgetting. New York: HarperCollins, 1997.

Short Stories

Flowers for the Broken. Seattle: Broken Moon, 1992.

Children's Literature

A Gift from Papa Diego / Un regalo de papá Diego. Illustrated by Geronimo Garcia. El Paso: Cinco Puntos, 1998.
Grandma Fina and Her Wonderful Umbrellas / La Abuelita Fina y sus sombrillas maravillosas. Illustrated by Geronimo Garcia. Translated by Pilar Herrera. El Paso: Cinco Puntos, 1999.
Sammy and Juliana in Hollywood. El Paso: Cinco Puntos, 2004.

Other

"Born in the U.S.A." In *Unknown Texas,* edited by Jonathan Eisen and Harold Straughn, pp. 389–404. New York: Macmillan, 1988.
"I Want to Write an American Poem: On Being a Chicano Writer in America." In *Without Discovery: A Native Response to Columbus,* edited by Ray González, pp. 127–143. Seattle: Broken Moon, 1992.

Further Readings
Reviews

Abos, Elena. Rev. of *A Gift from Papa Diego. Horn Book,* July–August, 1998, p. 478.

Ayres, Annie. Rev. of *A Gift from Papa Diego. The Booklist* 94, no. 17 (May 1, 1998): 1522.

Basinger, Julianne. "A Latino Novelist's Bilingual Art." *The Chronicle of Higher Education* 45, no. 13 (November 20, 1998): A9.

Brainard, Dulcy. Rev. of *Dark and Perfect Angels. Publishers Weekly* 242, no. 31 (July 31, 1995): 74.

Cole, Melanie. Rev. of *The House of Forgetting. Hispanic* 10, no. 9 (September 1997): 92.

Martínez, Demetria. "What a Moment, When the 'Voiceless' Speak!" Rev. of *Carry Me Like Water. National Catholic Reporter* 32, no. 23 (April 5, 1996): 16.

Monaghan, Pat. Rev. of *Calendar of Dust. Booklist* 88, no. 1 (September 1, 1991): 24.

Olson, Ray. Rev. of *Elegies in Blue. Booklist* 98, no. 12 (February 15, 2002): 986.

Olszewski, Lawrence. Rev. of *Elegies in Blue. Library Journal,* July 2002, pp. 85–86.

Rev. of *Carry Me Like Water. The Virginia Quarterly* 72, no. 1 (Winter 1996): SS23.

Rev. of *Grandma Fina and Her Wonderful Umbrellas. New Advocate,* Spring 2001, p. 177.

Welton, Ann. Rev. of *Grandma Fina and Her Wonderful Umbrellas. School Library Journal* 45, no. 10 (October 1999): 125–127.

Interviews

Dick, Bruce Allen. "Benjamin Alire Sáenz." In *A Poet's Truth: Conversations with Latino / Latina Poets,* pp. 202-214. Tucson: University of Arizona Press, 2003.

Hoyt, Jill. Interview with Benjamin Alire Sáenz. *Weekend All Things Considered,* Sept. 3, 1995.

Matuk, Farid. "Border Talk." *The Texas Observer,* March 28, 2003.

Luis Alberto Urrea

uis Urrea was born in Tijuana, Mexico, on August 20, 1955, and spent his early childhood there. After his father's early death, he spent his remaining childhood and teenage years living with his mother in San Diego. Urrea learned to cope with the harsh realities of living in a San Diego barrio filled with violence and crime by spending hours after school reading, writing, and composing rock music. Such interests—along with a caring high school teacher—eventually helped pave the way to college. After receiving a B.A. in English from the University of California, San Diego (UCSD) in 1977, he began working for relief organizations along the Mexican border. While he had already won recognition in college for his creative writing, he continued to work primarily with the relief organizations for ten years. During this period he kept scrupulous record of daily events, and this material would later feed into his first publication. To have the time to write this book, however, Urrea knew that he had to change to working in a profession that allowed time for writing. He secured a job teaching expository writing at Harvard University (1982–1986), where he was able to hone his craft as a writer and discover what would become his signature style: a poetic, razor-edged voice that cut through the skeins that mask reality. In 1993 Anchor Books published *Across the Wire: Life and Hard Times on the Mexican Border* to great critical acclaim. Here Urrea combined fact and fiction to recount with brutal honesty the lives of border peoples living across the wire and their struggle to survive absolute poverty. He followed this with another docu-journalistic book, *By the Lake of Sleeping Children: The Secret Life of the*

Mexican Border, which was also well received. In 1998 Urrea published a third testimonial-style book, *Nobody's Son: Notes from an American Life.* However, docu-journalistic writing is but one of his many forms of storytelling. In award-winning poetry, in his novel *In Search of Snow* (1994), and in his various ethnocritical naturalist books, Urrea uses imagery, character, voice, and point of view to powerfully evoke and affirm the experiences of those at society's margins.

Frederick Luis Aldama: So when did the light go on, and you knew you wanted to be a writer?

Luis Urrea: Well, it all started when I was growing up in a storytelling family in a *barrio* in Tijuana already filled with amazing stories and surreal visuals. After, we moved from Tijuana to *Barrio* Logan Heights in San Diego. (I joke with Juan Felipe Herrera: he had the lowlands and I had the highlands because we were up in Logan Heights.) At that time, Logan Heights was a pretty violent area—it still is—so I spent a lot of time on my own, hiding out, reading, and imagining.

I was thirteen when I really realized I wanted to write. One of the magical things that happened to me was I discovered my mother's old typewriter in the garage, and I hauled it out and got all the dirt and dust out of it and found out it still worked. It seemed like such magic to me, that you could type stuff; it looked so neat and clean.

During this time I had also discovered poetry. At first I really did not like poetry. Then one of my teachers told me to read Stephen Crane's poems, so I got the *Collected Poems of Stephen Crane.* I went crazy, man. I had never read anything like it. I was really impressed that they were short, little, tiny poems with these astounding twists and turns in them. And, because I was a rock 'n' roll kid, I had also just bought Jim Morrison's first book of poems. I also discovered John Lennon, Leonard Cohen, and Bob Dylan books. I felt like I had discovered the secret of the universe. So I started typing this crazy stuff up when I was thirteen, and my mom would sew it together and make books out of it.

This phase of being famous in my kitchen ended because my mother had heard that you should oil typewriters and so she oiled it with cooking oil. It destroyed the mechanisms, and because we couldn't afford to buy another one, I stopped typing. Of course, I continued scribbling on papers and in notebooks and things. By the time I got to high school, I really got serious about writing. I became *the* writer for my high school.

F.L.A.: In high school, was there someone who mentored you?

L.U.: Yeah, the person that really launched me in the life of the arts was my drama teacher. She was just this amazing, sophisticated woman who expected us to be smart and literate.

When I came into high school, I had gone through this kind of Malcolm Lowry *Under the Volcano* experience with my father. My dad had felt that I wasn't sufficiently *macho* to make it in the world. So he took me on a trip into Mexico, and we went all the way down to the bottom of Sinaloa, right near the border of Nayarit. After spending the summer there and traveling all over Mexico, he left me behind to grow up. I had this insane, debauched experience, but got really ill and nearly died. When I came back to the States, after a trip to the hospital, I began my first week of high school. It felt absurd after what I had just lived. So I fell in with this drama teacher and some brilliant, drug-soaked hippie seniors. We read Ferlinghetti's *Coney Island of the Mind,* Richard Brautigan's *Trout Fishing in America,* and Ginsburg's *Howl.* I was a straight-edge guy, no drugs, but I loved the world they were in—all this literate stuff.

F.L.A.: Did you study writing more formally once you got to college?

L.U.: When I got to college, there were two important events that happened. First, a literature class had assigned the *Norton Anthology of Modern Poetry*—which I had never heard of; it cost eighteen or twenty dollars, the most money I'd ever spent on a book—and as soon as I opened it and saw that I had the history of twentieth-century poetry in my hands, it completely changed my life. Second, I found in a used/damaged book bin Diane Wakoski's book *Motorcycle Betrayal Poems.* And I had never really paid attention to women's writing. I bought that book for a quarter or something and went completely crazy for it. Lots of my male friends detested the book; they were offended and even somewhat frightened by it, but I understood the rage in it.

It was at college that I first was exposed to Latin American authors, and I began to explore different kinds of writing. I started studying the formal aspects of Borges, Cortázar, García Márquez, Vargas Llosa, Unamuno, and Gabriela Mistral. It's ironic, but it wasn't until I graduated from college and started working as a teaching assistant in Chicano studies in San

Diego that I started to read Chicano literature. I knew it was out there, but I had not paid any attention to it because, even though I've got a college education, I was in a lot of ways self-taught. Having come sort of out of the street environment, I just learned as I went along. This is when I discovered Rudolfo Anaya and Alurista—a poet that blew my mind because I had never imagined code switching in writing. I was just like, "Wow, what is this? This guy's crazy." And then, you know, not only did he start code switching between Spanish and English and then Chicano slang, Spanish, and English, but then he got so extreme that he would use illustrations instead of words sometimes. I thought, "This is the best thing I've ever seen in my life."

In '82, I got airlifted out of California to go teach at Harvard, which was a whole other phase of reading, writing, and thinking.

F.L.A.: The science fiction writer Ursula Le Guin proved an important figure for you?

L.U.: I always say she was my discoverer. I was a college senior, and she came to teach at San Diego; it was the first time I had met a person who lived by their words. Here was this woman who was living the life of words, which I wanted to live but couldn't dream of doing. She taught me that it wasn't enough to just write words; you had to find a way to present them and to be professional. She also taught me new ways of thinking about things. It was a blessing to have someone I respected so much—and who was so powerful, wise, and brilliant—take you under her wing. She introduced me to Toni Morrison, which was incredible, and also published a story of mine in one of her anthologies; it was my first national sale.

F.L.A.: Some of your early work has been reprinted?

L.U.: There's a poem from those Alurista days in *The Fever of Being* called "Prima." And then there's the piece Le Guin published, "Father Returns from the Mountain"; that's in *Ghost Sickness* and in *Six Kinds of Sky*. They're pretty good, so I decided to keep them alive.

F.L.A.: "Father Returns from the Mountain" is very experimental—sort of metafictional?

L.U.: It's meta-nonfiction, but I didn't know it at the time. It's been published as poetry and as fiction. Oddly enough, after my father was killed in my senior year in college in a car wreck in Mexico, I had this horrible experience of having to buy his corpse off the Mexican police, and sit with the body for hours and hours in this room, just the corpse and me. When I got back from Mexico and went back to college, I found it extremely difficult to focus. I kept trying to write about it. A writing teacher of mine before Le Guin called me into his office and said, "You're hysterical and out of control. And you're trying to hurt me because you're upset that your father was killed." And he said, "If you want me to care, you'd better get yourself under control, and write this with utter control." And I was really hurt and angry, but later I knew that that was probably the best piece of writing advice I'd ever gotten. I learned something really hard about writing at that moment: why should a reader care? Yeah, everybody has a dad, and that's a sad story. But why should a reader care unless it's told memorably? (I ended up writing the piece I turned in to be considered for Le Guin's class; she took me into the class, and that ended up in her anthology.) The form I found was fragmented; it was an attempt to try to break up the traditional narrative flow and make it look somewhat like a shattered mirror, reflecting different surfaces at once.

F.L.A.: To support yourself as a writer, you've taught and worked a number of different jobs?

L.U.: I worked for years after high school in the Tijuana garbage dump, at orphanages in Mexico, and so on. Working as a translator for this relief group, I saw every imaginable horror you can trot out. I had been used to living in poverty. After my dad died, we were left with nothing. I went from this horrible, depressing world of poverty in San Diego down to the dump and seeing poverty and violence, death, and blood and horror. After a couple of years, I couldn't take it anymore. So I wrote a letter to my writing teacher, thinking this guy might be able to get me a job as a custodian at Harvard. I just needed to get away, maybe for a year, and then I'd come back and keep working with the poor. This guy obviously knew that I was a writer. And he asked me to send him any published works I had and a bibliography of anything I'd had in any lit. journals up to that point. And you know, I tell the story all the time in readings, but I was so dumb that I thought that you had to be a published writer to be a janitor at Harvard. I got the job, which was a shocker.

F.L.A.: Tell me a little about your stint at Harvard.

L.U.: It was a completely transforming experience, absolutely mind-bogglingly transforming for me. I arrived in Boston—this alien world—to begin a life on my own away from everybody I knew. I was suddenly in the cheapo bookstore basements all day every day, and wandering around Harvard and getting all this culture, and meeting people like John Irving, and seeing people like Eudora Welty and Norman Mailer speak.

But I had made this pact with myself to write about Tijuana and the people I had worked with, so I put all of my poetry and fiction writing aside to try to get *Across the Wire* published. I sent it out in 1983, but nobody, nobody, nobody would publish it. I felt like after a point I was becoming obsessed and maniacal. At that time Chicano writers weren't really visible. I was told to change my name so I'd sound Anglo, and all kinds of awful stuff. But I just kept plugging away, and fortunately it finally got published ten years after I wrote it.

F.L.A.: Tell me about the writing of your first novel, *In Search of Snow*.

L.U.: *In Search of Snow* began as a short story. The way it became a novel was kind of interesting. Eddie Olmos and his film partner, Tom Bauer, were touring *The Ballad of Gregorio Cortez* around the country and stopped off in Boston. I called the production office because I had seen the movie and thought it'd be really cool for my Harvard students to see it as a study in narration. Tom Bauer ended up coming to the class to talk about making movies. He asked if he could read some of my writing, so I gave him the short story. And he took it with him, and then called me and told me he and Eddie really liked the story, and that I should write a script. I told him I didn't know how, and he said, "Well, turn it into a novel first, and then we'll talk again." I never spoke to them again, but that made me decide, well, I can do this. So I wrote it as a novel, probably in 1989 or something.

After *Across the Wire* was finally accepted for publication, Lorna Dee Cervantes pushed me to submit *Fever of Being* to a publisher. It was accepted. So I decided to send out a revised version of *In Search of Snow*, which was also accepted. There was a moment when I thought, "Wow, I'm gonna own the world."

F.L.A.: How do you see your work within the book marketplace, within and/or outside ethnic boxes, within Chicano letters?

L.U.: Market has never been an issue for me. My books have been fairly obscure. Now, all of a sudden I'm finding myself sitting on a couple of books that might actually be big marketing things. I don't know what to do about that. That's interesting to watch.

The outside-of-the-box issue is interesting to me because I've always felt sort of outside of things. I'm interested in several genres, and I've been lucky enough to publish in all of them. I realize in some ways that's a marketing catastrophe because people don't know if I'm a poet, an essayist, or a fiction writer: "Are you a Chicano writer or not?"

In the Chicano movement I felt kind of outside because of the way I was raised and the way I understood that Chicanos were Mexicanos born here in the United States. I was born in Mexico. So was I really a Mexican author? Well, my mom was an American. Was I an American author? What was I? I don't know what I was. I still don't really know. So I decided that I really didn't like labels or boxes of any kind. I wanted to write what I wanted to write. And so I sort of pursued it that way. I don't think we should be trapped.

I always think a niche is a really good thing to have at a certain time in your career. But if you don't turn that niche over, so it's a step that you can climb up, it'll turn into your coffin. I think a lot of us have climbed up and claimed our rights as human beings in this world.

F.L.A.: As a writer, isn't the idea to have as many people read your work as possible?

L.U.: Yeah. Rudy Anaya once told me something that really touched me: "The personal is political. If you can make a rich, white America read about your little grandmother and feel as though she were their grandmother, then you have committed a prime political act in humanizing us as people to each other." I always held that in my heart. In writing *Across the Wire,* I took on this task to humanize people that no one—not Mexicans, Chicanos, or gringos—cared about: the garbage pickers in the Tijuana dump. It was a pretty hard task, but when you realize that they're human beings with their own dreams and desires—and you don't have to romanticize them, you don't have to prettify them, just tell their human story—it'll move people. That was a great lesson to me.

F.L.A.: You work in many different genres, such as poetry, investigative journalism, short stories, and so on. Does each process differ?

L.U.: The nonfiction stuff, like *Across the Wire* and *By the Lake of Sleeping Children,* was working with material from the people that was brilliant beyond my conception. But I also realized that there was another story that I couldn't tell in nonfiction, even though it was based on real things, and that was the deeper sense of what life would be like picking trash. So I took several incidents and vignettes and wove them together into a false day, a 24-hour period, and turned it into a fictional novella.

The novel, *In Search of Snow,* was just totally invented, though someone once pointed out to me that that book really is about all the parts of me. You know, there's the sort of Anglo, blue-collar kid. There's the Mexican American, you know, detribalized kid, as Jimmy Santiago Baca might say. Then there's the young Apache man. And all three of them are trying to work out their relationship to each other and to the world. The last part of *In Search of Snow,* when they finally get to the Garcia family home, is then finally explained in nonfiction in *Nobody's Son,* because those really were my godparents, the Garcias, who really lived. So to me it's this really rich tapestry of different facets.

Elements in my work cross-pollinate. Certain facets of the same story come out in all three genres. So I think perhaps the experience for me is so deep sometimes that I can't get it all. And it wants to be expressed in its full, sort of 3-D essence. And I can't always get it in just one. So I try and get it from different angles. And you know, the stuff in *Six Kinds of Sky* is all over the place. Some of it's personal experience. Some of it's just made up out of whole cloth.

F.L.A.: In *Nobody's Son,* self-discovery happens not in isolation from the world, but as a process of existing within nature and as a process of encountering others.

L.U.: I think we do learn in our friction against others. You go out in the world and rub up against it. And you find out what you're made of.

I've been really moved by nature writers, believe it or not. And the sense I got after a while was that we have forgotten that we are nature also. We think we're separate from nature, but I'm just as much a piece of nature as an elk or a bear. I just happen to be a person. We have this fallacy that has divided us from nature. And I remember being told by a Chicano poet friend of mine, "You know, nature writing," he said, "did you ever notice nature writing is all white guys? They're all guys that have enough money to have a Jeep and spend half a year wandering around, looking at plants." He said, "I don't have time for that. I've gotta live." And I thought, wow, it is a literature of leisure in a way. But then I thought, but that is *your* nature. *My* nature? You know, I come out of bowling alleys, and I come out of scrubbing toilets and cooking donuts, and that's my nature. I want to see the Vato Loco Tour of the United States: some crazy low-rider tour of America. Now, that would be cool.

F.L.A.: There's a moment in your writing when you turn your shoulder to Ed Abbey?

L.U.: I came to him pure of heart, you know? I didn't know anything about him. I found a beat-up, used paperback of *The Monkey Wrench Gang* in a used bookstore, and I read it, and I thought, holy crap, this is great. This is wild stuff. And then I read *Desert Solitaire*, and it was like somebody had defined something about the world that I hadn't been able to think about clearly: my connection with the land. I realized suddenly that my response to the land itself was both religious and sweaty, dirty—sexual, too. His kind of fearless tilting at windmills really appealed to me. And then all of a sudden I realized that he reviled us and thought we were scum. He didn't like Mexicanos. There's a little line in my new book, in *The Devil's Highway*, where I make a little gibe at Abbey because he had his friends bury him in that same area where those Mexicanos died trying to cross the desert border. He's, himself, a kind of illegal occupant of that area. And he chose to be buried illegally among the illegal walkers he so despised.

F.L.A.: You mentioned language and body, and at one point you say, "I have a barbed wire dissecting my heart." Can you talk a little about language and the body?

L.U.: Having grown up on the border, literally on the border, going back and forth across the border always felt like home to me. I did not realize until we left the whole *barrio* complex and moved to a white, working-class suburb that people didn't like Mexicans and that they didn't like Tijuana; it was filthy, foul, and embarrassing. I had no idea—until the words came. "Wetback" and "greaser" stuck with me. I thought somehow, somewhere on me, there was some kind of greasy patch of nauseating wetness that everybody knew about but me. I couldn't find it. I was just a kid, and that really stuck with me.

Language started rearing its ugly head also when my father tried hard to keep me 100 percent Mexican by speaking to me in Spanish, and my mother tried to keep me 100 percent American in English. My father called me Luis. My mother called me Lewis. So I was truly brought up on the border, in that I was brought up twice, as a Mexicano—reading, speaking, and listening to Spanish—and as an American-born. But there were gaps in the language, like with my relatives, who spoke a kind of *barrio*-speak.

Certainly, having chosen language as my tool and weapon—my art— it just became more and more important to me. And I find now, when I'm writing, people ask me, you know, "Are you going for an intellectual effect, or how do you write? How does language work for you?" And I can't explain it because it's almost mystical. I used to tell people that I try to write to a physical sensation that I can't express very well, but it's a sensation that I have. I know when I'm on because I can feel it physically. I know when I'm off because I feel physically uncomfortable; I know it's not right because the sensation in my heart or my gut is off.

F.L.A.: You use different techniques in your poetry, including Japanese haiku?

L.U.: Basho, Issa, Buson—those guys, you know, but the Chinese too. In college I studied Wang Wei, Li Po, Tu Fu, and then later Han Shan, "Cold Mountain." I think there's an Asian sensibility in the way I view the world here.

F.L.A.: Why photographs in *Across the Wire* and *By the Lake of Sleeping Children*?

L.U.: I just thought it's such a remarkable world that I wanted people to be able to see it as well as read about it. And that photographer, Jack Booth, had a very intense relationship with the people there. I took him, intro- duced him to them. He became really close to them. So I felt like that was his project as well as mine.

F.L.A.: The hymn to *vatos* in the book of photographs, *Vatos*?

L.U.: I actually wrote that poem in response to my nephew being killed (burned) by rival *vatos* down in San Diego. I was at the funeral, where all his homeys and his brother (who was dying of AIDS) had gathered along with the older generation. I thought, who's going to write a hymn or a prayer for any of us? So, I wrote "Hymn to Vatos" as a prayer, not just to gangbanger *vatos* and *cholos,* but to every one of our men. We are so criticized and so assaulted and so attacked that for us to do it amongst ourselves seems like the ultimate insanity to me. We will not accept our own brothers: the gangbanger, the drug addict, the *cholo,* the prisoner.

We won't even accept our gay brothers. What's wrong with us? So in a lot of ways that poem is a cry for us to open our hearts to each other, to love each other.

The book has caused a lot of people to feel discomfort because they think it's a pro–bad boy book. But it's really not, if you pay attention to the pictures and to the text. But the picture of the *cholo* is so incendiary still in our culture that it blinds us to everything else. There are moments, for example, in that poem that I tried to use for instruction, too, because I talk about men not being afraid to talk to their women. In other words, I'm trying to subliminally suggest that it's time for us to drop the *macho* stuff and listen—you know, listen to all of us, the ones that are handsome and the ones who are ugly. Sure, the bad, tough-ass guys, but our grandfathers, too. How about our priests? How about the gay men that you insult? Let's listen to each other.

F.L.A.: You tried your hand at drama with Jorge Huerta. Will you take that road again?

L.U.: God! We'll see. I was originally a drama major at UCSD. I had my own theater group, and I used to write the shows. Before *Across the Wire* came out, that UCSD drama group got in touch with me. It was Huerta's group. It was directed by Jose Luis Valenzuela, who went on to make the movie *Luminarias.* It was a really interesting experience to watch these guys from the improv theater troupe at the Tijuana dump; they wanted to see it, so I took them there. One of the women there started to have a baby, so we threw her in the van and took off and left the troupe behind. They were abandoned in the dump for, easily, eight hours. And, when we went back to pick them up, they had been carrying stuff all over the *barrio* and digging for shit, and, you know, they were totally immersed. So we took them home, and then we started doing this stuff. The play that I wrote was really pretty lame, I've got to admit, but some of the stuff was really interesting.

Yeah, I would do it again. I like that kind of stuff.

F.L.A.: Maybe you can tell me a little bit about your latest book, *The Devil's Highway?*

L.U.: "Devil's Highway" is the path that leads along the Arizona border with Mexico. It's an ancient footpath that has been notoriously bloody for its entire history: hundreds and hundreds and hundreds of people have died along this path. And the walkers who have to come across the border looking for work because of the border patrol's shutdowns in San Diego and Yuma, the south of Tucson, El Paso, and so forth, are forced into more and more dangerous areas. And so now they have to cross at places like the Devil's Highway. In May of 2001, a group of twenty-six or twenty-eight (no one's sure how many) men walked across the Devil's Highway and were heading from Sonoyta to Ajo, Arizona. And somebody illuminated them in a mountain pass with a spotlight. Nobody knows who it was but they ran, and unfortunately they ran west. And as they were running, they lost much of their water, and when they reconvened, their *coyote* tried to walk them back up to the pass that would lead them to Ajo, but they had crossed a mountain range without knowing it, and they got lost. And they slowly died a horrible, horrible, horrible death. And he, as *coyotes* are wont to do these days, abandoned them—he claims, to save their lives; they say, to let them die. Who knows? He almost died himself. And it was the largest manhunt in border patrol history.

Fortunately for me, Little, Brown contacted me and asked me if I was interested in doing this as a Trojan horse kind of a book. I thought it was a brilliant idea—in other words, write a men-in-peril book, along the lines of *The Perfect Storm,* but use the book to educate America, who still is very ignorant about the border, about what the policies are and what the reality is of the border. And I thought, that's a great opportunity to do it. And so I spent a while researching it and went down and had a really amazing, mind-bending experience, hanging out with the border patrol—which you can imagine, after all of my books, was a very eye-opening couple of days. And then I wrote it.

F.L.A.: Other projects?

L.U.: After spending twenty years working on huge epic novel, *The Hummingbird's Daughter,* it's finally coming out with Little, Brown. It's a historical novel about my great-great-aunt, Teresa Urrea, known as the Saint of Cabora. It's a historical novel about her sort of pre-Revolutionary work among the Yaquis and the indigenous people in northern Mexico. After that, I have another novel in holding, called *The House of Broken Angels,* that I want to get back to; it's actually kind of a taboo buster about the ripples of sexual abuse among men in the *barrio.* And I have a couple of books of poetry. I have stuff stacked up.

F.L.A.: There are so few writers who can actually make a living with their writing. Do you think you're at that point?

L.U.: I had a moment there when *Across the Wire* came out and sold like crazy, but I got paid very little for it. Then I won the Western States Book Award and got a wad of money; then I got a pretty good advance for *In Search of Snow* and had also sold my mom's house. So for just a minute I was *el vato rico*, you know? All of a sudden I was taking care of everybody and ended up with nothing.

In those days, people would ask me to come read for fifty bucks, and now they're offering me pretty good money to come read. It's not that I'm a venture capitalist or anything, but my life has changed—married with children—and my work has become better known. It's kind of an interesting science experiment to watch it.

Things are pretty good. Of course, teaching's important because it's one way of giving back, but there might be a time soon when I'll be able to make a living exclusively from my writing. And that's really exciting. It's really an incredible blessing. But it's a lot of pressure too. I know a lot of writers who write, period. And it's a very tense way to live if you have a family you're trying to take care of. If I didn't have a family—I have this saying that I tell people, that as long as I have a typewriter, a trailer, and my wife, I'd be all right. You can take away the trailer, and take away the typewriter. As long as my wife and I are together, I'm all right. But it's the children that I'm looking out for.

F.L.A.: What about Chicano writers writing and publishing today?

L.U.: I would say all of that incredible platoon of new writers is burning it up right behind me: Rane Arroyo, who's a wonderful poet; Manuel Muñoz and his beautiful book, *Zigzagger;* Rich Yanez; and Lisa Chávez, who's a killer poet—she's a Chicana/Alaskan poet writing from an indigenous perspective that's just amazing. Gina Franco has a really good book coming out from the University of Arizona Press, *The Keepsake Storm*. Karl Markham, even though he doesn't have a Chicano name, is a *vato loco* from Tucson. He's got a good book. So there's this whole new generation of wild, new, brilliant writers who are interesting to me because they're well versed in other stuff. José Skinner's got a book called *Flight*. He's my great hope. There's something really remarkable and grand going on in his work, his fiction. These folks are people who have been through the system, and they've been in different parts of the world. There are all these writers with this whole new vibrant, competitive edge out there. I'm looking back, and I'm going, "Wow, these guys are great."

Writings by the Author
Poetry

"Canción al final de un día de sombras," "la primavera nunca llega," and "prima." In *Literatura Fronteriza: Antología del Primer Festival San Diego-Tijuana, Mayo 1981,* edited by Alurista, pp. 57–61. San Diego: Maize Books, 1982.
The Fever of Being. Albuquerque: West End, 1994.
Ghost Sickness. El Paso: Cinco Puntos, 1997.
Vatos. El Paso: Cinco Puntos, 2000.

Novels

In Search of Snow. New York: HarperCollins, 1994.
The Hummingbird's Daughter. New York: Little, Brown, 2005.

Short Stories

"Mr. Mendoza's Paintbrush." In *Mirrors Beneath the Earth: Short Fiction by Chicano Writers,* edited by Ray González, pp. 301–311. Willimantic, CT: Curbstone, 1992.
Six Kinds of Sky: A Collection of Short Fiction. El Paso: Cinco Puntos, 2002.

Nonfiction

Across the Wire: Life and Hard Times on the Mexican Border. New York: Anchor, 1993.
By the Lake of Sleeping Children: The Secret Life of the Mexican Border. New York: Anchor, 1996.
Nobody's Son: Notes from an American Life. Tucson: University of Arizona Press, 1998.
Wandering Time: Western Notebooks. Tucson: University of Arizona Press, 1999.
The Devil's Highway: A True Story. New York: Little, Brown, 2004.

Essays

"Down the Highway with Edward Abbey." In *Resist Much, Obey Little: Remembering Ed Abbey,* edited by James R. Hepworth and Gregory McNamee, pp. 40–47. San Francisco: Sierra Club Books, 1996.

"None of Them Talk about Their Dreams." In *The Late Great Mexican Border: Reports from a Disappearing Line,* edited by Bobby Byrd and Susannah Mississippi Byrd, pp. 64–79. El Paso: Cinco Puntos, 1996.

Other

Un puño de tierra / A Handful of Dust. [Play.] Produced by Teatro Máscara Mágica, San Diego, February 1991.

With César A. González-T., eds. *Fragmentos de Barro: The First Seven Years.* San Diego: Tolteca Publications, Centro Cultural de la Raza, 1987.

With Gregory McNamee, eds. *A World of Turtles: A Literary Celebration.* Boulder: Johnson, 1997.

Further Readings
Critical Studies

Heide, Markus. "Transcultural Space in Luis Alberto Urrea's *In Search of Snow.*" In *Literature and Ethnicity in the Cultural Borderlands,* edited by Jesús Benito and Ana María Manzanas, pp. 115–126. Amsterdam/New York: Rodopi, 2002.

López Pulido, Alberto. "To Arrive Is to Begin: Benjamin Sáenz's *Carry Me Like Water* and the Pilgrimage of Origin in the Borderlands." *Studies in Twentieth Century Literature* 25, no. 1 (2001): 306–315.

Reviews

Aldama, Frederick Luis. Rev. of *In Search of Snow. East Bay Express Books,* September 1994: 13–14.

Auer, Tom. "Young Writers to Watch." Rev. of *By the Lake of Sleeping Children: The Secret Life of the Mexican Border. Bloomsbury Review* 17 (January/February 1997): 17.

Carroll, Mary. Rev. of *By the Lake of Sleeping Children: The Secret Life of the Mexican Border. Booklist* 93, no. 4 (October 15, 1996): 402.

Childress, Boyd. Rev. of *The Devil's Highway: A True Story. Booklist* 100, no. 13 (March 2004): 1118.

González, Ray. Rev. of *In Search of Snow. The Nation* 259, no. 3 (July 18, 1994): 98–102.

Kelly, Kathryn H. Rev. of *Across the Wire: Life and Hard Times on the Mexican Border. English Journal* 85, no. 1 (January 1996): 94–96.

Martin, Rebecca. Rev. of *Nobody's Son: Notes from an American Life. Library Journal* 123, no. 16 (October 1, 1998): 88.

Murphy, Richard J. Rev. of *Six Kinds of Sky. The Review of Contemporary Fiction* 22, no. 3 (2002): 167–169.

Uschuk, Pamela. Rev. of *Ghost Sickness. Parabola* 23, no. 4 (Winter 1998): 106–120.

Wall, Catherine E. Rev. of *Wandering Time: Western Notebooks. World Literature Today* 74, no. 3 (2000): 605.

Alfredo Véa Jr.

n 1950 Alfredo Véa was born to a teenage mother at the edge of Phoenix, Arizona. Raised by his grandparents and by the Filipino and Mexicano migrants that made up this community, Véa learned early about the power of language and the Yaqui worldview that would allow him to find a sense of belonging in a world filled with flux.

While his grandparents' admixture of Moorish, Yaqui, and ancient Olmec stories and beliefs mesmerized Véa, it would be years before he would find come to identify himself as a storyteller and writer of fiction. In the intervening years, Véa served in Vietnam as a radiotelephone operator, finished a B.S. in physics from the University of California at Berkeley (1975), and received a J.D. from Berkeley's Boalt Hall School of Law (1978).

Practicing as a lawyer and representing those at the racial and social fringes of society provided Véa with a sense of purpose through the 1980s. But he continued to feel a deep sense of lack: that somehow there must be another way to explore and represent U.S. ethnic experiences, a way that was more attuned to those shades of gray that were disallowed by judicial courts and legal theory. In response, Véa wrote and published his first novel, *La Maravilla* (1993), which follows the early life of Beto as he comes to terms with his mixed Yaqui and Spanish heritage. Following the success of *La Maravilla*, Véa published *The Silver Cloud Café* (1996), in which he delved deeply into the archives of Mexican and U.S. history to bring to life the bloody Cristero Wars and the invasion of the Philippines within the framework of a story set in contemporary San Francisco. Véa used the murder mystery genre to extend his narrative scope to include characters who bridge different times and national spaces: from the Philippines to Mexico to San Francisco and California's Central Valley. In 1999 Véa published *Gods Go Begging,* a story about Vietnam, but one that does not focus merely on victories and losses. Instead, it powerfully portrays the pains and pleasures that his multiracial characters learn to share within and across the wires of a prison fence. As he interweaves the destinies of characters such as an Army chaplain, a high-ranking North Vietnamese infantry officer, and an African American sergeant, Véa imagines alternatives to war. Alfredo Véa's novels are deeply learned and wide in historical and literary scope. His beautifully wrought, complexly organized imagined worlds, brimming with multifaceted characters, powerfully enrich Chicano-penned fictional forms and contents.

Frederick Luis Aldama: You're a practicing criminal defense lawyer and a novelist?

Alfredo Véa: I'd never written anything—not even a short story—before *La Maravilla.* In fact, it was this death penalty case in the Central Valley that inspired me to write *La Maravilla.* The courtroom, the jury, the judge, and the two defense lawyers were all so incredibly racist toward my Mexican client, and the trial such a sham, that I started writing the novel.

At first I thought it was going to be an angry novel, but it really didn't turn out that way. During the writing process, I learned how to omit a European presence and archetypes from this little town, Buckeye, to see how a story would work with a bunch of Mexican, African American, Anglo Oklahoma, and Filipino characters. The writing was so engaging that it was also like I'd finally found an instrument I could play. When I finished writing the book, I actually didn't intend to do anything with it. For me it was more of an exercise—a way to exorcise those racist demons I'd encountered in the courtroom, like Coltrane on the sax or something. But a friend sent it to the agent Sandra Dijkstra without telling me. Next thing you know, I have an agent that wants to represent me and a contract in the mail.

After finishing *La Maravilla* I wanted to write more specifically about the racism and anti-miscegenation towards Filipino and Mexicano farmworkers in California's Central Valley. After César Chávez and the United Farm Workers' strikes, I kept waiting for an aggressive turnaround that would give field-workers labor rights and more respect, which would lead to the developing of a Mexican American intelligentsia. I waited as well for some Chicano writers to come along and really raise the bar in representing this experience. But I never really saw it happen, so I wrote the book as a response to this. I wanted to explore all these ancient Filipino and Mexican traditions that were mixing on these fields. I wanted to capture those incredible confluences of energy and thought. I wanted to write this history and culture. I wanted to tell Mr. Redneck, if you delete the Mexicans, you don't have any country music—to put it in their face intelligently and through the power of narrative.

F.L.A.: In *La Maravilla,* you name your protagonist after Einstein, Alberto, and you mention scientific principles everywhere.

A.V.: Yeah, I loved Albert Einstein when I was a kid. And when I went to college, I studied physics, getting a B.S. in physics from UC Berkeley. I've always been involved with physics as far back as I can remember. My grandfather was, in his own way, a metaphysician. I write about physics in *La Maravilla* to honor my Yaqui grandfather—and my Catholic Spanish grandmother; they used to argue with one another about my soul. My grandmother baptized more than thirty times, just out of fear that my grandfather's worldview might be more powerful than the Catholic faith. Of course, they were both right. It was a combination of the Indian and Spanish soul that would survive through *mestizo* Mexicans like myself.

F.L.A.: Clearly, your early experiences growing up in migrant farmworking communities in California and Arizona have informed your fiction. How did you manage to get out of this exploitive system to be able to go to college and then later become a lawyer and a novelist?

A.V.: When I was a teenager, I worked in the wineries in Livermore; they had a great high school there for the smart kids of all the scientists that were working at the Lawrence Science Labs. Here I was, this migrant worker kid that was completely unsocialized, in a high school filled with smart white kids whose fathers are scientists. I didn't wither, though. I had too much drive. I read a lot more than any of them. And I did really well. I didn't do it all on my own, though. There was a teacher, Jack Beary (I dedicate *La Maravilla* to him), who encouraged me to think for myself. Once I finished high school, and after picking vegetables in Arizona for a season, I went to Berkeley.

After a semester, I got drafted. I spent a year and a half in Vietnam at the end of the 1960s. After Vietnam, and before returning to Berkeley, I went to France for two years. After my experiences in Vietnam—the incredible lies that led to incredible carnage—I wasn't ready to return to the States. I needed some distance from our country; I needed some time and a place to think for a while. That's my grandfather's Yaqui influence: get away and go think. You can be alone in the middle of the desert and not be lonely. In France I got a job as a janitor at the Fontain Bleu Cooking School. Every night I would sit in the cafés and talk with other French veterans of Dien Bien Phu, of the war of Algiers, and of World War II to help clear my head and get some comparative historical perspective. I was the only Chicano I ever saw over there.

Finally, I returned to finish my degree at Berkeley, but after Vietnam, I was sickened by what people had done with physics. So I switched tracks and studied law at Boalt [Hall, UC Berkeley's School of Law]. At the beginning of *Gods Go Begging,* I write: "The fruits of physics have been harvested here."

F.L.A.: Why the decision to become a criminal defense attorney?

A.V.: In 1981–82 there were only one or two Chicano lawyers practicing in San Francisco. I felt it was important to try to do something for my people. Many of those being tried were exactly like people that I saw in Vietnam: uneducated people with two-hundred-word vocabularies that were being victimized and manipulated by larger exploitive systems.

F.L.A.: In *Gods Go Begging,* you tell the stories of those that are at the social margins, who learn to transcend their everyday, restricted vision of the world and see eye-to-eye.

A.V.: The minute the language disappears, there's no difference between a Mexican and a Cambodian, say. All the assumptions just evaporate. It's amazing how similar everybody's lives actually are. We all have the same kinds of concerns.

F.L.A.: In your novels, you often invent figures that police borders and people when the more natural predisposition of your characters is to mix languages, bodies, and cultures.

A.V.: The old mythologies and grand narratives don't work anymore. Of course, you've got to look at the old ones first to see what they've done. In *Silver Cloud Café* I fictionalize the abominable Cristero religious war in Mexico that had brown people killing brown people. We need to look long and hard at the past to be able to make new, positive narratives in our present and future.

F.L.A.: In all your novels, your characters try to cross cultural, racial, and linguistic borders. In *Silver Cloud Café,* you even invent a character, Manuel, who operates the drawbridge that ultimately brings two worlds together.

A.V.: First, it's pleasing to know that somebody's really understanding what I'm trying to do in my books. I've been a little bitter about the literary academy, who don't seem to get my novels. Worse still, the Chicanos don't seem to get my work. It seems that they're trying to build a little enclave of trendy Chicano writers. Like Cisneros, whose writing isn't all that special, but because of this Chicano critical cult, she's really got a megalomaniacal thing happening.

F.L.A.: You write novels that don't fit the Chicano/a mold?

A.V.: They might fit into Chicano literature in about ten years, fifteen years from now, but today people don't recognize them as part of the Chicano canon. Later, maybe the Chicano literary critics will realize that they don't really know how to debate the role of literature and art—that their arguments fall far short of those debates that took place during the Harlem Renaissance with Langston Hughes and W. E. B. DuBois sitting around arguing about whether or not the black aesthetic should be utilitarian and for the sake of the people or not. But as a result of the kind of gatekeeping in Chicano letters, my novels aren't allowed to be a part of this canon. But I just keep writing.

F.L.A.: You craft narrative fictions with a real attention to language and detail as well as infusing a massive amount of historical and cultural knowledge into your novels. How do you manage this? What is your writing process?

A.V.: There's a period before writing when I read for three or four months in and around material that has to do with what I want to write about, and this idea is still vague and broad, like divesting European archetypes in one book to incorporating them whole-hog in another, or talking about the historical connection between America and Europe in another.

The novels come out of this desire to show how the whole world is a lot more than you think it is. *Silver Cloud Café* and *Gods Go Begging* are at their core saying, "Look at the world and love it because it is so complex and deep." They also come out of a desire to reimagine historical events—to make them visible even. In the novel that I've been working on, I wanted to write about women, and then it turned into a profound exploration of misogyny in our culture that traces back to slavery. So I've read these historians who say that if there hadn't been African American women in America, there would have been no love life on the frontier at all. And people have no idea that Santa Anna was screwing a *mulata* named Emily Morgan in a silk tent, wearing red Turkish underwear and smoking opium, and lost the entire northern Mexican territories to the U.S. in the 1848 war. The story and the woman, Emily Morgan, disappeared. She was in history for one day. In my new novel, I'm telling her story.

I also experiment with narrative form as I write. I usually start to write a novel by writing a poem for each chapter. In chapter 13 of *La Maravilla*, I wrote in an anapestic Aztec poetic form. Now, that was tough to do. In this new novel, I used more of an operatic, recitative song form to structure my chapters.

When I conceive of my narrators, I try to figure out ways to give them another kind of power beyond the usual omniscience. I also think a lot about the implied audience when I'm inventing my narrators. If you abide by that rule that great European writers adhere to, that one must lift the audience as opposed to simply leaving the audience where it was when the story began, then you're going to write good novels.

F.L.A.: Death is central to your novels: not just the genocide in *Gods Go Begging*, but also the grandparents' telling their stories from their grave in *La Maravilla* and the murder that begins the unfolding of the mystery in *Silver Cloud Café*.

A.V.: I'm obsessed by it. That veneer that smoothed over the presence of death in our society was scratched—removed even—after I returned from Vietnam. At first, it was difficult to live with this clarity, no longer assuming that I'd be here tomorrow, or that any random individual walking the streets will be here tomorrow. Back from Vietnam, life and death had new meaning. I no longer took it for granted that everything would turn out well; I no longer had faith in the inherent good of humanity. This was all taken away forever once Vietnam exposed this raw nerve end.

I have this same dream—sometimes twice, three times a week—that I'm on a conveyor belt with people ahead of me and behind me. The way I read it, my life is no better today than the life of an Egyptian who died five thousand years ago. The way the world operates today, we're not progressing toward a better life. So the best I can do is to write about and capture what I see around me in the world today, and yesterday, to look deep within myself to probe historical meaning and the human condition as critically and as imaginatively and powerfully as possible.

Vietnam not only exposed raw nerve endings to the world; it was like being pulled out of the womb again. After that I became obsessed with scratching the surfaces that delude us.

F.L.A.: Can you talk about the way you detail different spaces in your novels?

A.V.: When I write, I want people to know where they are in my invented worlds, what's around them. This comes from my interest in French Impressionist painting and those stories my grandparents would tell me that would fill out my imagination with precise locations and shapes and people in my imagination; their stories were so calming and so comforting—and so involved.

The story is of absolute importance. I really take offense at modern books that don't respect narrative—that don't believe that as a writer you need to paint a picture on the page for your reader. For me, reading is still an extension of an oral tradition. It's storytelling, so you're still responsible for providing all the details to bring your reader into your world. You've got to weave that harbinger in to get your reader to listen, for example. I remember listening to storytellers in India that would hold their audiences captive for twenty-four hours. Like in Homer's epics, they'd employ a variety of devices to keep their listeners engaged—the mnemonic, for example. Or there's Dickens, who makes such a complete picture in your mind with a novel like *A Tale of Two Cities.* Nabokov, too: some critics complained that he was being wordy, underestimating the reader's intelligence and misreading his technique for inventing captivating fictional worlds. When I write, then, I'm most interested in using narrative techniques that will most powerfully captivate my readers.

F.L.A.: Your characters experience the trauma of being uprooted, yet it is this uprooting that opens the possibility for the unexpected encounter, the collision of cultures.

A.V.: Unfortunately, in the United States a Puritan, Manifest Destiny ideology has justified the forced dislocations of native peoples historically.

John Winthrop said that a white man (this is, by the way, one of the first usages of that word *white* to identify a raceless status) is obliged by God to conquer an uncivilized, empty land. This, of course, blatantly disregarded the native Indians' presence and natural, civil, and legal right to this land.

We're seeing similar dislocations and genocides today. Instead of Mexican Americans having legal and civil rights, we're disappearing because of lack of access to education, lack of employment opportunities. In our place, Taco Bells are mushrooming. As every day passes, we're getting one step closer to becoming a weightless culture, a culture void of any racial and ethnic history and bodily content. That's why people are increasingly turning to mysticism. They don't want to go to church, but they do want mysticism. They want pyramids on their crotches as well as quartz crystals and gemstones to fondle. All this meaningless, esoteric stuff to fill up that void left with the social erasure of Chicanos, blacks, Asians, and so on, that is a result of mass consumption in our capitalist, globalized world. That's why people drink tasteless Budweiser and tasteless Folgers coffee.

If globalization wins, Budweiser wins; tastelessness wins. People don't understand that market culture is not culture; it's marketing of product to generate consumer interest and a dollar profit. There's nothing organic about it. That's why I write about real forms of cultural formations: the confluence of musical forms as bodies collide, for example. That's why the emphasis on the unexpected: to move as far away from the fingered, premeditated, and deliberate mass production of nonculture in our world.

F.L.A.: Where does Chicano literature stand in all of this mass-generated, mass-consumable culture?

A.V.: I've had correspondence with Gabriel García Márquez after he read *La Maravilla* and talked to Octavio Paz just before he died and had long chats with Carlos Fuentes, and what struck me about these writers is their sense of being Latino writers who take an active part within a larger social and political fabric. What we need in the U.S. with Chicano writers is the formation of an intelligentsia. To do this, we need Chicano writers to look beyond themselves, to write with a larger sense of purpose—not, say, as politicians, but as writers interested in the art of their craft. They need to read and learn from Nabokov, Dostoevsky, García Márquez, Faulkner, and Eugene O'Neill, for example. Chicano writers need to stop writing about the last tortilla. Good art is good art; good fiction is good fiction, and we must strive to produce this. I mean, when someone tells me Tupac is as good as Miles Davis, my ass! Give Tupac a trumpet and see what he does. What's he going to do to replace twenty-five years of experience on a trumpet, practicing every goddamn day on an instrument? Or a Coleman Hawkins or something? You can't replace virtuosity. Virtuosity is a starting place for writing and for music. Look for some virtuosity (writers I've mentioned are a good start), be courageous, and then start writing. That's all I've got to say.

Writings by the Author
Novels

La Maravilla. New York: Dutton, 1993.
The Silver Cloud Café. New York: Dutton, 1996.
Gods Go Begging. New York: Dutton, 1999.

Further Readings
Critical Studies

Alaimo, Stacy. "Multiculturalism and Epistemic Rupture: The Vanishing Acts of Guillermo Gomez-Peña and Alfredo Véa Jr." *MELUS* 25, no. 2 (2000): 163–185.
Cantú, Roberto. "Alfredo Véa." *Dictionary of Literary Biography*, Vol. 209, *Chicano Writers*, pp. 281–285. Detroit: The Gale Group, 1999.
———. "Borders of the Self in Alfredo Véa's *The Silver Cloud Café*." *Studies in Twentieth Century Literature* 25, no. 1 (2001): 210–245.
Christie, John S. "Crowding Out Latinos: Mexican Americans in the Public Consciousness." *MELUS* 26, no. 2 (2001): 267–271.

Reviews

Augenbraum, Harold. Rev. of *Gods Go Begging*. *Library Journal* 124, no. 12 (1999): 142.
Joyce, Alice. Rev. of *La Maravilla*. *Booklist* 89, no. 13 (March 1, 1993): 1158.
Pearl, Nancy. Rev. of *The Silver Cloud Café*. *Library Journal* 121, no. 14 (September 1, 1996): 211.

Interviews

Biggers, Jeff. "More than Measuring Up: An Interview with Alfredo Véa." *Blooms-bury Review* 20, no. 1 (2000): 5.

Porter, Kathleen Sullivan. "The Amazement of Reality: An Interview with Alfredo Véa Jr. *Hayden's Ferry Review* 22 (1998): 81–92.

Alma Luz Villanueva

lma Luz Villanueva was born on October 4, 1944, in Lompoc, California. Raised in San Francisco's Mission District by her Yaqui maternal grandmother, Villanueva learned early of the trials and tribulations Mexican women face within a sexist and racist society. Deeply connected to her maternal Mexican roots—she never met her father, who was of German ancestry—Villanueva came to appreciate the healing power of art and storytelling. Her maternal grandfather was also a great influence, with his love of writing and metaphysical musings. Art and storytelling would become essential to Villanueva in her post-coming-of-age struggles, as the loss of her maternal grandmother left her fending for herself in San Francisco at a young age. These difficult life circumstances prevented her from finishing high school. She married and had a son during this period. However, with three children and much life experience under her belt, Villanueva was finally able to carve out a place for herself as a writer. On a small farm in California's Sierra Nevada, Villanueva began dedicating long hours to the honing of her creative writing skills. She was especially attuned to nature and the cycles of life, death, and rebirth. She continued to dedicate long hours to her craft—the writing of poetry, novels, and short stories—which led her to an M.F.A. program at Vermont College in 1984. She has since become one of the most productive Chicana writers in the country, publishing poetry, novels, short stories, and essays that variously explore themes of gender, race, and sexuality as they connect back to an earthly spiritual sensibility. In her first collection of poetry, *Bloodroot* (1977), and her first novel, *The Ultraviolet Sky* (1987)—to mention only a few of her many works—she experiments with form and voice to complicate our sense of the universal forces of life and death in all aspects of our lives. She affirms the strengths and values of Latina women in their deep rootedness to cultural traditions and nature. Her work has won national recognition, including the American Book Award and an award from the Before Columbus Foundation.

Frederick Luis Aldama: You've had extensive experience publishing with small presses. Why not go with the bigger trade presses?

Alma Luz Villanueva: Bilingual Press has been wonderful as a publisher for me. I do publish with many "large publishers" as well—in anthologies and textbooks, for example. Right now, I don't have an agent, but I continue to publish my work with regularity. Also, Bilingual acts as my agent many times, as do I. (I'm getting good at it.)

I think I've been fortunate, as my work was picked up fairly quickly and then published with awards early on, which brought attention to my work. The most recent anthologies include *The Best American Poetry 1996, Prayers for a Thousand Years, Inspiration from Leaders and Visionaries Around the World, Caliente! The Best Erotic Writing in Latin American Fiction, Letters to J. D. Salinger, Under the Fifth Sun, Her Words: An Anthology of Poetry to the Great Goddess, Contemporary Hispanic Quotations, Snapshots, Understanding Poetry,* and many other anthologies.

I've found publication and readership definitely expanding since 1980, and I feel it's my duty—and challenge—as a writer to write inside/outside any boxes I might find myself stuck within or locked out of. It's my creative journey, not a prescribed role. I have much hope and excitement for new Latina/o fiction, and for all new global fiction. "We are not the mainstream; we are the ocean," says Ishmael Reed.

F.L.A.: How have institutions such as M.F.A. programs helped or hindered your career?

A.L.V.: I found my M.F.A. program to be elitist and racist, but decided to persevere and am glad I did. The M.F.A. program I teach in now, at Antioch University in Los Angeles, is the one I would have wanted to be a student in, a very different experience. Yet my M.F.A. program became a challenge to me, to speak out when I witnessed racism or was targeted in any way, so it may have been the exact program I needed at the time to evolve further as a writer, to stand my ground. (I will omit the name of the college, please.) If I can contribute to a journal or magazine in a creative way, I find it to be a pleasure. I've written book reviews for *Ms.* magazine, for example, as well as poetry/fiction in *Ms.*

Teaching is the balancing part of the spectrum of my "hermit writer," and I love the exchange with student writers. Of course, awards and reviews are icing on the cake after the long work of solitude, the writing of fiction/poetry. It's inspiring and really necessary to connect to my readers, as when I visit colleges and speak directly to students who read my work: wonderful. I'm now receiving letters from students who are reading *Luna's California Poppies,* wonderful letters.

F.L.A.: Do you imagine an audience when writing?

A.L.V.: As I write, I don't imagine an audience; I'm too immersed in the fictive dream, or the dictates of the poem. Only later does it come to me that someone will read it someday. I think when I first began to write poetry, for example, I was just so grateful to begin the poem, to hear to the end, and to receive an answer I longed to hear. This is why I truly write. It continues to be the same, yet I hope my words are for the world and will continue to reach readers long after my spirit self has moved on.

F.L.A.: In your poetry collections, such as *Mother, May I,* you move between Spanish and English but mostly use English. What is the intended effect?

A.L.V.: Spanish was my first language, but when my grandmother, Jesús Villanueva, died, I no longer spoke Spanish on a daily basis. I feel like, though I write in English, I "feel" in Spanish, and then switch to some Spanish words for emphasis. Actually, my grandmother also spoke Yaqui. I have memories of it, but I've retained nothing of it, except that it sounded like water.

F.L.A.: Can there be politics in aesthetics? I think here of poems of the earth, women, children, and animals, and also those like "Former Lebanese Prime Minister Saeb Salam Dismisses . . ." or "Child's Play."

A.L.V.: I have a series of poems titled "Dear World in Its Tenth Year" that I call my "bitch moaning poems." Who can ignore the genocide of Bosnia, Rwanda, Tibet? These concerns embody themselves in my work.

F.L.A.: The body is firmly situated in the world in your work? I think here of your poem "On Realizing I Am Not Emily Dickinson."

A.L.V.: With the above in mind, I'm also a mother of four grown children, each one a healer in their own right. I was not a writer that had the luxury of absolute solitude—someone to clean and cook for me. I was the housekeeper, cook, and daily mother for forty years.

F.L.A.: What have been some major influences on your writing?

A.L.V.: I love Native American flute/chanting (I play it a lot as I write; it floats me into the dream) as well as Brazilian music, Bach's cello concertos, Sting, U2, Stevie Wonder, and many of the new women writers/singers. I'm inspired by a global vision of art, literature, music, and film. I simply love the new film *Frida Kahlo*—very daring, visionary, and visually exciting. I take inspiration from feisty women and heartfelt men, or perhaps that merging of both. I love the work of Laurens van der Post (his *Heart of the Hunter* has much wisdom on every page); the autobiographical *Earthly Paradise* by the French writer Colette; Herman Hesse; Isabel Allende's work, and her *Paula* that's so utterly honest and brave—a gift.

F.L.A.: You work in several different genres—novels, short stories, poetry. Does each have its own process? And within each genre—as with, for example, poetry—you use different forms?

A.L.V.: My poetry always guides my fiction, but the process is obviously different. However, poetry was the journey to finding my own unique voice. Poetry is my "truth teller," my "bullshit detector," and so as I work on my novels, I'm always writing poetry as well. The novel is a very long dream, working vividly on my own. This is also the advice I give my writing students, that until they've claimed their own unique voice, they're still practicing (which is why writing practice is so crucial: that's how we evolve as writers), and that when they do claim it, they will know the difference, as the reader knows the difference.

F.L.A.: What about your choice of titles: *Mother, May I? Bloodroot,* and so on?

A.L.V.: I find that my book titles have to do with earth and sky, which are grounded in my themes. Each book has its own structure (that play with form and content), and it's up to the writer to find it. Until you do, you're not quite in the flow of the work. When you find it, it's as though you're following an arrow in flight to its target.

F.L.A.: You use a variety of different styles and techniques to engage your readers. I think of your experimenting with typographic representation and narrative form in *Luna's California Poppies.*

A.L.V.: *Luna* had its own particular challenges because it's largely written in the voice of twelve-year-old Luna, so I had to give up total authorial control to embrace this kid's point of view: how she really thought, talked, and spelled. I haven't been twelve in a long time, but I loved remembering that spirit.

F.L.A.: You portray good and bad men, but usually from the point of view of women.

A.L.V.: I've reversed the gaze many times in my novels and stories. I've surrendered to my male characters to feel/see who they are, and I will continue to do so. As for the blood image, it's a very feminine image, as in fertility. With patriarchy it's been hijacked into a symbol of war/violence/ domination: blood. I meet many men, including my grown sons, who agree with this, who remember the fertility of blood. Hoorrrayy for these men!!!

F.L.A.: You portray an array of different characters but usually focus on women's struggles: prostitution, sexual abuse, difficulty coming of age, and survival. I see this in *Weeping Woman: La Llorona and Other Stories,* which is dedicated to your daughter, Antoinette.

A.L.V.: My daughter actually told me of a dream of seeing a beautiful woman taking her black shawl off to catch the rain, and I was struck by the healing quality of her dream, so I dedicated this book to my daughter. (She's head nurse in critical care and a wonderful healer.) These stories came to me from a journey to the secondhand store in Santa Cruz, Califas: a box of battered shells I found. As I held them, I saw an old woman, very strong, walk into me, staring directly into my eyes; she made me weep. Then the stories came, some out of thin air, some encouraged from our daily global news.

F.L.A.: Is the story of Luna in *Luna's California Poppies* part of the formation of a young Chicana feminist worldview?

A.L.V.: As children we naturally think/feel this way, and so my hope is that Luna will be a reminder of that time now.

F.L.A.: What is the relationship between your vision of Chicano literature and its engagement with mainstream culture in your poetry and fiction?

A.L.V.: Every word, every book will find its way in the world—as in Ishmael Reed's words, "to the ocean." But the nonwhite writer may have to be especially persistent, a pain in *las nalgas* to the end—and with joy and beauty as well, as we go.

F.L.A.: There's a fusion of opposites (eroticism versus violence, for example) in your novel *Ultraviolet Sky?*

A.L.V.: I love this question because that was my ultimate answer as a writer—that arrow that I follow, page by page, to "the end." Unfortunately, in our world, in this time, this is the experience of many women, and many women experience a truly brutal sexual violation, as in the womb of genocide and war. My experience obviously pales, but I feel it as a writer/poet. Sensuality, Eros, is a beautiful, natural aspect to us all, and I think that no matter what happens to us, it's our human right to reclaim it, to be fully alive.

F.L.A.: Memory, the body, and language are important in your work?

A.L.V.: Again, the natural wisdom of the body—sensuality, Eros, connection to the earth—becomes evident in my work because that's how I experience being alive, truly alive. And so my experience/truth is conveyed in what I write.

F.L.A.: You present many different themes—womanhood and girlhood, the presence of nature, family—in your work?

A.L.V.: I think I have many themes as well as multilayered themes, but my central theme remains my "arrow." I feel fortunate to have brought up three sons—to have witnessed the absolute beauty of the young boy to the grown man—as well as my daughter—to have witnessed not me, but her own self, her girl self, becoming clear. I've told each one, I wouldn't have missed them for the universe (measles, mumps, teenhood included).

My grandmother was an herbal healer (as was her mother and her mother), and to see my daughter now as a healer, as well as my sons, the family intent continues. My thirty-seven-year-old son, for example, teaches high school chemistry and is also a family counselor: the teaching inspired him to counsel families. And my youngest son, who's twenty-three, is now a journalist with a passion for the oppressed, to tell their stories. I'm proud of them all, needless to say.

F.L.A.: You've been writing since the late 1970s (*Bloodroot* and *Mother, May I?*), through the 1980s (*Naked Ladies, Life Span,* and *The Ultraviolet Sky*), and into the 1990s (*Letters to My Mother, Desire, Luna's California Poppies, Vida*). How do you see your work evolving?

A.L.V.: Again, it's that challenge of finding the form for each new work that comes my way, and I know it's the same for every writer. I think as I live, grow, and evolve, so does my work: each poem, each story, each novel. That's the mystery and the joy of it. I look forward to the further journey.

F.L.A.: Has your sense of writing and publishing changed?

A.L.V.: All I know is that I will write until I leave this body. Of course, I'm grateful for every book I've published, and I wait for *la vida* to surprise me, as it always does.

F.L.A.: What are you working on now?

A.L.V.: I'm about midway through a novel in progress. A new book of poetry has just been accepted for publication, *Soft Chaos,* so perhaps in 2006 it will be out. And I'm very slowly working on a craft book, all the things I've had to make conscious for my students—how to do it—to pass it on. And my next novel has started to come to me, so I'm taking notes. It seems to be taking place in Mexico/U.S.A.

Writings by the Author
Novels

The Ultraviolet Sky. Tempe, AZ: Bilingual Press / Editorial Bilingüe, 1987.
Naked Ladies. Tempe, AZ: Bilingual Press / Editorial Bilingüe, 1994.
Letters to My Mother. New York: Pocket Books, 1997.
Desire. Tempe, AZ: Bilingual Press / Editorial Bilingüe, 1998.
Luna's California Poppies. Tempe, AZ: Bilingual Press / Editorial Bilingüe, 2000.

Poetry

Bloodroot. Austin: Place of Herons Press, 1977.
Mother, May I? Pittsburgh: Motheroot, 1978.
Life Span. Austin: Place of Herons Press, 1985.
La Chingada. Tempe: Bilingual Press / Editorial Bilingüe, 1985.
"La Chingada." In *Five Poets of Aztlán,* edited by Santiago Daydí-Tolson, pp. 140–163. Tempe, AZ: Bilingual Press / Editorial Bilingüe, 1985.

Short Stories

Weeping Woman: La Llorana and Other Stories. Tempe, AZ: Bilingual Press / Editorial Bilingüe, 1994.

"Golden Glass." In *Hispanics in the United States: An Anthology of Creative Literature,* edited by Francisco Jiménez and Gary D. Keller, Vol. 2, pp. 70–72. Tempe, AZ: Bilingual Press / Editorial Bilingüe, 1982.

Further Readings
Critical Studies

Daydí-Tolson, Santiago. Introduction. In *Five Poets of Aztlán,* edited by Santiago Daydí-Tolson, pp. 9–58. Tempe, AZ: Bilingual Press / Editorial Bilingüe, 1985.

Morales, Alejandro. "Terra Mater and the Emergence of Myth in Poems by Alma Villanueva." *Bilingual Review / La Revista Bilingüe* 7, no. 2 (1980): 123–142.

Nericcio, William A. "A Decidedly 'Mexican' and 'American' Semi[er]otic Transference: Frida Kahlo in the Eyes of Gilbert Hernandez." In *Latino/a Popular Culture,* edited by Michelle Habell-Pallán and Mary Romero, pp. 190–207 New York: New York University Press, 2002.

Ordóñez, Elizabeth. "Body, Spirit, and the Text: Alma Villanueva's *Life Span.*" In *Criticism in the Borderlands: Studies in Chicano Literature, Culture, and Ideology,* edited by Héctor Calderón and José David Saldívar, pp. 61–71. Durham, NC: Duke University Press, 1991.

Perles Rochel, Juan Antonio. "Autoexilio chicano en *The Ultraviolet Sky* de Alma Luz Villanueva." In *Exilos femeninos,* edited by Pilar Cuder Domínguez, pp. 277–282. Huelva, Spain: Instituto Andaluz de la Mujer, 2000.

———."Sexismo y violencia en *Naked Ladies* de Alma Luz Villanueva." In *El sexismo en el lenguaje,* edited by Fernández de la Torre Madueño and Maria Dolores, pp. 283–292. Málaga, Spain: Diputación Provincial de Málaga, 1999.

Sánchez, Marta Ester. "The Birthing of a Poetic 'I' in Alma Villanueva's *Mother, May I?:* The Search for Female Identity." In *Contemporary Chicana Poetry: A Critical Approach to an Emerging Literature,* pp. 24–84. Berkeley: University of California Press, 1985.

Tatum, Charles M. *Chicano Literature: A Critical History.* Boston: Twayne, 1982.